REDWOOD WRITING PROJECT

Uncommon Sense

Uncommon Sense
Theoretical Practice
in Language Education

JOHN S. MAYHER

New York University

BOYNTON/COOK PUBLISHERS

HEINEMANN
PORTSMOUTH, NH

BOYNTON/COOK PUBLISHERS, INC.
A Subsidiary of
HEINEMANN EDUCATIONAL BOOKS, INC.
361 Hanover Street   Portsmouth, NH   03801-3959
Offices and agents throughout the world

© *1990 by John S. Mayher.*

We would like to thank the following for permission to reprint material appearing in this book:

Page 40: From *Education under Siege: The Conservative, Liberal and Radical Debate over Schooling* by Stanley Aronowitz and Henry A. Giroux. Published by Bergin & Garvey, 1985.

Pages 153–54: From *Relevance: Communication and Cognition* by Dan Sperber and Deirdre Wilson. Published by Basil Blackwell, 1986.

Pages 169–70: From *The Jolly Postman or Other People's Letters* by Allan and Janet Ahlberg. Copyright © 1986 by Allan and Janet Ahlberg. By permission of Little, Brown and Company.

Library of Congress Cataloging-in-Publication Data
Mayher, John Sawyer.
    Uncommon sense : theoretical practice in language education / John S. Mayher.
        p.   cm.
    Bibliography: p.
    ISBN 0-86709-247-5
    1. English language—Study and teaching (Elementary)   2. English language—Study and teaching (Secondary)   I. Title.
    LB1576.M397   1990
    428.4071'2—dc20   89-31482
                                                                                    CIP

Front cover art: Todd Siler, Mind without Borders (Metaprint), *1988. Mixed media, collage and lithography on paper, 30" x 44½". Private Collection, courtesy of Ronald Feldman Fine Arts, New York.*

Designed by Vic Schwarz
Printed in the United States of America
94 93 92 91   9 8 7 6 5 4 3 2

Contents

Foreword

As Larry Cuban (1984) has shown, American schools have changed little in terms of pedagogy over a one-hundred-year period. Progressive educational ideas, by and large, have never really taken root in classrooms, not even in the teaching of English, the subject in which there has probably been the most radical theorizing over those one hundred years. I'm sure that research would unearth similar findings in the United Kingdom, Canada, Australia, and New Zealand, which, with the United States, make up the core of the International Federation for the Teaching of English, founded in 1983. What is it that so persistently reinforces pedagogical inertia in our schools?

John Mayher, in a wide-ranging and deeply reflective consideration of this question, begins and concludes with the view that "educational common sense" is the opiate which has dulled teachers' hearts and minds, a common sense which, in soluble form, renders itself transparent in the daily lives of teachers. It is the *un*common sense that comes from fearless reflection on action for which teachers must struggle, knowing still that truth will always be tangential and that educational common sense will always insidiously infiltrate even the most open-eyed investigation of what is.

Tenaciously, with erudition, and speaking in a clear, personal voice, Mayher strips away layer after layer of prejudice, misconception, and habit which constitute so much of English teaching in America and beyond. His is not, however, the commentary of an academic spectator. There's an autobiographical, confessional tone to the whole exposé. Mayher shows himself as voyager on a journey of continuing reconstruction from his early days as a young tyro at Homestead High School, fresh from his college baptism in the fonts of literary criticism, to the present, where, as a University Professor, he continues daily to discover new insights in his quest for uncommon sense.

From my perspective in the Antipodes, and as one who has had the privilege of observing English teaching in all the founding member countries of the International Federation for the Teaching of English, I see Mayher speaking not only about an American phenomenon. His is a treatise about teaching in the Western English-speaking world and so will reverberate with English teachers everywhere. It is my judgment, however, that the American education scene is the most steeped of all in debilitating educational common sense. American teachers need to respond to Mayher's call to arms if they are to be rid of their mind-forged manacles. "Teachers at all levels," he says, "need and must demand higher levels of professional autonomy . . . . Achieving this change will require political action of a sort which American teachers have traditionally shied away from." (p. 20)

A feature of Mayher's treatment of the theme of uncommon sense is his unobtrusive breadth of reference. With seeming ease and without ostentatiously parading his wisdom, Mayher synthesizes for us an enormous corpus of literature across a wide frontier—the gurus of English literature from Matthew Arnold, through Leavis to Moffett, Britton, Barnes, Applebee, and the newly prominent Australians, Watson and Thomson; the radical, educational uncommonsense critics from Dewey through to Holt, Kozol, Postman, Aronowitz, Giroux, and Goodlad; the psychologists—Pavlov, Skinner, Kelly, Vygotsky, Smith, Donaldson; the linguists—Sapir, Chomsky, Halliday, Lakoff; the philosophers—Polanyi, Kuhn, Rorty; and, as well, enriching interdisciplinary insights from the likes of Donald Schön, whose book, *The Reflective Practitioner*, has obviously been strongly inspirational.

Detective style, Mayher takes us firmly and surely behind the transparencies of much taken-for-granted practice, where, in a new light, we are taught to see the flawed common sense of that which is now apparent—the tracking system, the transmission of knowledge as if children learn what we teach, and the assembly line "bottom up" aggregation of skills taught in parts. Mayher shows how even the students themselves collude in the reproduction and consolidation of practices which are, in fact, educationally toxic, even when they find these practices obnoxious. "The kids' conviction that the normal paraphernalia of schooling is an essential ingredient of learning was deep and powerful even if they also knew they couldn't or wouldn't do the drills and fill in the required blanks." (p. 53)

Compared with so many other books written by academics on English teaching, this is a work where the classroom is never far away. Mayher keeps grounding his commentary through recognizable anecdote and reference to the experience of teachers. To balance this classroom perspective, he also grounds his work in another significant way. He is very clearheaded about the sociopolitical context of schooling. He understands well how the rhetorical work of a William Bennett or an E. D. Hirsch, coupled with a fundamentalist national politics, provides scaffolding for the palace of common sense.

Here's a book for which I would reserve the word "generous." It's a rare privilege to be able to eavesdrop on an uncommon mind at work, especially one which so scrupulously takes account of the eavesdroppers and makes accessible and warm what has too often been remote and cold in the past. Mayher's work is of the essence of art which conceals art. At the end of our chat with him, we have been taken effortlessly through more than two decades of his learning in order to emerge devastatingly disturbed by the work's unfolding truth.

Both for those who would aspire to be English teachers and for those who, like me, have tried to be, this is a book which will be at the same time healingly integrative and pleasurably explosive. It will be fun putting it all together again, when you set down Mayher's book and take up uncommon sense.

GARTH BOOMER
Associate Director-General
of Education (Curriculum)
South Australia
Department of Education

Acknowledgments

Everyone who starts to write recognizes immediately that the ideas they are expressing derive directly or indirectly from a great intertextual conversation. While I hope there are some new ideas here, as well as some new expressions of old ideas, in many cases I can no longer tell which are which. While I have tried to cite those sources from which I directly drew some of the ideas here, I must also recognize that there are as many uncited sources as acknowledged ones, not because I have deliberately tried to ignore them, but because they have become so deeply embedded in my pesonal construct system that I no longer recognize their source. I must, therefore, both recognize and apologize to all those who see their ideas recycled here as my own. There have been too many books, articles, and conversations to remember them all, and in some ways incorporation, not imitation, is the sincerest form of flattery.

Among those who stand out for their uncredited as well as some of their credited ideas are: Noam Chomsky, Louise Rosenblatt, Frank Smith, James Moffett, Carl Rogers, John Dewey, James Britton, Neil Postman, Gordon Wells, Donald Graves, Janet Emig, John Dixon, Jerome Bruner, and Donald Schön.

The autobiographical quality of this book has made me focus anew on the teachers I had throughout my education from the beginning through graduate school. My first two teachers, who started me off in uncommonsense directions, were my mother, Dossie Sawyer Staples, and my grandmother, Dee Winslow Sawyer. Once I left home, like most American students, I had largely

commonsense teachers in school, but there were also exceptions—
teachers who managed to transcend the ordinary and encourage
me as an uncommonsense learner. In formulating the ideas expressed here, therefore, I have been grateful for the opportunity to
learn with and from:

Marion Howe (Grade 5), Elizabeth Norwood and Edward
Wyman (Grades 7 and 8), Clinton Ely and Richard Gurney (High
School), Clay Hunt and Frederick Rudolph (College), Bernie
O'Donnell, Royall Gettmann, Howard Maclay, J. N. Hook, Israel
Scheffler, James Moffett, John Mellon, Wayne O'Neil, and Noam
Chomsky (Graduate School).

Like any teacher, I have learned more from my students than
they have learned from me. While there have been too many years
and too many students to list them all, I am grateful to them for
their support throughout my evolution as a teacher. Many of the
incidents in the book have been directly derived from my experiences of working with them, and I hope any who come across it will
recognize my appreciation of their contribution to my education.
One of my recent classes also read the preliminary version of this
text in manuscript, and I further appreciate their comments which
have, I hope, clarified and strengthened it.

I have also been particularly fortunate to have shared the
experience of teaching and learning with a wide variety of professional peers. I've learned from our conversations, from our team
teaching, and above all from their example. Particularly important
over the years have been:

Carole Sherrill, Mary Smith, Bernie Hubbard, and Jim War-
ren, with whom I team taught English at Homestead High School;
Scott Thomson of Homestead and Cubberley High Schools, who
showed me that a school administrator can be an educational
leader; Harold Vine, Marilyn Sobelman, and Margot Ely at New
York University, who continue to show me that we can change
what we do and how we do it; from around the country, my
brother, Bill Mayher, who has helped me learn to care for kids, Dan
Kirby of the University of Georgia, Jim Collins from SUNY Buffalo,
and Bill Smith of Pittsburgh, who have shared with me their questions as well as their answers; and since I've been fortunate to work
with people teaching English around the world, I must add Jimmy
Britton, Myra Barrs, and Geoffrey Summerfield of the United Kingdom, Judith Newman of Canada, and Barbara Kamler, Pat Diamond
and, especially, Garth Boomer of Australia, to the list.

As a teacher of graduate students, I have been particularly
fortunate in having students who have continued to work with me
professionally as peers after their student days were over. It is
consistently rewarding for a teacher to run into one's former stu-

dents as they emerge as leaders in our field. Again it is hard to list such people without fear of inadvertently leaving someone out, but they have my continued gratitude and respect.

With specific reference to the sources of inspiration and help which enabled me to start and finish this book five people stand out for special mention.

Elaine Caret is the closest equivalent I know to the ideal uncommonsense teacher. She proves every day in a commonsense high school that uncommonsense teaching can be done and does succeed. Without her example, I'd be much less confident than I am about the real world possibilities of the uncommonsense approach.

Cindy Onore, once a student and now a professional peer at the City College of New York, not only used the manuscript of the book with her students and gave me valuable feedback from them and from her, but exemplifies in her teaching the kind of uncommonsense approach to teacher education that should become the standard for our field.

Gordon Pradl and I were graduate students together and have been colleagues at NYU for nearly two decades. Throughout that period we have struggled together to explore the ideas expressed here, and without our conversations there simply would be no book. As an editor-reader he also helped prune the worst excesses of my prose although neither he nor my other readers can be held responsible for my final choice.

Rita Brause is another former student and now a faculty member at Fordham University. Rita and I have researched together, written together, and talked together so often during the last fifteen years or so that I could never fully sort out which of these ideas are hers and which are mine. In addition to her critical reading and response to early versions of this manuscript, she consistently provided logistical and moral support throughout its composition, made more important by the fact that its first draft was completed while I was abroad. Ours has been an ideal professional and personal collaboration.

Nancy Lester sits squarely at the core of my personal and professional life. There wasn't a single day during the writing of this book when she did not provide inspiration—from the earliest conversations about it to the final critique of each successive draft. Her own dedication to the process of teacher change through inservice education and her understanding of both how difficult and important it is has been a model of how these issues must be approached. Her unwillingness to settle for the second-rate, her conviction that there are fundamental beliefs which cannot be compromised, and her unceasing attempts to enact her principles has given me confidence that these ideas deserve to be heard. Living and learning with her has been the greatest experience of my life, and it is to her that I dedicate this book.

J. S. M.

Eze-sur-Mer, Alpes Maritimes
Portsea, Victoria
Bayview, New South Wales
Wellfleet, Massachusetts
New York, New York

CHAPTER 1

Introducing
Uncommon Sense

Although this book stresses the importance of understanding learning, it also takes teaching and teachers very seriously. As a learner, a teacher, and a teacher-educator, I have experienced the powers of good and bad teaching, the manifold challenges of doing it well, and the awesome complexities of understanding all of the contextual factors which influence why and how we teach. Such a complex art cannot be described in simple terms, and the problems we face do not admit simple solutions.

If this book has a single theme, it is that schools must be dramatically changed if they are to fulfill their educational mission in a democratic society. Teachers are the only people who have the power, the commitment, the desire, and the capacity to be leaders in the process of change. But to take on such leadership roles we must substantially change our conceptions of the nature and processes of schooling. Doing so will not be easy, since most of these conceptions are based on assumptions that have not been the subject of sufficient professional scrutiny and analysis. Questioning such assumptions requires both reexamining and reinterpreting the meaning of our own learning experiences in and out of school by looking at them through new theoretical lenses.

As teachers we have too often not been questioners. We have believed it was more important to have answers than questions. We have let others determine our curricula, our teaching strategies, and the texts we use. We have resisted change by claiming that "*they* won't let me do it," without recognizing our own role as part of the "they." Or we have incorporated new approaches into the old system, so that teaching the writing process, for example, becomes a kind of long workbook whose only substantial difference from earlier ones is that the blanks to be filled in are longer.

The world in which we operate has real constraints: tests our students must pass, administrators who value the lesson plan more than the students' learning, schedules which bring us too many students for too short periods, and a student population increasingly affected by drugs and violence. These systemic problems will never be changed unless we begin to retake control of the schools we work in. And to retake control we need a new perspective— here called *uncommon sense* —on the nature of the problems we face, the goals we are trying to achieve, and the means by which we can help our students develop all of their powers as language users.

Acquiring such a new perspective is not a short or easy process. There are no quick fixes for real problems. Accordingly, this is not a short or easy book. Further, neither this book nor any book can do the job by itself. That task will require individual and collective efforts to reconceptualize who we are and what we do as teachers. The struggle will not be an easy one, but most of the professional teachers I know are neither afraid to work hard nor to go the extra mile. Their complaints are not about working too hard, but about the institutional barriers which have been created and which limit their effectiveness and constrain their autonomy.

Making the transition from commonsense to uncommonsense teaching won't be a smooth process. There will be missteps, false starts, and frustrations along the way. We will have to abandon some of the certainties which now inform our practice and learn to look at our students' learning in new ways. Students, parents, administrators, and the public must also be reeducated if uncommonsense practices are to become common. We will need, particularly, new means of uncommonsense assessment if we are to show all parties concerned the quality of learning which can result from uncommonsense teaching. Along the way teachers may have to wear a commonsense disguise in some schools in order to experiment with uncommonsense approaches.

Commonsense schools were created by people like us. Despite the powerful constraints under which we operate, people like us can work to change them. It won't be easy, but it's worth a try.

Toward Uncommon Sense

Everywhere I look these days I see common themes: humans as meaning-makers in a social context; interpretation as a constructive and reconstructive activity; mind in society; relevance theory; transactions (reader/text, writer/text, viewer/film); whole language education; *both* inside-out and outside-in learning; apprenticeship as a model for teaching and learning; critical literacy for a democracy; the language of possibility; transformative intellectuals; reflective practitioners.

I see all of these elements as the keystones of uncommon sense: learners going beyond the information given; language being learned in use; the power of narrative in learning, in memory, and in development; the normally creative use of language; and a focus on learning not teaching. But as I play with the items on such lists, it occurs to me how much they run counter to much of the *educational common sense* embedded in our culture, particularly in our views of schooling: teaching, learning, order, and discipline.

Common sense isn't uniform, nor is it a coherent body of doctrine. Clifford Geertz (1983) has shown both its internal contradictions and why it will always have them. But it's part of what counts as normal—as "reality" in a culture. In this sense, it's an aspect of what I've called "Theory 1"—the unanalyzed (and often unconscious) mental explanation of the ways things work in the world (Mayher 1982). This makes common sense very powerful because it's socially sanctioned. Since it's internalized by all of us, it structures our perceptions and, therefore, our actions.

Despite its power and cultural support, this commonsense system isn't frozen. We can change our minds. We can notice things that don't fit, and when we do, we can change our commonsense belief system. Often we don't, of course, but the point is that we *can*. In fact, the very systems that give us our early rules of the way things are seem to be the same systems that give rise to challenges. As we seek for deeper, more encompassing rules, we often notice anomalies, exceptions, or contradictions. Noticing them can trigger quite massive realignments of our mental systems. Or, to put it another way, we can tell ourselves a new story and thereby both reinterpret the past and change our expectations for the future. The very inconsistencies of common sense may help in this regard, since their conflict occasionally becomes noticeable as, for example, when "revenge is sweet" meets "let bygones be bygones."

The potential for individual and group deviations from a uniform allegiance to common sense means that at any given moment we can find resistance to the status quo if we look for it. As we explore the common sense of language education in our culture, we shall see that the uncommonsense alternatives I am proposing have been developed by a number of people whose only common characteristic may have been a capacity to question received wisdom—to ask why and not be satisfied with a conventional answer. To accomplish that, the book's structure essentially contrasts the common sense of traditional practices and beliefs about language education with a position I'm calling uncommon sense, based on contemporary theories and research on language education. My position on these issues has been developing for twenty-five years and is still being modified as I write this, so I don't expect it to be regarded as either fixed or rigid.

My goal is change: change of mind, which will, I hope, lead to a change in behavior. To accomplish the changing of minds is a formidable thing to attempt. It is hardest of all with adults who have developed a repertoire of more or less successful strategies for interpreting the world and coping with its problems and don't want to be bothered reexamining them, much less changing them. I'm further handicapped by the fact that one of the cornerstones of my uncommon sense is that *I know I can't tell, transmit, or teach anything about this directly, because my uncommon sense of learning denies the worth of such a procedure.* Language won't permit me to implant my ideas in your head directly, but language is all I've got at my disposal. Worse still, I'm confined to writing, so that all the factors which might help me if I were speaking to you directly—charm, warmth, and personality (you can take my word for it)—aren't available to help.

My words can only be part of the impetus, since you have to create meaning from them, and then you have to do the changing. So my function here is to make what is familiar and taken for granted about schools and schooling look a bit strange by giving you some new lenses to look through. With luck the lenses will correspond to some aspects of your previous system of perception, partly because this won't all be new stuff to most readers and partly because I've tried to find ways to connect the old and the new by means of other—usually nonschool—teaching and learning experiences.

Most changes don't come as blinding revelations like the one on the road to Damascus that changed Saul to Paul, but are more gradual and incremental. Let me illustrate my own change process with an example that was marked by both a critical incident and a slow evolution in understanding. During my first year of full-time high school teaching, I was teaching tenth grade English in a California suburban high school. It came time to have "The Poetry Unit" (an instance of common sense!), and I helped my fellow teaching-team members (team teaching was, and remains, uncommon sense) pick out (more common sense) some poems for the class to read. Among the poems I picked was Robert Frost's "Stopping by Woods on a Snowy Evening." I didn't think deeply about it, as I recall. But I remember choosing it because I liked it, I understood it (or thought I did, which in 1962 was the same thing),

I had seen and heard Frost read it, I could tell some Frost stories (the teacher as entertainer, another example of common sense, except for the New Critics, whose common sense didn't permit such war stories), and I was sure it would be accessible to my group of fifteen-year-olds.

So the day came, I told my Frost stories to general approval, and then I dramatically read the poem aloud. At that point I tried to get a discussion going which I anticipated would clarify the tricky passages (why all this talk about who owns the woods?) or make the students ponder the metaphysical significance of the theme. I was a competent (if mostly unconscious) New Critic and felt confident about my ability to Brooks and Warrenize a poem. But nothing happened. There were awkward silences among a group that was normally eager and talkative. If I asked a factual question, they could and would answer it, but there was no energy, no speculation, no spark.

Then came the flash: Kitty raised her hand and asked, "Why did he stop? Wouldn't he just want to get in out of the wet?" And Anne added, "What's so appealing about snow falling anyway?" It was too late to really save the day (or the poem), but I finally understood that what I, as a product of the snow belt of central New England, had taken for granted—the experience of a silent snowfall in the woods—was not shared by my students. They were Californians! Only three out of thirty had actually seen snow fall in such quantities that it stuck, and none of them had ever lived anywhere which featured substantial snowfalls.

The sudden flash, of course, was that what I had assumed would be easy and accessible was exotic and opaque. What came only gradually, and is still emerging, is a recognition that *all success-ful reading experiences—not just this poem, or poetry, or even just "lit-erature"—depend on the reader's capacity to bring relevant background and experiences to bear.* Once I realized the role that background experience played in reading, I never again saw the problem of text selection in the same way. The external, familiar world had not changed—same kids, same classroom, and, of course, the same words on the page—but my lenses were different, and I saw things I'd never seen before. With luck, you've had some of these flashes yourselves and some of your commonsense ideas have changed as a result of such critical incidents.

Toward Reflective Practice

I'll be challenging some of the common sense of professional education, and in particular, of teacher education. The common sense of the education of practitioners has traditionally been based on an approach to education which Donald Schön (1983) has called "technical rationality." This means that the professional activities of architects, doctors, engineers, or teachers are most appropriately conceived of as applying theory and the knowledge generated by research into it to the problems of professional practice. So, for example, research into the virus that causes a disease, undertaken in the context of a virus theory of disease, can lead to a vaccine which produces antibodies to the virus and thus protects the body against it. The practice of the health professional, therefore, consists of acquiring the necessary knowledge about the virus and the vaccine, and then providing it in an appropriate form for those at risk from the disease.

There's no question that many aspects of professional practice have benefited substantially from such technically rational solutions. Diseases have been prevented or cured, bridges and buildings have been built, and so on. The research that has been done on the underlying causes and effects of such problems has led to impressive technical and technological solutions. But despite these undoubted advances, the picture of technical triumph is far less clear today than it seemed only a few decades ago. Technical solutions have frequently brought new problems as fast as they have solved old ones, in part because they were usually conceived without a full understanding of their long-term consequences. DDT killed a lot of agricultural "pests," but it also began poisoning the whole ecosystem, thus having a disastrous impact on lots of nonpests. Dams have tamed the Colorado River, only to bring new problems of silt and salt which threaten to poison the very crops they are irrigating. Every new highway seems to create more instead of less traffic congestion. And even in medicine, the relative costs and benefits of improved medical technology have created new and complex questions about the worth of human life and the appropriateness of using every means possible to prolong it. What we clearly need is an ecological approach to change, which is still uncommon rather than common sense for too many people.

Furthermore, average working professionals—doctors, teachers, economists, or engineers—frequently find that the problems they confront in their real practice are much more muddy and complex than the straightforward ones that are capable of technical solutions. Research problems must be cleared of all their real-world debris in order to be studied, but real problems cannot be "controlled" so simply. Patients, students, businesspeople, workers, and clients of all sorts have families and personal histories; they are enmeshed in a web of complex social and natural forces; and they just don't behave as simply (or as rationally) as the technical theories suggest they should or will. For many professionals—including teachers—there has been a growing disenchantment with technically rational solutions for the real problems they face daily in the classroom, and a consequent growing skepticism that university theory and research, still largely dominated by technical rationality, will help them much.

This skepticism is especially understandable in a social context which values university professors—the seekers, keepers, and transmitters of the disembedded knowledge which is the cornerstone of technical rationality—over elementary and secondary schoolteachers. Even within universities, this hierarchy of values has elevated the "pure" seekers in faculties of arts and sciences above their "applied" colleagues in the professional schools. This has the unfortunate and ironic result that education professors—including me, at least some of the time—have sought to move closer to their academically more prestigious colleagues by doing research and "generating knowledge" which is less and less directly applicable to the professional context of the schools.

While some of this research and theory development has had important implications for the theory and practice of education, and, in this context, of language education, it can rarely, if ever, be thought of as knowledge which can be *applied* directly to educational problems as the technical rationality model suggests. So although I draw on much of the theory and research that has been conducted in that tradition, I try to do so throughout while recognizing that applying it requires a different sort of knowledge, what Schön (1987) calls "a new epistemology of practice" (p. 1). Central to this new epistemology is "artistry."

> Artistry is an exercise of intelligence, a kind of knowing, though different in crucial respects from our standard model of professional knowledge. It is not inherently mysterious; it is intelligible in its own terms; and we can learn a great deal about it—within what limits, we should treat as an open question—by carefully studying the performance of unusually competent performers.
>
> In the terrain of professional practice, applied science and research-based technique occupy a critically important though limited territory, bounded on several sides by artistry. There are [additionally] *an art of problem framing, an art of implementation, and an art of improvisation*—all necessary to mediate the use in practice of applied science and technique. (p. 13, my italics.)

By trying to reclaim artistry as a domain of knowledge and inquiry, Schön is trying to turn the conventional hierarchy of knowledge on its head and explore both how such knowledge works in practice and how people should be educated to perform it. Essentially, this derives from what Schön (1983) had characterized as "reflection-in-action," which combines both knowing and doing in a transactional relationship through which the doing affects the knowing and the knowing affects the doing. The result is a new synthesis of personal knowledge for the reflective practitioner which is greater than either alone.

The uncommonsense theory developed here will require the kind of artistry of implementation that Schön identifies. Its utility will depend upon the competence of professionals to frame problems appropriately so as to exploit whatever usefulness it has. One of the reasons I pay so much attention to commonsense theories and approaches is that since they dominate the process of framing the problems we are trying to solve, they seem to lead inevitably to commonsense practices as a way of solving them. *If we can see the problems we face in new ways, new solutions may be forthcoming.* And whatever the worth of the uncommonsense theory as a guide to reflection-in-action, uncommonsense teaching places a special premium on the art of improvisation. Built on a recognition that teaching and learning are too complex to be sequenced and planned too far in advance—not to mention at too great a distance from the classroom, as when the attempt is made by districts and states, textbook publishers and test makers—uncommonsense requires teachers who will be always improvising, always creating a climate for learning through the art of teaching.

Substantial change will not be easy to accomplish in any event, but it will not even be attempted by teachers and students without an equally dramatic change in their understanding of *why* language develops as it does and of the real constraints which govern its use. Fundamental to this understanding is one of the cornerstones of the uncommonsense position, the belief that language develops through genuine, purposeful use. For many of us this is not a new idea, having been articulated over twenty years ago in Dixon's *Growth Through English* (1967), and in other forms in the work of John Dewey and in many of the early position statements of the National Council of Teachers of English (NCTE). Yet its full implications have rarely been understood and even more rarely employed as the basis for changing the language education curriculum. Indeed the capacity of schools to fit even good new ideas into the commonsense framework cannot be underestimated. This capacity to domesticate new ideas into commonsense practices has been one of the principal reasons nothing much has changed even after decades of attempts at progressive reform.

This uncommonsense theory is offered, therefore, not as a theory to be applied mechanically to pedagogical problems but as one that tries to help frame those problems in new ways. It's also presented as a step toward a reform of the professional education of teachers, an attempt to recognize the importance of studying effective learning and teaching with a focus on the kind of reflection-in-action which combines knowing and doing, technical knowledge and artistry. If professors and teachers are to work effectively together to change the theory and practice of schooling, they must utilize the kind of mutual respect that reflective practice requires.

The Roles of the Readers of This Book

As readers I hope you can play a series of games. Game 1, the *Reflecting Game,* involves identifying with, recalling, sharing, and reflecting on those experiences which led to our common sense. It involves both reminiscing and identifying the interpretation we've made of our experience. This is one of the games I'm playing as a writer as well, so with luck my autobiographical excerpts will help you get in touch with your experiences both when they are similar and different. Here I hope you'll be able to say: "Yes, this is the kind of thing that I've experienced, or believed, or understood in the past if not necessarily in the present." This progress toward becoming a reflective practitioner involves comparing our knowing with our doing, our beliefs with our practices, and exploring, with artistry, the connections among them.

Game 2, borrowed from Peter Elbow (1973), is the *Doubting Game.* Here you're invited to challenge your own educational common sense, to wonder if common sense is sensible after all. Readers who from my perspective are successful will at least keep open the possibility that their commonsense beliefs may be in need of revision. And clearly the doubting game should be played with my statements as well, although I'm attempting to make them as unassailable and persuasive as possible! One of the functions of the best aspects of our noneducational common sense is to aid in playing the doubting game, but that doesn't make it easy to challenge our own commonsense positions.

The third game is the *Empathy Game,* which involves comprehending my exposition. "What is he talking about?" you may ask, or "Why is he making that connection?" or "Where does that idea come from?" This approach doesn't involve accepting or adopting my position, but rather attempting to understand why I have come to the beliefs I am expounding and exactly what those beliefs are. Doing so will also involve you in the reflecting game, and except for the necessity of separating these strategies for rhetorical purposes, it seems clear that they function more or less simultaneously during that process of meaning making we call reading.

Another game is the *Believing Game* (also adapted from Elbow). Believing does not, again, mean adopting, but rather projecting the ideas you're interpreting into the world of your experience as though they were true. For example, what would a first-grade classroom be like if there were no explicit teaching of reading, no workbooks, no basal readers, no leveled reading groups, no reading aloud of a common text, no phonics rules, no sequence of skills? How would children learn to read? What would be happening? What materials would be required? Some of these methods I will discuss explicitly, but since the common sense of our educational culture indicates that all or most of them are essential to beginning reading instruction, changing these teaching and learning behaviors will involve the imaginative projection of an alternative set of classroom structures and strategies.

Unless this book has absolutely no effect on you, your new set of beliefs will involve a personal synthesis of your old ones, my challenge to them where it makes sense, and your own emerging constructs of how they can be of use in your professional life. This stance of reflection-in-action is an ongoing process which will begin only when you finish the text. If this book is to have any lasting effect, it will do so only after its ideas have been tested in the crucible of your experience.

One final approach to the book might be thought of as the *Sharing Game*. One of the serious problems impeding change in commonsense schools remains the professional isolation of teachers. Since the shared culture of teaching remains powerfully supported by many of the implicit commonsense beliefs and practices explored here, changing that culture requires professional collaborative talk among teachers. As teachers we need the opportunity to share our tentative formulations of new ideas and approaches and our attempts to implement them in our classrooms. Finding likeminded colleagues to work with, and working to restructure schools to encourage and permit more time for such collaboration, may be the best hope for actually achieving the kinds of substantive changes recommended here.

Another way of looking at these games is to think of what you're doing as what scientists call "thought experiments," in which you test my ideas against what you think would happen in the real world. While such experiments are useful as part of the reading process, they are ultimately no substitute for primary research undertaken in our own classrooms. Such research need not be experimental in a formal sense, but it does require a concerted effort first to uncover the biases and assumptions which may be coloring our observations, and then to try to observe classroom life in as systematic, objective, and unbiased a way as possible.

For me, classroom research is really just a way of characterizing the kind of learning-through-teaching which characterizes good teaching (Mayher and Brause 1983). That is, effective teachers start their planning with a more or less explicit hypothesis about how a particular activity or set of activities will promote student learning toward a specified goal. As the activity is proceeding and after it is complete, we evaluate its effectiveness by determining how well or poorly it helped our students achieve the learning we were trying to promote. We then modify our initial hypothesis so that when we try to teach the same thing the next time, we do so in a somewhat different way depending upon our assessment of the efficacy of our methods.

As I've been writing this book, I've also continued to engage in the struggle to become the kind of uncommonsense teacher I'd like to be. I still haven't achieved all of what I'd like to, and my own classroom research tells me that I talk too much, that I'm still frustrated by the schedule imposed on my classes, and that I'm still torn between my old, but comforting, commonsense beliefs in the efficacy of "covering the material," and my growing recognition that my students learn only when *they* uncover it, not when I cover it! I've been gradually evolving toward uncommonsense practices during the twenty-five years I've been teaching, and I'm not there yet. The process of change is a long one for most of us, and it's longest of all for those who have been successful at commonsense teaching. Giving up the familiar is never easy, but doing so can be one way to make teaching the kind of rewarding and challenging business it can be.

CHAPTER 2

The Roots of Common Sense

When I graduated from college in 1961, I'd decided to become an English teacher. I'd been drifting in that direction during my four years as an undergraduate. I'd gone to college thinking that I'd be a nuclear physicist, but calculus and freshman physics had disabused me of that notion, and I migrated through history, to American studies (my actual major), to lots of English courses. These last courses were, as common sense dictated, all literature courses, organized primarily historically (The Literature of the Renaissance), biographically (Shakespeare), or sometimes generically (Modern Poetry).

I'd also been writing for the college newspaper, ending up as its editor, and during the summer before my senior year I'd had a terrific job as a reporter for a real daily newspaper. I decided on teaching rather than reporting because I liked the personal contact; and the common sense of journalism at that time was that it took too long to get off obituaries or the police beat and on to writing more interesting stuff. On this point I was wrong, since a substantial number of people who worked with me on the college paper rapidly worked themselves into interesting journalistic positions after graduation, but despite that I've never regretted my choice.

English Teaching: Circa 1961

But what did it mean to be a *teacher*, or more precisely, a secondary school English teacher? My constructs of what that

13

meant were based on having been a student. At this time I'd had no teacher education courses, and except for some informal observing and teacher aiding at the local high school, I'd done no teaching at all. So what I had to do was project from what I'd experienced on one side of the desk to what it would be like on the other. Like many—but, surprisingly, not all future teachers—I had always liked school. I'd been good at it; I knew how it worked; and I felt comfortable there. So the generalized good vibrations I felt about staying in the comfortable world of the school were part of my attraction to English teaching.

This sense of security was combined with the general altruism of youth, which was being strongly reinforced at the dawn of the Kennedy era by the plea, "Ask not what your country can do for you. . . . " Kennedy had assured us that the youth of America could rejuvenate the world; the Peace Corps had been founded—and I decided to teach high school. It was certainly a more noble and self-sacrificing course than becoming a banker or a lawyer, I thought, but why an *English* teacher?

The crucial factor here is that what an English teacher did was very clear to me: He taught literature, had kids write about it, corrected their essays, and, especially for the less able or younger students, taught grammar, usage, spelling, and punctuation. In addition to spelling there might be some vocabulary-building exercises, including roots, prefixes, and suffixes, and, on occasion, some work on formal or informal public speaking. English teachers also served as advisers for the student newspaper or yearbook or as directors of the school's plays. It was, after all, common sense.

This commonsense view of the career I had chosen was based on a broad consensus, since it was pretty generally shared by school people, by parents, by educational publishers, by students, and by the leaders of the profession as a whole. My first methods course, for example, was taught by Professor Edward Sauer using his newly published methods text, *English in the Secondary School* (1961), which articulated this general approach to defining the subject and the English teacher's role and was completely complementary to the commonsense view I already held. I was grateful for the practical advice of both book and course, but I don't remember any of it as being particularly startling, except that he expanded the definition of literature to include books written specifically for adolescents, a genre that had been only marginally a part of my personal reading history and never had been part of my schooling.

The widespread agreement on this conception of English teaching can be seen in the nearly universal use of historically based literature anthologies and prescriptive grammars. *Adventures in American Literature* (eleventh grade) and *Adventures in British*

Literature (twelfth grade) dominated the literature market so thoroughly that other competing series tended to be clones. The idea of using paperbacks in the high school literature program was regarded as a daring innovation, the sort of thing one wrote articles about for *The English Journal*. *Warriner's English Grammar and Composition* series was similarly pervasive with books that differed so little in format and substance from grades 7 through 12 that students had learned to count on regular days of essentially the same grammar and usage drills from year to year. The literature books emphasized chronology and, in the earlier years, genre, and therefore encouraged teaching *about* literature. They provided material for teaching and for testing, and both the grammar and literature texts made English seem to have a content to be taught and learned for the tests. The anthologies usually included the obligatory Shakespeare play throughout high school, and they often consisted mostly of bits and snippets from the approved masters, as well as elaborate notes and introductory comments on whose contents students could also be tested. Enduring and safe, semi-classics like *Silas Marner, A Tale of Two Cities, Treasure Island,* and the like were either included in the anthologies or available in class sets. The weight of these tomes may not have done much for the minds and hearts of American youth, but they certainly built up their muscles as they wrestled them out of their lockers and carried them to class.

This conception of English teaching appealed to me partly because I was good at what was being taught. I was reasonably confident of my abilities as both reader and editor. In particular I could read and write about literature. Actually being a writer was not really a prerequisite for English teaching in the commonsense context, but in my case my general confidence as a writer made up for my somewhat shaky grasp of how to use the comma—my own *bête noire* as a high school writer. Speaking and listening seemed completely nonproblematic to me, certainly not something one "studied," although I had done some debating in high school and college. So I was sure I had the right stuff to do the job, which is always a reason to be attracted to something as a potential vocation.

More important, however, I thought the job was important, but here I would have been much less articulate about why. Sure, I knew reading and writing were important for an educated citizenry. I'd read my Jefferson, and I was convinced that the American experiment in democracy would fail without a literate, even a critically literate, population. If I'd been pressed as to why English should be required of all students, which I don't recall ever happening, I'm sure I would have mumbled something along those lines and would have been happy to let the connection between the commonsense view of English teaching and such a critically literate body politic remain vague. I might have added something, too, about bringing out deeper humanistic feelings, developing moral values, and enhancing an appreciation for the aesthetic side of life. The implicit moral purpose of English teaching circa 1961 was based on the assumption that reading the great works of the literary canon would enrich the spirit and enlighten one's taste as well as sharpen the mind.

My initiation into the profession went quite smoothly, therefore, on the theoretical and philosophical side. There didn't seem to be much to talk about, and it wasn't talked about very much. The practical side was a little more bumpy, since Billy Blanco and Richard Chobanian weren't always as eager to receive their dose of high culture as I was to dish it out. But that only strengthened my conviction that the problem I faced was learning how to cope with the day-to-day realities of schoolkeeping, not theorizing about what it was all for anyway. So *I was certified to teach as I had been taught:* to bring democratic literacy skills and an elite cultural heritage to the youth of America.

I've begun this section with a fragment of my autobiography for a variety of reasons, including the time-honored desire to make the book interesting enough for you to turn the page (such is the power of even a quasi-narrative). It also helps to emphasize that I began teaching very definitely as a commonsense teacher. But the most important reason for including my own experience here is to emphasize that thinking about the nature and goals of language education cannot be done in a social, cultural, and historical vacuum. Each of us comes to our commonsense beliefs about what is normal, or even about what is real, in a particular culture at a particular time in its development. We do, to be sure, experience that culture in somewhat idiosyncratic ways, but even these individual experiences are undoubtedly influenced by our gender, our ethnic background, our socioeconomic status, and the educational opportunities it affords us, and even by such apparently irrelevant factors as our height. So the experience encapsulated above undoubtedly reflects to some degree the perceptions of a tall, WASP male who grew up with a secure economic outlook in the Eisenhower boom years and had an elite liberal arts education.

My perception of what secondary English teaching was for, therefore, undoubtedly had some biases built into it, including the fact that I never questioned whether or not there ought to be such a subject. But both my later reading of the crucial documents of the period, and the similarity of perceptions I found among my colleagues when I moved from the East Coast to the West Coast and actually began teaching high school full time, lead me to believe that these perspectives were widely enough shared to deserve the label of common sense. There were other points of view around, of which I had not heard, and there were some unresolved difficulties which needed attention. But most of these were regarded as technical problems of how to do what we were trying to do better rather than issues which raised serious questions about the philosophical and theoretical underpinnings of our activities.

Hierarchies of Schooling

Before I return to these issues and explore further how my common sense on these questions has changed, I need to deal briefly with one important area: the relations between primary, secondary, and tertiary (higher) education. The title of this chapter refers to language education, and yet up to now I've only been talking about teaching English, and secondary English at that. It seemed clear to me at that time that there were meaningful and real distinctions between the three levels of education. That was commonsensical then and is, for most people, common sense now. Although I'm not sure that I thought about what elementary school teachers did, it was obvious to me that they did not teach English with a capital E. Higher education people did, and indeed most secondary teachers of that era more or less openly yearned for the day when they would be freed of all the grammar and composition trivia of high school so that they could devote full time to the higher pursuit of capital L literature, which was the stuff of college English.

Since I implicitly bought into one of the most powerful beliefs of educational common sense—that people who taught older and brighter students were superior to those who taught younger and slower ones—I would have paid little attention to a book discussing the nature of language acquisition, of beginning reading or writing, or any other of the concerns of primary school teachers. Conversely, I regarded insights into the teaching of literature in higher education as providing useful approaches to my tasks. Indeed the climate then current, expressed by such documents as the Commission on English's *Freedom and Discipline in English* (1965), which was the first professional book about the nature of English teaching that my high school colleagues and I ever took seriously, explicitly stated that high school literature teaching should be a mirror of and a preparation for the study of literature in universities.

A great commonsense divide in schooling existed, and largely still exists, between elementary and secondary schooling, so those who were teaching or preparing to teach elementary school were cut off from the concerns of secondary and higher educators and vice versa. This separation derived historically from the fact that everyone was supposed to need an elementary education, but secondary education was, in the nineteenth century, available to, and believed necessary for, only a relatively small elite. Since elementary education was supposed to be devoted to the "basics," it seemed quite natural for it to develop along skill-oriented lines. While secondary school teachers taught content, elementary teachers taught reading skills, penmanship, punctuation, spelling, and the like. Given this divide, elementary teachers would be no more likely to have concerned themselves with problems of literature and rhetoric instruction than would secondary and higher education people to have worried about beginning reading and writing, except, in the latter case, to complain about the inadequate preparation of the students with whom they were dealing.

One of the crucial tenets of my current uncommonsense position on language education, however, is that while there are differences among pupils at different ages, *the basic similarities of the processes of language development, and therefore the requirements of language education, are essentially the same from kindergarten throughout the rest of schooling, indeed from birth to death.* I state this here because it seems crucially important that readers who teach or intend to teach at any level of education learn to recognize these commonalities. Rather than ignoring stories about children at a stage different from the one we teach or believing that they have no application to our situation, we will have to try to see the process of development as a continuum in which both the past and the future educational lives of our pupils play a fundamental role.

The commonsense hierarchy of prestige, which accords greatest respect to those who teach the older and the brighter, is at best merely false, and at worst pernicious. A more realistic position is that the hierarchy should be reversed, since older and brighter students usually present fewer challenges to teachers, but the most accurate view would probably be that *all levels provide significant challenges and all are extremely difficult to do well.* Such a hierarchy is pernicious in its effects on the self-esteem of both the teachers and the pupils who find themselves at its base. It's hard to feel good about who you are or what you do if the weight of the institution labels you as second- or third-rate. And it can be most disastrous for all if beginning teachers, as well as those whose competence is suspect, are routinely given such "low-level" classes to teach, as too often has been the case. I was lucky, and my potential students even luckier, that I wasn't given an entire program of low-track classes when I began teaching, since I would have taught them very badly. But there's no doubt that such classes had (and have) the least prestige and are the least likely to receive the innovative attention of the best teachers that students on higher tracks receive.

What is crucial here, however, is to explore how this prestige hierarchy came to be part of common sense, and to see why it continues to exist. In my experience such a hierarchy operates both within and across schools. It is least clear in primary schools, although elementary teachers often express comfort at dealing with younger children and a fear of the subject mastery which would be required at the secondary level. I've already noted the tendency of secondary teachers to yearn for the groves of higher academe, and even within schools the plum teaching assignments are usually the advanced placement, enriched, or honors classes. In universities, graduate, and particularly doctoral, teaching has always outranked teaching mere undergraduates. In some places this is institutionalized by having a separate graduate faculty of senior and high-powered scholars. Virtually everywhere in higher education where there is an opportunity to do so, freshman composition—the economic lifeblood and yet most despised course in the English department— is relegated to the graduate-student apprentices.

Although there are undoubtedly many reasons why the hierarchy developed and persists, the central one for our purposes in this chapter derives from the commonsense belief that *the function of schooling is to* transmit *knowledge and skill from expert practitioners to the young*. If this premise is accepted, then it follows that the most highly esteemed teachers should be those with the most highly specialized knowledge to transmit. Since more specialization and expertise are required as one goes up the educational ladder, it becomes sensible to value the graduate school scholar more highly than anyone else in the educational system, and, by analogy, to value the specialist more at every other level of schooling.

Another factor that sustains the hierarchy is the reality that teachers in higher education are much more autonomous in determining how to spend their daily time and energy than teachers in primary and secondary schools. No graduate professor would tolerate being required to turn in lesson plans, to bring a doctor's note if she were ill, or to punch a time clock, all freedom-restricting and therefore deprofessionalizing constraints which have been imposed routinely on public school teachers. In particular the choice of approaches to teaching and of the curriculum are much more firmly in the hands of university faculties than in schools. But like the other aspects of this hierarchy, if we question the commonsense assumptions upon which they are based, we see that alternative possibilities exist. If there is no inherent reason these differences must exist, then it seems clear that teachers at all levels need and must demand higher levels of professional autonomy.

Attaining these will be an important step toward creating a context within which uncommonsense teaching can operate.

Achieving this change will require political action of a sort which American teachers have traditionally shied away from. Only in the past few years have teachers even begun to voice collective concern for increasing their autonomy. American teachers have developed effective strategies for collective action only in regard to salaries, and even this activism is of relatively recent vintage; when I started teaching, collective bargaining by teachers was illegal nationwide. But until teachers can jointly recognize that curricular control is their most important right and responsibility, schools will continue to be run without substantial concern for the educational processes which should be their only real mission.

Subject English

Parallel to the development of the belief that more specialization is better than less was the development of the academic specializations themselves. Although this process had been happening fairly steadily since antiquity, English teachers frequently forget that the inclusion of English studies within the higher education pantheon is of very recent vintage. The teaching of reading and writing were always considered basic ingredients of primary education, but once these skills were acquired, it was generally believed that they needed little more academic attention, and none at all in a higher education system where language and literature study was limited to classical languages. Acquaintance with literature written in English was assumed to happen at home, and the study of Latin grammar and composition was expected to be sufficient to assure the mastery of an effective English prose style.

A full treatment of the history of English teaching in higher and even secondary education would take us too far afield here, but I will sketch some of the sources of the commonsense position and provide some suggestions for further reading. One cause derived from the steadily growing number of students who began to avail themselves of secondary and higher education during the second half of the nineteenth century and especially during the first half of the twentieth century. This expansion of post-primary student population was most dramatic in the United States, but it eventually became a factor in the rest of the English-speaking world as well. This increase in the numbers of students in high schools and colleges inevitably meant a widening of the socioeconomic stratum from which such students came. The higher levels of education, formerly reserved for the social elite, therefore began to be more accessible to and highly regarded by the middle and eventually the working classes as well. The effects of this broadening of the student population were complex (for some discussion see Chapter 5 of Powell et al. [1985] and Hampel [1986]), but from the elite perspective of the existing schools and colleges, the new cadre of students needed to become more familiar with the English literary tradition and to master the standard version of the written language. Both these demands emphasized the importance of English studies as part of the core of secondary and higher education, since socialization into the higher culture was a central part of the educational mission at both levels.

The second major factor derived from the related concern for inculcating appropriate moral values in the young. The decline of religion in industrial societies raised fears of a moral decline, and beginning with Matthew Arnold in late Victorian England, the reading of literature was offered as an effective and appropriate substitute for religious instruction in developing an understanding of the moral life. Literature also provided a concomitant opportunity to educate the aesthetic sensibilities of the young. Although this position was developed most fully in the United Kingdom, especially by F.R. Leavis and his students and colleagues, it had echoes in the United States in everything from the McGuffey Readers, which were filled with texts teaching moral and patriotic lessons, to the ideas of T.S. Eliot and the development of the New Criticism. (For further discussion see Mathiesen [1975] for the United Kingdom; Applebee [1974] and Ohmann [1976] for the United States; and Watson [1981] for Australia.)

There was, as well, a continuing concern with literacy skills, and particularly with writing skills, once it was clear that first primary and, later, secondary education had not "taught" them adequately. College professors have been complaining about their students' low level of writing ability—by which they have usually meant an inability to spell, punctuate, and employ standard grammar and rhetorical forms—almost as long as there have been colleges in the United States, as Wallace Douglas (1976) has shown. In some American universities the first pressure which created English departments came from this perceived decline in literacy skills, and courses in composition for entering students became widespread by the end of the nineteenth century.

Despite the earlier failure of schools to develop these skills with an approach that was based on the commonsense position that they could be acquired first in order to be used later, college composition courses were organized in exactly that spirit. Only this time college English professors were convinced *they* would succeed because their knowledge of (mostly classical) rhetoric would ensure that this time the students would really learn to write. The classical tradition was by no means abandoned with the inclusion of English in the curriculum. Latin composition continued to be the model of good prose, and Latin-based prescriptive grammars of English continued to have a powerful influence on nineteenth century composition instruction. They still provide the framework for most school grammar and composition books in use today. The view of writing instruction as a low-level technical problem of acquiring skills helped to contribute to the higher degree of prestige accorded to literature teaching which became part of the common sense of subject English.

The need to educate more—and different types of—students and the association of literature with high culture and a higher morality created the need for a specialized priesthood and began the process of professionalizing the teaching of literature. This was further accelerated by the fact that as literature departments grew in universities they had to compete for prestige and resources with the sciences and social sciences, which were growing in power and respect through their apparently direct associations with the rise of technology and of the economic and social complexity of the industrial world. English scholars needed to make discoveries and advance knowledge if they were to be able to hold their heads up in faculty club coffee klatches. Therefore subject English had to become more specialized and esoteric, even in some respects scientific, in order to continue to hold its own in the academic marketplace.

This growth of professional literary scholarship in itself might have been harmless enough if it hadn't affected literature teaching as well. In this century literature teaching in universities has moved steadily toward the initiation of student readers into the professional priesthood. Literary texts were presented as mysterious entities which only the initiated could properly understand, and neophytes were expected to defer or even deny their own personal encounter with the text until it had been explicated by the professorial expert. This led, naturally enough, to the students' perception of their task as literature students as not to interpret texts independently, but to regurgitate the approved interpretation provided by their teacher and the other professional scholar-critics who had already unraveled the text's mysteries. Such an approach had the additional advantage of providing the security of asking questions which had "right" answers, which seemed to bring additional, even scientific, rigor to English studies. The fact that nothing questioned means nothing gained too often was lost on these literary experts, since they rarely thought much about the effects of their pedagogy.

This situation was bad enough for university English majors, but it began to have disastrous effects when those English majors went on to become secondary English teachers. They (to be fair, I should say we) were often confused and bewildered when the students we encountered proved hostile, recalcitrant, or just plain bored with their teachers' hard-won insights into the mysteries of the metaphysical poets or the linguistic and moral subtleties of Shakespearian tragedy. It's no wonder that such teachers preferred older and more academically inclined students who, if they didn't fully believe in the new religion, were willing enough to play the game in hopes that it would lead to their admission to an elite institution of higher learning. This general set of beliefs not only characterized my education, but structured my initial approaches to literature teaching as well.

Related to this development of an academic discipline called English, which was almost entirely concerned with literature, was the development of a clearly defined consensual canon of great books. These works were believed to embody what Matthew Arnold (1873) called "the best that has been thought and said in the world," and to constitute the high culture that the school was to transmit to the young. Once again we see the commonsense metaphor of education as transmission, but here I would like to emphasize that the commonsense view of the content of the secondary English curriculum derives in large part from the development of subject English in colleges and universities. The centrality of a high-culture view of literature and the secondary and instrumental place assigned to language and composition studies is a direct reflection of this set of priorities. And, given the hierarchical nature of the educational system, the function of the lower schools was centered on the preparation of students for the higher levels.

The combination of the priority accorded to the high culture embodied in the literary canon, and the difficulties associated with getting the unwashed masses to embrace it enthusiastically, had the further effect of convincing higher English academics and their acolytes in the secondary schools that only an elite percentage of the population was capable of being fully initiated into the literary culture. Such a set of beliefs rapidly becomes a self-fulfilling prophecy, of course, whether institutionalized in a separate school system for the elite, as in England, or in the tracking within the more comprehensive high schools that emerged in the United States. The tracking system and the skills and drills curriculum offered to the bottom track reflected these beliefs and became enshrined as part of educational common sense. Such curricular distinctions were solidly in place when I began teaching, and they still characterize the typical curriculum of American high schools as can clearly be seen, for example, in Powell et al. (1985) and Sedlak et al. (1987) and in the recent recommendations of William Bennett for the ideal curriculum of his fictional James Madison High School.

What Sedlak and his colleagues observed is that the whole curricular structure of the secondary school can be characterized by their title, *Selling Students Short*. Similar observations were made by Goodlad's team (1984) for both elementary and secondary schools, and it seems to be a consistent theme of acute observers of what is happening in contemporary schools: that students have become disengaged from the school curriculum. It just doesn't seem to them to contain much that is worth learning, and little attention is paid to any motivation for learning other than the threat of tests and the promise of better grades for more effort. While this is particularly problematic for the least able and for the large group that makes up the middle ability range of the school population (the group that Powell and his colleagues characterized as the "unspecial"), it has permeated the whole enterprise except for the very few who find something in school to get excited about. And this excitement is more likely to be found in the periphery of the school curriculum—in the band or the glee club, the art room or the shop—than it is in the academic core.

Some observers and critics of the schools have called for a return to what they perceive to have been the higher standards of the past (see, for example, Ravitch and Finn [1987] and Cheney [1987], as well as the earlier report of the National Commission on Excellence called *A Nation at Risk* [1983]), but from the uncommon-sense analysis made here, such a golden age of high standards never existed except for a small minority of students. The problem of developing the potential for excellence of all students is one of the core issues facing today's educators.

English and "The National Interest"

The major problems that were perceived to exist in this commonsense framework of language education in the early sixties were not that the approach might be somehow misconceived, but that it wasn't being implemented effectively. This perceived lack of effectiveness had been brought to public awareness by the Soviets' launching of the first Sputnik in 1957. Our assumed technological superiority had been rudely challenged, and the spotlight of blame was quickly shone on the schools. These crises of confidence in the schools are cyclical phenomena. It should be emphasized that such periodic examinations of how schools are doing are both inevitable and useful, even though they usually involve more than a little hysteria and don't always lead to constructive change. Without some public and political perception that everything isn't hunky dory in the world of schools, however, there would be neither pressure nor opportunity for change.

Within the world of English teaching, the first flush of the Sputnik crisis brought little concern, since the problem seemed to reside more in the province of science and math education than in English. But since reading ability clearly underlies the ability to understand science texts, and since English teachers had inherited from their Latin teaching ancestors the claim that the study of language and the writing of clear and effective prose were intimately connected with the ability to think, it wasn't long before English and language arts teachers were under public scrutiny as well. And once it became clear, through the passage of the National Defense Education Act (1958), that federal money was available for teacher education and curriculum development in those areas that were deemed essential to the national defense, then English teachers wanted to join the gravy train along with their colleagues in the sciences. They eventually achieved their goal through vigorous lobbying by the NCTE and the publication by James Squire and some colleagues of *The National Interest and the Teaching of English* (1961, with a second report in 1964), which argued that since literacy skills were crucial to all aspects of education and every profession, even the most scientific or technological, English should be included within the purview of the NDEA.

One important aspect of that successful lobbying effort should be noted, however, and that is that although most secondary school English curricula were strongly literature-centered, the argument on behalf of the importance of English to the nation barely mentioned literature. The argument was made on behalf of literacy skills; and yet not only were these not the central concerns of English teachers, even more ironic, they were not things that English teachers were very good at promoting. Few techniques were available to help develop student writing abilities except the discredited teaching of prescriptive grammar and the similarly ineffective "assign-and-correct" mode of composition instruction. But the claim of essentiality was based not so much on the idea that English teachers were doing these things well, as on the notion that it was important to do them. The problem, therefore, was to upgrade the performance of the profession.

The effect of this renewed attention to English was not conceptually revolutionary, however, but was used to attempt to increase the professionalism of secondary English teachers within the commonsense framework. The discovery that lots of people teaching English had not been English majors was one condition put forward to explain poor instruction, and the remedy for that was to provide secondary teachers with advanced courses in the "content" of English. Parallel federally- and foundation-supported efforts would attempt to further develop, rationalize, and give a sound academic foundation to the English curriculum.

Equal blame for poor educational performance was attributed to the pernicious influence of institutions for teacher education and their supposed continuing devotion to the progressive educational concerns of educating the whole child instead of teaching academic subject matter. Courses in methods of teaching came in for particular assault as academics in faculties of arts and sciences looked with horror at the emphasis on teaching teachers how to teach rather than on mastering the content of the subjects they were teaching. This attack focused most directly on the preparation of primary school teachers, who had always been expected to be masters of all the academic trades, but it was now claimed that they didn't have the academic background to do so. But even secondary teacher training was derided as being at best a watered down version of the real stuff of the academy.

There was certainly more than a little truth in many of these criticisms, and indeed the preparation of teachers had, and still has, many serious defects. Most of these derived more from the continuing low status which was accorded to schoolteachers and therefore to those who prepared them than from weaknesses in their subject matter preparation. They derived further from the belief in the technical rational basis of professional preparation, which accorded the most prestige to the "pure" theories of the arts and sciences which were presumed to provide the knowledge base to be applied to practical professional problems (Schön 1983). Advanced academic knowledge of the discipline being taught is, at best, only a partial and in some ways a completely wrongheaded solution to the alleged problems of poor instruction. This is particularly true if the content and methods of instruction in higher education bear only a tangential relationship to the concerns of primary and secondary teaching, as is the case in English. High school and college English departments have the same title, but their focus and concerns are quite divergent.

Ironically, in some ways teachers were better than their training during that period because education in the fifties and sixties continued to attract the best and the brightest of American women, since so many other professional doors were closed to them. As those doors have been opened in recent decades, women have deserted education for more prestigious careers. One reason the status of teaching must be improved is to attract talented women (as well as men) to the field once again.

The Tripod Curriculum

The conceptual framework for improving English teaching in response to Sputnik can be seen most clearly in the previously mentioned *Freedom and Discipline in English*. Prepared by a Commission on English (1965), dominated by higher education professors appointed by the College Entrance Examination Board, the document clearly emphasized that the purpose of high school education was preparation for college study, and therefore that the definition of English should be in the hands of higher education academics. There was some attention paid to the needs of the noncollege bound, but in general what they were supposed to need was either a watered-down version of the high culture curriculum (since they were not going to have a further dose of it in a university), or remedial attention to skills so that they would be at least minimally literate and therefore able to function as democratic citizens. Although the *Freedom and Discipline* approach was more determinedly academic and focused on higher education than was common in American schools, it was not a radically new conception of the goals or nature of English teaching. It continued the effort by higher education institutions to determine secondary school instruction which had begun with the report of the Committee of Ten in 1893.

The curriculum they endorsed and which was reflected in the book's sections was that of the tripod of literature, language, and composition study. The tripod metaphor sought the strength associated with three-legged stools, but the committee paid little attention to how these three facets of English study were to be unified, except to recommend more writing about literature and that language study be done, where possible, in the context of the student's writing. The structure of their report and its separation of the three subjects it reflected, actually encouraged the independent treatment of each aspect. The commonsense pattern of secondary English instruction was thereby endorsed, and teachers could go on —as most still do—teaching literature, grammar, and writing in separate compartments, usually on different days of the week, and letting whatever integration is required happen in the minds of the students rather than in the practices of the classroom.

Literature

One of the principal thrusts of *Freedom and Discipline* was to continue to expand the importance of literature teaching and, especially, of literature study as it had been developing in higher education. This approach was somewhat ironic in view of Squire's contemporaneous argument in *The National Interest* that literacy skills, not literature, were the primary goal of English teaching, but it accurately reflected the focus of higher education English departments—and higher education English professors wrote the report. Literary criticism was the order of the day, and secondary teachers and students were to become practitioners of this arcane art. A sample critical essay by a professional critic was even included as a model to be emulated, and teachers were encouraged both to become more expert critics themselves and to pass that knowledge along to the aspiring scholars that their students were assumed to be.

While the goal of increasing the depth and power with which students read literature seems unobjectionable enough, the actual effect of the literary and critical emphasis, still within the framework of content, was to increase the teacher's role as expert interpreter and to reduce the chance that students would be empowered to make their own sense of what they read. The basic teaching structure continued to be whole-class teaching of teacher-selected texts. And the class format and the kinds of literature tests that were given continued to encourage students to memorize the "facts" of the text ("Where did Silas bury the money?" or "How was the witches' prophecy fulfilled in *Macbeth*?") or, if interpretation was required, to restate an expert interpretation previously provided by the teacher, by a literary critic, or by the growing number of *Cliff's Notes*.

All this seemed commonsensical enough, since teachers and professional literary scholars probably *can* read more expertly than ten- or fifteen-year-olds, and if we had expert knowledge to pass on, why should we be hesitant to do so? And, indeed, if expert reading practices are thought of as strategies for encountering and making meaning from texts, there may be considerable virtue in having the teacher model how we proceed as readers. The major drawback to this approach as it was implemented, however, was that the products rather than the processes of literary analysis tended to be presented (and tested); students were rarely encouraged or allowed to encounter texts on their own to develop their authority as readers. Where an initial encounter was permitted, the structure of the subsequent literature class was usually based on the teacher's more or less gradual demonstration of superior understanding of the work, thereby squashing all dissenting views.

Whatever the theoretical merits or demerits of the commonsense approach to literature, its most evident failure can be seen in the fact that it has not produced generations of powerful readers who continue to enjoy reading literature on their own after they have left school. The best research documenting this has been done in Australia by Jack Thomson (1987), but similar findings can be derived from readership surveys in the United States, which show that there was no golden age of American literature appreciation. (For a discussion see Suhor [1988].) What Thomson found in Australia, what the readership surveys have shown, and what is particularly insightfully documented in a study by Janice Radway (1984) of readers of romance fiction, is that although the secondary school curriculum has continued to focus on the canon of approved classics, teenagers and adults predominately like to read texts that are considered by English teachers to be of lesser quality. While there may very well be value in such reading—and I certainly enjoy it myself on sunny summer days—it is not what the commonsense approach to teaching literature as articulated in *Freedom and Discipline* sought as a goal.

Indeed the long-term evaluation of any approach to teaching rests not in whether or not students can pass the tests or write the critical essays we demand of them in school, but in how their schooling influences their adult capacities, attitudes, abilities, and choices. If students leave school believing, for example, that poems are mysterious objects which provoke pain and confusion more than pleasure or enlightenment, then they are very unlikely to make the reading of poems part of their reading repertoire after they have escaped the requiring reach of their English teachers. And they are less likely to feel a need or desire to make literature part of their children's early experiences. If the long-term goal of literature teaching is to promote lifelong reading, as it is from the uncommonsense perspective, then any approach which makes that less likely to happen must be critically scrutinized.

Composition

The limited or even harmful effects of commonsense English teaching can be seen even more dramatically in the failure of commonsense writing instruction to produce a population of competent, confident, and comfortable writers. While serious literature may be subsequently merely ignored by most school graduates, writing is more often than not viewed with fear and even panic. While many people do manage to find pleasure in reading as a pastime, even if the texts are mostly escapist fiction, writing, for most of them, is a chore to be avoided if possible and one to be done quickly when it cannot be, as if it were bitter medicine to be swallowed as fast as possible. If asked, most high school and all college graduates will more or less cheerfully claim that they are pretty good readers, but almost every group of adults I've ever worked with had strong doubts about their abilities as writers.

The first thing that should be noted about commonsense writing instruction is that there really was—and is—very little to it.

That is, what has passed for writing instruction has been either more or less careful teacher marking, correcting, and commenting on student writing, or instruction in the formal features of writing: grammar, punctuation, spelling, and the approved structure for paragraphs and essays. Teacher comments and corrections were intended to provide a basis for improving the next paper to be written, since only rarely were students expected to make revisions of the paper that had been so marked. Rules of grammar and punctuation and maxims about beginning paragraphs with topic sentences and having an introduction, a body, and a conclusion were designed to provide guidelines and a framework which would help student writers control the written system. While endless hours were devoted by teachers to these commenting practices, research has shown that they are largely ineffective in helping students learn to write. (For a summary see Brannon and Knoblauch [1982] and for some analysis see the NYU dissertations of Ziv [1981], Peitzman [1981], Onore [1983], and McCracken [1985].)

There were very few opportunities for student writers to choose personally meaningful topics to write about or personally meaningful readers to address: Virtually all writing was done on teacher demand, on teacher-set topics, in teacher-determined forms, and written almost entirely for the teacher, who functioned as grader and judge. The major limitation of teacher comment as a means of writing instruction was that the paper was usually so devoid of interest to the student writer that on receiving the comments back from the harried teacher, he or she was unwilling, even if it might have been possible, to abstract from the idiosyncratic comments on paper A to some general principle which might have been helpful in composing paper B. I remember being greatly affronted when students didn't even look at the comments I'd so laboriously made, just checked their grade and tossed the paper in the wastebasket. Even that was not enough evidence to shake my faith in the practice or its commonsense justification. I usually blamed the student!

Further, if the comments were mostly focused on the formal features of the paper, as was usually the case, such marks implicitly emphasized that the major concern of school writing was not what you said but how you said it. This was justified by the commonsense view that one first learned to write by means of school assignments, so that when the time came to write in the real world, the tools for doing so would be at the writer's command. One of the responses to the demands for better writing instruction in the post-Sputnik era in which I was involved was the creation of a new composition curriculum which consisted entirely of recommended assignments for students to complete. I remember four of us work-

ing diligently one hot summer to frame a sequence of such assignments with careful attention to their rhetorical genre demands
—narration, description, persuasion, argumentation, and exposition—and being concerned mostly about giving students an opportunity to practice using comparison and contrast, supporting
generalizations with examples, and so on. Although we tried to
make the topics interesting, it didn't really matter in our scheme of
things whether or not school writing was itself meaningful for the
writer; what counted was acquiring the skills necessary to be able
to write later, in college or in the working world.

The prevailing perspective held that if such skills could be
developed without writing at all; by doing grammar exercises,
memorizing spelling lists, learning punctuation rules, so much the
better, since that would be the most efficient possible method. In
fact, too much attention to meaning was generally thought to be
a drawback, since that tended to encourage students to employ
forms or set themselves writing problems which outstripped their
skill capacities. And for most teachers and students, these drills
and exercises really were believed to be writing instruction, since
they were supposed to lead to the mastery of the formal features of
standard written English. Again, research has shown that they do
not fulfill that instrumental role, as I discussed in my doctoral
dissertation (Mayher 1970).

This mechanical aspect was, and is, the major element of the
public's common sense of language teaching. When parents, business people, and politicians complain about the failures of English
teaching, their major complaint is with our failure to teach people
to spell and punctuate, not with their lack of capacity for clear and
powerful expression, and certainly not with our failures in developing literary appreciation. Even students, particularly those who
have had problems with writing and have found themselves in
remedial writing classes, are usually convinced that what they need
is a good dose of grammar and spelling instruction and that this
will somehow solve their problem. People may not like having
papers bled red by English teachers, but they are convinced that
such practices are essential to their success. The English teacher
who doesn't assault student texts is criticized as soft or lazy, while
those who do are often held by students in the highest esteem as
someone they may not like, but who is giving them the real stuff.

Even otherwise quite progressive English teachers frequently
feel guilty if they don't engage in this ritual. This feeling stems
partly from their own adherence to the commonsense endorsement
of its importance, and the associated belief that error correction is
the route to improvement, and partly from a kind of fear that if they
don't do it, they somehow are letting down the side of literacy. It

is almost as though there is a great English teacher in the sky looking over their shoulders as they read student work, one who threatens a thunderbolt if too many spelling errors or comma splices slip
by. Such English teachers seem to believe that not calling student
attention to errors will develop bad habits, which will become more
and more deeply ingrained and therefore virtually impossible to
root out, even though research shows that this is not the case.

Language/Grammar

For many of these teachers, errors of grammar and usage seem
to be yet another sign of the moral decay and decline in standards
which everywhere pervades modern mass culture. They (we?) see
themselves as the last bulwark against a rising tide of barbarism
which threatens to engulf an increasingly permissive society. One
such teacher, writing in an inservice course about the importance of
teaching grammar, made an explicit connection between the lack
of grammar instruction and the concomitant decline in standards in
schools and the narcissistic pursuit of pleasure through purchas-
ing designer jeans, listening to rock and roll, and using drugs,
which she found so horrifying in her relatively affluent suburban
students.

No one would deny that there are serious problems in our
society, but a causative relationship between holding the line on
error correction and such problems seems far fetched. It is, however, widely accepted, but given the fact that the complaints about
student incapacities to master such conventions have been a constant feature of educational criticism for over one hundred years,
the antiquity of such complaints makes it hard to keep believing
in the commonsense view that there really was a golden age of
literacy when everybody learned these things to which we should
return. In a time of rapid and accelerating change, a nostalgic belief
that things were better when we supposedly paid more attention
to form and structure is very appealing, and it continues to be a
powerful force affecting the nature of schooling and its language
education components.

The continuing pressure to teach more grammar is one of the
most enduring aspects of the common sense of language education. It was ratified in *Freedom and Discipline*, even though there
were disclaimers about the ineffectiveness of doing so outside the
context of student writing. The root cause of the concern for grammar instruction stems from the oft-noted fact that language usage
is one of the surest signals of social and educational status. The
capacity of language to send such signals and the capacity of language users to interpret them makes almost all people linguistically

insecure once they venture beyond the boundaries of their home and neighborhood.

Given these linguistic insecurities and the development of a mass educational system, one of whose missions was to ensure more equal access to further education and economic success, the commonsense belief developed that there was an instrumental connection between knowledge of the rules of language (i.e. grammar and usage) and success in using it appropriately. It was surely common sense that if you wanted to speak and write like a member of the successful segments of society, the surest route to doing so was to learn the rules they followed. And, beginning in the eighteenth century with the work of Bishop Robert Lowth (1762) and Lindley Murray (1790/1800) and continuing through the nineteenth century into our own, a plethora of prescriptive grammars were written which prescribed the socially appropriate linguistic rules for the rising, but linguistically insecure, middle class to follow (for discussion see Baron [1982]). While the problem was and is a real one, the "solution" usually aggravated rather than solved it.

Such grammars were often woefully inadequate as descriptions of the linguistic features involved. In many cases they failed to accurately reflect the nature of English by insisting that the elegant version of English was more like Latin, a language where infinitives cannot be split—because they are one word not two—and where there are no multiple purpose words which sometimes function as prepositions—and therefore cannot end a sentence—and sometimes as verb particles—where they can and often do. The classic parody of the stylistic absurdities produced by such "rules" was Winston Churchill's: "There is some nonsense up with which I will not put." (How many of you noticed, or were offended by, the split infinitive two sentences back?) The inaccuracy of such grammars is not as important, however, as their confident tone. They were taken as authoritative by teachers and students alike, so that the connection between knowing the rules of language as encoded in them and mastering linguistic appropriateness to achieve educational and economic success became deeply embedded in educational common sense.

One of the things that makes me recognize that the project I am now engaged in is a formidable one is that the power of grammar instruction to effect change in language use has been one of the most heavily and steadily researched areas of education, yet every single study has shown little or no connection. From the 1890s to the present, study after study has been conducted to explore the direct instrumentality of grammar teaching. They have been conducted by people who believed there was a connection, and so it is likely that whatever biases they had would have tipped the balance in favor of grammar's instrumental role. And yet a connection has consistently failed to appear; in study after study the students who know their grammar best just don't write (or speak) any better than their less knowledgeable peers. In fact, if an effect shows up at all, it is usually slightly negative. (For discussion see Hartwell [1985] and Hillocks [1986]. For reviews of the research see Braddock et al. [1963], Mellon [1969], and Sherwin [1969].)

Further, these studies are, as educational research goes, relatively well-known. Their challenge to the commonsense position has made them newsworthy both within and without educational circles. And yet, despite the fact that they have had considerable impact on the people who have been instrumental in forming the uncommonsense position, they have rarely dented the common sense of either educators or the public at large. There are many reasons for this, including the depth of the insecurities alluded to above, the strength of the conviction of a connection between linguistic and social manners, and a feeling on the part of insecure writers that they would be all right if they'd only really learned their grammar when they were in school. The particular hold of this belief on commonsense English teachers may have been strengthened by a confusion of correlation with causation by teachers who did learn their grammar at the same time they were learning to write and, quite understandable, believe that mastering the former led to success in the latter.

My sense, however, is that the deeper reason for this continuing conviction is that teachers in particular and the public in general have never had an adequate understanding of the nature of language, of language learning and development, or, indeed, of learning, through which insights they might be able to understand why no such instrumental connection could be expected to be found. The beliefs about language and learning held by prescriptive grammarians made such a connection seem commonsensical, and when they failed to find it, they more often than not looked for technical explanations for its nonappearance, still sure in their hearts that it really was there. It may not be likely that my attempt in this book to place this connection in a different context will be any more effective than the noble band of scholars and teachers who have argued this position before, but I hope that if the nature of the debate can be changed, it may allow us to see what legitimate role language instruction can and cannot have in schools.

Nothing in the uncommonsense position should be taken to mean that linguistic form doesn't count or isn't important. The debate is not between people who have high standards and care about form and those who are sloppy and unconcerned with linguistic propriety.

The dispute is properly construed much more in terms of means than ends, particularly if those ends are viewed from a long-range perspective. The way we write and speak and spell and punctuate does count, but it is vitally important to remember that the most significant reason it counts is not a matter of linguistic etiquette or even appearing to be middle class, but of making it easier for readers to make meaning from our texts.

I don't want spelling errors or comma splices to mar the surface of this text, because I know as a reader that they distract and confuse, and I need all the surface smoothness I can muster to enable my readers to get on with the job of meaning making.

And as a writer, I know that confusing *there* with *their* or *to* with *too*, or leaving out commas, or mangling syntax will defeat my communicative intentions as surely as will muddled thinking or infelicitous examples. But I also know several other things: I don't need to worry overmuch about these problems when I'm composing this draft, because I'll have a chance to go back to it and rectify whatever errors I can catch. I know further that I can call on others to help me do so, and that this will not only not be cheating but is standard practice for all writers. And perhaps most important, I understand that whatever facility I have in doing these things did not derive from my study of grammar, even though I've studied more grammar than all but a minute fraction of the population. They derived, instead, from meaningful use, and I am still learning them. *The instrumental role of meaningful use as a means of learning provides one of the sharpest contrasts between the theories underlying uncommon- and commonsense practice.*

Common Sense Meets Personal Growth

The tension reflected in the different priorities assigned to literature teaching and literacy skills in the two documents I have been discussing, *Freedom and Discipline* and *In the National Interest*, was the key internal conflict of commonsense English teaching in the mid-1960s. When the American leaders of English education met with their British peers at the first international conference on the teaching of English, held at Dartmouth in 1966, the American concerns were directly focused on the question of *"What is English?"* They hoped to find a way to reconcile the tensions they felt between the public pressures to teach skills and their desire as English teachers to pass on the cultural heritage through teaching the literary canon. The American participants at the conference were somewhat astonished, therefore, to find that their British colleagues were not asking that question at all, but were concerned, instead, with "*How* is English?" That is, how can the ability to use English in all four modes be developed in all learners?

The British perspective as described by John Dixon in *Growth Through English* (1967), his report on the Dartmouth meeting, centered the focus of concern for language education on the individual language learner. Called *the personal growth model of language education, it stressed each learner's linguistic capacities and concerns for meaning making through language.* The capacity to use language was seen as the greatest of human resources for making sense of the world, for communicating to others about it, and for learning; and the function of language education was to provide the means of facilitating the growth of the individual's language capacity.

This position's central challenge to the American version of common sense was the idea that "language is learnt by operation, not by dummy runs" (Dixon, p. 13). This proposition, which had developed from a variety of sources, including the study of language development and the nature of reading and writing, directly confronted the commonsense view that it is both necessary and more efficient to learn to read and write through exercises, drills, workbooks, and other dummy-run activities in order to be able to do so later meaningfully. Meaningfulness and the student's purpose in using the language had to become the primary determiner of whether or not a particular learning experience would be effective in promoting language development. It further challenged the cultural heritage position by making it clear that it was the meaning the learners made from the texts they read which would determine how they responded to them, not the teacher's or the higher education expert's sense of why they were significant or important.

A further dimension of the personal growth model of subject English was its insistence on imagination and creativity, not as aesthetic frills or the province of the cultural elite, but as a vital part of the linguistic and human capacities of all learners. Imaginative and creative work had always been suspect in the commonsense tradition as not quite serious enough, not the hard stuff of the world of facts, rules, and ideas. Common sense had developed a sharp dichotomy between cognitive (good) and affective (suspect) kinds of learning, but the personal growth position was not only arguing for the centrality of the educated imagination but also insisting on the inseparability of the cognitive and affective domains. It makes many teachers uncomfortable to think about the education of feelings or of the creative powers of their students, but once we recognize that every sentence contains both cognitive and affective elements for both its maker and its interpreter, the importance of the connection begins to become clear.

That commonsense English was not one of the creative subjects was eloquently testified to by a fifteen-year-old girl writing in
1969 about what she did and didn't like about school. She wrote:

> I enjoy, and do well in, the creative subjects like art, music,
> and history. I don't like subjects that aren't creative like sci-
> ence, math, and English.

Her teacher queried (in red ink!):

> Can't English be creative?

And she replied (in pencil):

> Sorry, not for me.

Given the dummy-run quality of commonsense English instruction, it's hard to argue with her even when we wish, along with her
teacher, that it wasn't true.

Whereas the traditional conception of the English curriculum
had derived its content *a priori* from the list of skills that must be
mastered or from the literary canon, the personal growth approach
maintained that we must start with the concerns of the students
and with the competencies they have already mastered before they
arrive in our classroom. The content of English, therefore, is of relatively less concern than the processes of meaningful language use
which alone will develop those linguistic capacities further. Students must read, write, speak, and listen in purposeful and active
ways if they are to develop; therefore the content of English derives
primarily from the needs of the learner as a language user and as a
thinker, creator, imaginer, learner, citizen, and future parent.

This does not mean that *teacher* knowledge of the cultural
heritage, of the nature of language, or as a result of the ways to
facilitate language development is any less important as a result;
indeed it is probably more so. What it demands, instead, are teachers with a wide repertoire of knowledge and skills who can deploy
them appropriately as needed. The security and comfort provided
by the preset curriculum in which one knows in the fall what the
year will entail is gone forever, since until one has met one's students, it is impossible to determine what they will need or will want
to work on. Given the need to allocate texts and avoid duplication
within a school system, some general parameters or constraints
for the sake of curricular organization will still be needed, but the
American dream of the curriculum where the content of each day
can be determined before the first bell rings for the year has to be
dismissed as the illusion it has always been.

Despite the reality that the actual processes of instruction have never fitted all that neatly into the boxes that the curriculum said they would (partly, of course, because such curricula were usually written by people who weren't actually teaching the children, like my composition committee, or determined by textbooks written by people even farther removed from the school), teachers have often been frightened by the apparent lack of predetermined structure and sequence in this approach. One of the major securities provided by the commonsense tradition has been its apparent confidence that there was a predeterminable sequence of content and activities which was to be followed for all students. The more cynical defenders of the tradition have sometimes claimed that this was necessary since teachers can't be expected to think for themselves. It is certainly true that many teachers haven't had much experience in doing so (any more than their students have!), but there is no reason to believe that once we try it, our superior knowledge of the students we are actually teaching won't enable us to do better than a textbook publisher in Chicago, or the curriculum supervisor in the district office, at determining what and how to teach.

To do so effectively, of course, we will need a different kind of education, or reeducation in the case of experienced teachers, than has traditionally been provided. The final success of the implementation of an uncommonsense approach will depend upon teachers recognizing and developing their own expertise as students of the language and learning processes in their own classrooms.

The Impact of the Personal Growth Approach

Dixon's exposition of the personal growth model had a powerful impact on many of the graduate students in English education in the United States, including me, and it has had some effect on teaching practices as well. But it has not, for the most part, really dented the commonsense position on the nature of language education. There were some significant exceptions, most notably in the work of James Moffett (1968a and 1968b), but long-term effects have been very sparse. Personal growth has had more impact in some other areas of the English-speaking world, most notably in New Zealand, Australia, and the United Kingdom itself, but even in these countries, the practitioners who were influenced by these theories have remained a minority. The power of the commonsense tradition has continued to be influential, and surprisingly uniform, around the English education world.

Despite my emphasis on the skills and cultural heritage models as characterizing the common sense of English teaching, there were other traditions in language education in America which meshed better with the process and developmental aspects of the personal growth approach. Springing in part from the progressive tradition, and particularly from the writings of John Dewey, earlier eras of secondary English teachers had developed what they called life experience curricula which had many similar goals and methods to those of the personal growth model. (For discussion of these cycles see Applebee [1974].) And the National Council of Teachers of English had traditionally resisted the overacademic emphases of its colleagues in the Modern Language Association, which consisted mostly of English scholars in higher education. (For discussion see Hook [1979].)

In primary schools, the progressive's emphasis on teaching children rather than subjects has never been completely abandoned, although the attacks of such critics as Rudolf Flesch in *Why Johnny Can't Read* (1955) on what he called the look-and-say method of reading instruction brought a renewed emphasis on phonics instruction, as did the creation of the so-called linguistic approach to reading by Leonard Bloomfield and Clarence Barnhart (1961). Whether in phonics, linguistics, or basal reading programs, children in American primary schools were largely reading texts as things to be decoded, not as meaningful encounters. And the texts themselves were mostly committee-written and controlled for their level of difficulty, using such criteria as their linguistic structures and their vocabulary in conjunction with a skills approach.

During the immediate post-Dartmouth period, a renewed attack on the mindlessness and inhumanity of American schools was mounted by such neoprogressives as Jonathan Kozol (1967), John Holt (1964), Herbert Kohl (1967), and Neil Postman and Charles Weingartner (1969). For a time it looked as if education might be one of the venues where lasting social change would emerge from the social and political turmoil of the Vietnam era. It certainly seemed to many of us that there was a real chance for such changes to occur, and lots of experimental programs were set up which called into question a wide range of commonsense beliefs about the nature and purposes of schooling. I was involved for a time with one of them, the creation of a community-controlled alternative high school in East Harlem in New York City (such were the buzzwords of the time), which opened for students in February 1971 with me as a volunteer teacher. Stanley Aronowitz, who was one of the leaders of the school, describes what it was like and what went wrong. (For a fuller discussion and analysis see Aronowitz and Giroux [1985], Chapter 4.)

At Park East we shared all of the misconceptions of the rest
of the movement. We attributed [student] alienation to the
"straight curriculum" of the public schools, their authoritarian
style of leadership, and the failure of schools to inspire teachers to dedicated pedagogy. Our view was that the curriculum and governance had to be (a) relevant to students' lives
by becoming more practical without succumbing to the anti-
intellectualism of vocational education, (b) become less rigid
to allow students a wider range of learning options, (c) involve students as well as parents in the processes of school
governance. Of course, we made no political analysis of the
reasons the old curriculum was inadequate or administration
had become arbitrary. We attributed its inadequacy merely
to the fact that it was imposed from above, without regard to
student needs. In short we accepted the canons of student-
centered education but, at the same time, made the claim that
such an orientation had outcomes that would satisfy the concerns of parents, college admission officers and employers.
We claimed that students could master the three Rs without
recourse to teaching and curriculum styles that "turned them
off." We accepted the implicit assumption that a "caring"
learning environment was often the sufficient condition for
motivating students to learning. At no time in our rumina-
tions over the crisis in learning did it occur to us that the
problem might be broader than the power of the schooling
environment. We assumed that good teachers and excited
students, given their autonomy by an activist but non-direc-
tive administration, and political support from parents and
other community organizations, would reverse the tendency
of schooling to grow more distant from education. . . .
  Of course, we were wrong. (pp. 58–59)

Aronowitz goes on to analyze the failures of such schools in
sociopolitical terms, and he and Giroux are very persuasive in their
arguments that until educational reformers come to understand
and bring appropriate pressures to bear on the political context
in which schools operate, there will be little hope for schools to
really affect either their students—particularly the traditionally dis-
enfranchised that Park East tried to reach—or society at large.
Their perspective and that of others who, like them, have discussed
the political and ideological structure and content of schooling,
must be included as part of the uncommonsense perspective. Indeed the vigor and power of the so-called "back-to-basics" movement, another way of characterizing much of common sense, which
dismantled whatever reforms had been successfully achieved dur-

ing the later 1970s, was greatly enhanced by the fact that the commonsense goals of schooling were not adequately addressed within the political context of the time.

As a teacher at Park East and as a supervisor of student teachers there, I was mostly concerned with finding a curriculum and a teaching approach which would engage the students and thereby, in effect, entice them into a commonsense tradition. I, too, had more failure than success, but in retrospect I realize that my failures, and those of many of the student teachers I worked with at the school over the next few years, stemmed in part from our lack of understanding of effective alternative means or ends for language education. We were only halfway toward uncommon sense: we did care a lot, and that helped, and we brought kids in contact with books that they cared about and enjoyed reading, and that helped too. What we didn't accomplish was to help students find a means of more fully developing critical powers of literacy. They needed this if they were to find the capacity to both critique and participate in the power structure of the world in which they lived. And while we were, as Aronowitz and Giroux point out, most successful with those who were already self-directed and orally competent, we had much less success with those who (in their words) "needed a *reason* to become educated in the ways of industrial or post-industrial society. [For them] there was nothing self-evident about the canons of mathematical calculation or of bourgeois humanistic traditions" (Aronowitz and Giroux, p. 60). Their common sense was not ours, and we didn't have enough else to offer except our energy and concern.

Contemporary Common Sense: Cultural Literacy and Excellence

As this book is being written, the primary manifestations of common sense in the debates about schooling are exemplified by the call for increasing the knowledge base of American students with the clear implication that this will raise the level of excellence they attain. What is ironic in this debate is that while it is really a renewal of the old tensions between the skills and cultural heritage positions whose uneasy alliance makes up common sense, both parties to the debate blame progressives from Rousseau to Dewey to the more recent neoprogressive movement of the late 1960s for what has been perceived as a decline in standards and the growth of ignorance. From the uncommonsense perspective, what seems to be happening is that the advocates of more traditional content in the school curriculum (exemplified, for example, by Ravitch and Finn [1987], Cheney [1987], and William Bennett) are attacking the progressives for what really are the results of the earlier conservative response to progressive proposals: the heavy and largely content-free skills emphasis of the back-to-basics movement.

That these concerns have struck a responsive chord with the American public, or at least the American book-buying public, can be seen by the emergence and long and successful run on the best-seller list of two books addressing these concerns: Allen Bloom's *The Closing of the American Mind* (1987) and E.D. Hirsch's *Cultural Literacy* (1987). Bloom's book is concerned mostly with higher education, and with elite higher education at that. But the enthusiasm which greeted his nostalgic case against the relativizing of American values, his sense that the morals of Western culture have been eroded by a do-your-own-thing, anything-goes philosophy, and his disparagement of American students (and most of his faculty colleagues) as barbarous cowards who have caved in to intellectual anarchy has shown that there is a profound discomfort among at least the elite of this country that things are out of hand and getting worse.

Hirsch's concern is that we have lost or are losing the common cultural background that is essential to the ability to read anything from the classic texts of our cultural heritage to the front page of today's newspaper. In addition to learning everyday words like *run* or *love* or *breakfast*, the meanings we construct as language users also depend upon a specific set of concepts (and their associated labels) which are specific to each particular culture. In a sense, of course, so are the everyday words, but the American cultural relevance of such words as *democracy, baseball,* or *assembly line,* of such proper names as *Thomas Jefferson, Babe Ruth,* or *Henry Ford,* or of such phrases as *manifest destiny, unassisted triple play,* or *workers of the world unite* are much clearer and more specific. Sharing the general mental models or schema of a culture is an important aspect of becoming a member of it, and it is clearly part—although only part, since criticism is as important as conformity—of what schooling is all about even in cultures where schools don't look much like ours.

Hirsch is right in insisting that such cultural literacy is an important aspect of learning to read, and, although he doesn't dwell on it, learning to use language in all other modes as well, but he is wrong in his conception of what it is and how we acquire it. Where Hirsch goes right is in his sense that in order to read the literature of a culture, broadly defined to include virtually any written text, readers must share a set of associated schema or mental models of such things in our culture as democracy, baseball, and assembly-line production. Hirsch goes wrong in two ways: first in his insistence that there is one and only one culture worthy of acquisition in a complex, multicultural society like ours, and secondly in his sense of how we acquire our own individual mental models of the culture. The first mistake has garnered most of the rage that the book generated, for Hirsch had the temerity to include a list of items which the subtitle of the book characterized as "what every American should know." Hirsch has been rightly criticized for various biases inherent in the list, in particular for its seeming to give undue attention to the importance of white Anglo-Saxon males. And it seems clear that his list is also generationally biased to emphasize those things that were experienced by, and of value to, educated adults born before the Second World War. But even a broader and more encompassing list would still miss the point that our mental representation of the culture is not structured in the form of an out-of-context list, nor do we learn or acquire it in such ways as Hirsch suggests.

By presenting his list, Hirsch seems to be suggesting that what is essential is not a real experience of, say, reading Shakespeare, but a kind of superficial acquaintance with key names and concepts sufficient to recognize them when they are used in a text. Further, it seems to be his view that one should acquire cultural literacy first—preferably when young and eager to memorize lists —and then use it when one reaches higher education. (In some ways Hirsch's complaint is an extended example of the all-too-common bemoaning by college professors of the lack of appropriate background experience in the undergraduates they teach.) While the problem may be a real one, the solution is not to increase list memorization in schools but to recognize that genuine cultural literacy only derives from meaningful encounters with the cultures one is to become literate in.

The problem *is* real enough, since commonsense schools, particularly those which have based their approaches to reading instruction on the back-to-basics, skills-before-substance approach to reading instruction, really have not given their pupils much experience with the central texts of our culture, whether they are children's literature or more adult fare. Commonsense secondary schools have tried to compensate for this by running students rapidly through a bits-and-snippets exposure to cultural heritage, but they have usually done so in ways which encourage little meaningful engagement with the texts chosen, and by giving fact-based recall tests which demand memorization of the periphery of literature (names, dates, schools of thought, and so on). This can all seem pretty normal to American commonsense teachers (and students), but it horrified Ken Watson of Australia when he visited an American high school class and saw the "Brahmin poets"—Holmes, Lowell, and Whittier—"covered" by a one-time-only reading of one poem apiece, with little time to engage with any of the texts because they apparently all had to be "done" in that period. (I was even more chagrined than Ken when he told the story because it sounded all too familiar to me from my own early teaching.)

Cultural literacy must be understood as a two-way street; its acquisition, like the acquisition of the rest of language, is dialogic, based on both the learner's growing sense of what she wants and needs to understand about the world she lives in and the culture's prior experiences about how best to convey this. That is, in part at least, the basis upon which curriculum decisions are and ought to be made, but all curriculum decisions are subject to either implicit or explicit negotiation between learners and teachers (and, more generally, the school). It is important to notice in this context that cultures are fluid, that they can and do change, and that the culture appropriate for one generation may not suit its successors. One hopes for some continuity in such matters, and certainly one of the great potential benefits of helping children learn to read is to assure that they won't be isolated from either past or present cultures. The ease with which today's children master the culture of computers, compared to the reluctance and terror the machines often provoke in their elders, is a powerful illustration of the process of cultural change at work.

As in the case of the rest of our vocabularies, the vocabulary and concepts of our culture are highly structured, interrelated, and complex entities which must be acquired in meaningful contexts if they are to be productive. No amount of memorizing lists or running pell mell through a cultural heritage anthology will do it; lists are not even a sensible way to conceptualize how our cultural constructs are organized. Children can and do learn the facts and labels for them with ease and power in contexts where doing so is important to them. Consider, for example, the relative cultural literacy of adolescents and adults in such domains as rock-and roll music, or horror movies, or surfing. The problem is to try to make the so-called high culture of the past as relevant, as vital, indeed as interesting, as the daily teenage culture of fast food, designer jeans, and television sitcoms. Accomplishing this is not easy, but if we genuinely value such things, then we can and will find a way to do so. But the way will not be through lists, or out-of-context memory exercises; the way will be to find a path which brings them meaningfully alive in the contemporary reality of children and adolescents. And if we can't? Then maybe their importance has been overstated.

The contemporary debates about the nature of what children learn and how teachers should teach remind us once again what schools and teachers have too often forgotten, that educational issues are frequently political issues in the sense that they are debates about the nature and future of society which go far beyond the walls of classrooms. What teachers and students do, individually and collectively, matters both within and without the school itself. The uncommonsense position is political in that it is committed to democratic educational values that promise all children the right to an education which will develop their full potential as language users to a level of critical literacy. It is also political in the sense that it recognizes that many of the people who express or act on commonsense assumptions do so because they are either worried about the possibility of turmoil that such a critically literate citizenry might present, or because they are convinced that such attainments are beyond the powers of all but a small fraction of the student population. Both views tend to support the excessive concern for the top echelon of American students which has marked both the Sputnik-inspired era of school criticism of the late 1950s and the fear of foreign, particularly Japanese, technological and economic power that inspired *A Nation at Risk* and gave rise to the current spate of school critiques.

If a new progressive movement is to succeed where the neoprogressive movement failed, it will need, in addition to a political analysis, an alternative conception of language and literacy education which meets societal demands for high standards of literacy without compromising our concern for meaningfulness and developing the critical competencies students need in their roles as future citizens. The Jeffersonian foundations of American education demand such critical competencies, and as many observers pointed out during the Irangate crisis, the deeper problem was not whether Ronald Reagan was in control of policy and events during it, but why the American public had ever thought he could be or would be, based on his record both as Governor of California and in his first term as President. The failure of schools to develop a critically literate public of the sort Jefferson had in mind may not be the only explanation for America's continuing inability to critically scrutinize candidates and officeholders, but it certainly plays a significant role. The uncommonsense approach suggested here will provide just such an alternative.

CHAPTER 3

Commonsense
Learning

Although I began as a commonsense teacher, I can now recognize that while I'd been a pretty good student in commonsense schooling environments, I hadn't been, myself, a completely commonsense learner. In particular I had a strong capacity to try to make schoolwork meaningful whenever I could, and in retrospect I know that I was most successful when I could do so. Sometimes this approach got me in trouble, like the time when I was to do an oral report for Mrs. Wilson in sixth-grade Geography about a trip from Boston to New York. The chapter in our textbook described the trip by way of the Boston Post Road and discussed the eighteenth-century postal system which had kept the colonies in touch with each other and had been so essential to developing intercolony unity. It was this contact which enabled the colonies to share their grievances against the British and eventually led to both the Revolution and the forming of the United States. This description was interesting enough stuff, and I had enjoyed reading it—all the more so, probably, because the eighteenth-century road ran near Worcester, Massachusetts, where I grew up, and its twentieth-century descendant, part of U.S. Route 20, still ran nearby. But because the material had been thoroughly covered in the chapter which the whole class had been assigned to read, I decided that my oral report would take a different route. I'd describe the trip by train along the shore route from Boston to New York via Providence and New London.

This made the project much more interesting to me. I researched the new route, including a description of the train, the cities and countryside which would be seen, and some of the history of both Rhode Island and Connecticut. I prepared some illustrations—carefully mounted on colored construction paper—and a map large enough to be seen by the whole class. When I started to give the report and said we were going by train, Mrs. Wilson had seemed a little nervous, but since one could also go by train over a route similar to the Post Road, she still wasn't sure what I was up to. But as soon as it was clear that I was heading for Providence rather than Worcester, she cut me off, told me to sit down, and explained to me (and to the whole class) that I'd done the wrong sort of report. What she'd wanted, she said, was an oral report on the material in the chapter on the Post Road. There could—even should—be some additional research, but the format and information of the book was to be the model.

Although I remember very clearly the humiliation I felt more than thirty-five years ago, I still don't know whether or not her assignment had been sufficiently explicit to preclude my uncommonsense response. I remember being just as sure that I was right as I'm sure she was positive that I had done the wrong thing. What was (and is) clear, however, was that she intended me to make a commonsense response to the assignment—to recapitulate and regurgitate the text—and that I had not done so. Since she had the power in that situation and there was no appeal, I did the report over two days later, this time taking the commonsense path.

What I learned from it, I now realize, was that commonsense teachers make commonsense demands, and that students had better learn to play the school game by its commonsense rules. I was, by that time, sufficiently secure as a learner not to let the commonsense limits of schooling completely constrain my learning, but I'm sure that others might not have been so independent. In retrospect it seems clear to me that one of the real dangers of commonsense schooling is that it places significant limits on what children are supposed to learn and makes it either unnecessary or, as in this case, risky, to go beyond them. Having a school curriculum that builds a floor all children should achieve makes a certain amount of sense, but when that floor also becomes the ceiling, the effects will be disastrous.

One facet of being the kind of commonsense teacher that I was when I began, however, was that I had not reflected very deeply on the nature of learning. It was another area where my ideas had been formed primarily by my experience as a student, when what seemed centrally important was the content to be learned; the only learning problems I had personally confronted were those of how to remember the material being taught in order to pass the test on it. Even my confrontation with Mrs. Wilson seemed to me to have been a dispute about appropriate content, not about the relative merits of independent versus regurgitative learning. If there were other learning processes involved, they had escaped me, and if the commonsense constructs of learning I had developed were potentially problematic, such problems were not in the forefront of my awareness. Indeed, given the way common sense is built, it couldn't be otherwise.

As I started teaching, I soon became aware that some students were learning more easily than others and that some material seemed easy for students to learn and other concepts seemed more difficult. Even this awareness didn't cause me initially to question my ideas about learning. Like most commonsense teachers, my team-teaching colleagues and I focused most of our attention on trying to organize and present the material in more effective ways, usually by having a different starting point or a better sequence or otherwise modifying the content to be taught. Since our goals were to transmit information about the cultural heritage and develop skills in language use, we discussed in our planning process such issues as, for example, how much historical or biographical background the class would need in order to read Emerson and Thoreau, and then explored how best to present it. We then lectured to transmit the background we'd decided was essential. It was rare for us to consider any change in the kinds of learning processes the students would engage in, and even when we did so, as when we decided to read *Billy Budd* aloud rather than having the students read it on their own, it was a decision that was more likely to be made on the basis of making the material presented as accessible as possible, than on careful consideration of how one really would go about learning to read or write better. We never really questioned *the fundamental tenet of commonsense schooling: that students learn what teachers teach.*

And like many other believers in the common sense of schooling, we attributed most of the problems students had to limits on their own capacities and/or lack of willingness to work hard. Like most commonsense teachers we didn't question the tracking system under which we taught, because we believed both that some kids were innately smarter than others, and some were lazier than others. The smarter kids were properly segregated from their less able peers, we felt, because otherwise their progress would be slowed and their achievements restricted. The less skilled (who were also frequently the laziest, in the sense that they were least likely to do the required work) had to be taught separately both to prevent their contaminating the good apples in the school barrel, and because they needed more consistent monitoring to assure that they did the work. For them the focus of instruction was appropriately skill- and drill-centered, since they needed this extra help to achieve the skill levels needed for graduation. The fact that this extra drill didn't actually seem to help much, and that students almost never moved out of the lower track, didn't worry us because it confirmed our self-fulfilling belief that these kids really weren't as capable as their peers.

Commonsense Metaphors for Learning

One of the clearest ways of uncovering the largely unconscious commonsense constructs of learning that teachers and schools operate with is to examine the metaphors we use to characterize learners and learning. These include: the learner as empty vessel to be filled with the content of education, the learner as maze runner who needs to master the basics of complex processes by learning them separately and in an appropriate sequence, the learner as sponge who absorbs information and squeezes it back out when appropriate, and the learner who practices through drills to develop good habits and avoid bad ones. One thing common to all these metaphors is that learning involves responding to stimuli, or ingesting undigested information. Another common metaphor for learning, that of nutrition, does suggest some digestion, but the actual processes of schooling often work against digestion by requiring the material being fed to the learner to be regurgitated on tests before it has been absorbed.

Stating these metaphors so baldly may not be as revealing as looking further at our commonsense language about these processes. Learners are frequently characterized as having a large or a small capacity in their mental vessels, or as having different levels of translucency: Some are bright, others are dim or dull. Some of us have minds like steel traps which retain the information we receive, while too many of us find ourselves characterized as sieve-like, the information sluicing on by us. Even the notion of exercise, so central to schooling, implies that mental workouts are required to ensure the development of both skilled performances and good study habits.

The concept of skill itself is not usually recognized as metaphorical, but when we look carefully at how it is used to characterize such things as our abilities to pound a nail and play a scale, to recognize an initial consonant blend, or to write a paragraph with a topic sentence, we can see that it provides only a loose conceptual cover for a multitude of different types of processes. What these competencies share in the commonsense view is the notion that complex processes and abilities are to be understood as consisting of a set of simple skills which can be separately mastered. This idea in turn gives rise to the notion that some skills are basic, and to the belief that the way to acquire the complex wholes is to master the simpler parts and then put the whole thing together.

It seems so completely commonsensical to proceed in this bottom-up direction when learning to read or write or play the piano, or even to solve quadratic equations or to understand the causes of the First World War, that the normal patterns of schooling have consistently been organized to reflect such sequences. Indeed the only major debates that have tended to occur about how to do this most effectively have been about what the optimum skill sequence is and when it should be begun, not about whether or not such a sequence is the best characterization of the learning processes involved. The organizing metaphor involved here might be characterized as that of erecting a building, where it seems natural enough to start in the basement with the foundations and move upward toward the roof.

What is frequently forgotten in the building metaphor is that before the foundations are laid, there must be an overall conception of what the building will be used for and how it should look. Insofar as schooling is concerned, this is not usually recognized as a problem, since the teachers collectively are supposed to know the purpose for which the skills are needed, and the student-workers need only take it on faith that a building will eventually result from what may seem to be pointless activity. This may or may not work well in a mass-production assembly line—there are, apparently, some severe problems even there—but it seems even less clearly effective as a blueprint for human learning. In practice, this fragmentation can lead to even more disastrous effects, since many individual teachers have only a sketchy understanding of the relation of the skills to be mastered in their particular grade or subject to the whole building. The activities practiced in, say, Grade 5, may not actually be foundational to the same building as those of Grades 3 or 7.

Together with the bottom-up sequence from simple to complex, the commonsense view of learning has also, consistent with the empty vessel metaphor, emphasized the centrality of outside-in processes of development. Whatever children bring to the learning encounter is discounted in favor of an emphasis on what the environment, and particularly the instructional environment of teachers and texts, brings to bear. Indeed, as Phillida Salmon (1985) has pointed out, the reason we have schools for children is "the assumption that because they are still young, they do not as yet know much" (p. 23). This, in turn, is tied to another commonsense notion: the development from ignorant, incompetent childhood to knowledgeable, competent adulthood which seems to be borne out in our own experience and supported by our adult memories. Some of us may, at times, also remember that this wasn't the way it seemed to us as children or, particularly, as adolescents, when we were sure we were often more competent than adults gave us credit for. Whether or not we were right, as I still think I was in my confrontation with Mrs. Wilson, or wrong, as I'm sure I often was in other contexts, this difference in perspective is not part of, or even recognized in, commonsense schooling.

The outside-in, "teacher-knows-best" emphasis of schooling is supported by the commonsense view that learning is predominantly a deliberate and usually conscious process. We know when we are learning, goes the commonsense account, and we must work—even work hard—to do so most effectively. It may be pleasant enough once we have learned something—we can feel good about having mastered the times tables, the phonics rules, or the difference between *their* and *there*—but doing so is likely to be quite tedious, boring, and painful. The commonsense equation seems to be that if it's painful, it's productive; if it's fun, it's trivial and a waste of time. This conception of learning provides a rationale for the emphasis in schools on memorization, drills, and exercises as we struggle to learn the labels for the parts of speech and to analyze the structure of a model paragraph. And if no one enjoys doing it very much, not to worry, because the competence thus acquired will stand us in good stead when we leave school and move onto building the real buildings of our real lives.

One of the most powerful examples I've ever read of the pervasiveness of these commonsense views among students as well as educators was the description by James Herndon (1968) of his first year of teaching. He was teaching in what has euphemistically come to be called an inner-city junior high school, meaning that most of the students in it were black and poor. Like their supposedly more advantaged peers, these children had already learned what school was "spozed to be" and were somewhat disconcerted by Herndon's uncommonsense teaching approach. Through a credentials mix-up, he was taken out of the classroom for a month in the middle of the year and replaced by a substitute. When he returned his students greeted him warmly but with some trepidation for, as they complained, "She was a *real* teacher." They had had homework every night and quizzes every day. He looked in the gradebook and discovered that, sure enough, there was a long string of marks for each child. Most of them, including those of the speaker, were zeros, however, and when he asked the class about that, they agreed that they hadn't actually done the work but had found it very comforting to have had such a teacher, since having such things required was, in the words of the title of his book, "the way it spozed to be" (Herndon 1968, p. 101ff).

The kids' conviction that the normal paraphernalia of schooling is an essential ingredient of learning was deep and powerful even if they also knew they couldn't or wouldn't do the drills and fill in the required blanks. Its even more powerful hold on educators, who both could and did play the school game well, should not be a surprise to any of us, since it has been long recognized that such experiences are the most powerful factor in shaping teachers' constructs of teaching and learning. And for teachers, such constructs have been further supported by most of the learning theories which have formed the staple of the educational psychology course required for certification. While I think it would be wrong to place too much emphasis on the role of such courses in shaping teachers' constructs of learning, the fact that these courses largely have not challenged the commonsense view helps explain why there has continued to be such a cultural consensus on these issues, with professionals and nonprofessionals alike holding essentially the same commonsense views.

The power of these commonsense metaphors for learning and the drills-and-skills practices that support them provide one of the most impenetrable barriers to changing the patterns of schooling. Even when teachers want to change, the administrators they work for and the students they work with may be made so uncomfortable by new patterns of instruction that they will fight to return to the old system. Changing patterns of learning and teaching in an individual classroom may be very difficult, therefore, without changing the structure of instruction and its associated testing process as a whole.

Behaviorism: Support for Skills and Drills

Although many of these beliefs and practices grew out of our commonsense experience of learning in commonsense schools, they did get academic and theoretical support from behaviorism. This theory was initially developed by the Russian psychologist Ivan Pavlov using his salivating dogs, but it was further developed and applied to an American educational context by John Watson and, particularly, by B. F. Skinner. The fundamental postulate of this theory of learning was that learning involved a process of operant conditioning, in which learners were reinforced (essentially rewarded) for producing appropriate behavior. The paradigmatic examples of such learning were hungry rats learning to run mazes efficiently to get to their food reward as quickly as possible, or pigeons learning to peck their way through a complex sequence of flashing lights for the same sort of reward. There were some explorations of negative reinforcement by, for example, administering electric shock whenever the maze runner inappropriately turned left instead of right, but although this was found to have a strong initial effect, it didn't seem to produce the same level of long-term learning as positive reinforcement and had other adverse effects such as discouraging the rats from trying the maze at all.

One of the potential difficulties facing behaviorist accounts of learning, the extrapolation of results derived from studying rats and pigeons to explain the process of human learning, was essentially dealt with by ruling out any concern for the internal structure of the learning organism. The name "behaviorist" itself reveals this methodological approach: The only thing that need be and can be accounted for is what people (and rats, dogs, pigeons, and so on) *do*. We have no access to and need have no concern for such invisible qualities as motives, intentions, or mental states. In fact, for Skinner, as he argued most powerfully in his influential *Beyond Freedom and Dignity* (1971), concerns with mental states and structures gave rise to what he characterized as a series of harmful myths, like human freedom and dignity, which had, ironically, actually enslaved human beings by denying them the chance to develop the full potential which only a behavioristically structured technology of behavior could ensure. His utopian (?) novel, *Walden Two* (1948), is a powerful and frightening evocation of what such a world would be like, made even more scary by its uncomfortable resemblance to the schools we know so well for those of us who haven't given up on the ideas of freedom and dignity.

Behaviorism developed in part in response to the inadequacies of earlier introspectionist approaches to psychology, which had hoped to account for human mental properties by having people report what they were thinking and feeling. Clearly there were serious problems of reliability in such reports, and behaviorism's throwing out of the mental baby along with the introspectionist bath water was also supported by the rise of the positivist approach to scientific evidence. This view essentially believed that only observable phenomena were subject to objective verification. Both positivism and behaviorism were skeptical of explanatory theories based on deduction; they insisted instead on the primacy of bottom-up inductive accounts of complex processes which excluded both unobservable inferences and the idea that intentional states could be appealed to as the cause of behavior.

This is probably the best example I know of a conflict between the common sense that people develop on the basis of their experience and the educational common sense that informs and underlies schooling. All of us believe that we often, if not always, base our behavior on our intentions, and that we represent those intentions somehow in our minds. Although the precise nature of how such intentions and other mental states interact with behavior is not fully understood, they are nevertheless recognized as a central factor in the uncommonsense learning theories which have been developed to challenge the behaviorist/positivist account. In this case, I hope that readers can call upon the common sense of their own learning history—particularly their ways of learning outside schools—and explore how it conflicts with the commonsense behaviorism of traditional teaching and learning. When we are learning for our own purposes outside a school setting, we don't choose to run the equivalent of mazes but instead keep our attention focused throughout on the ability we are trying to develop or the knowledge we are trying to acquire.

In schooling, however, this kind of experimentally based common sense becomes uncommon. The educational commonsense notions of externally controlled (outside-in), atomic skills (bottom-up) learning achieved through drill and repetition continue to dominate. Although teachers and even textbook writers may not be deliberately choosing behaviorist practices, the commonsense approaches they use do conform more closely to behaviorist than to more cognitivist, uncommonsense accounts of the teaching and learning process.

The effect of behaviorism on schooling was to further reinforce the prevailing tendency to view learning as the acquisition of a step-by-step sequence of skills. Analysis could break down complex processes like reading into a set of behaviors that must be mastered, and these could then be sequenced from simple or basic skills on up to more complex ones. This approach could be extended in the case of reading to an analysis of texts themselves, so that they too could be presented to learners in a simple to complex order. Such analysis is the source of readability formulas and the classification of texts by grade-level difficulty. And since such internal or mental concerns as meaningfulness or the reader's interest in the texts were ruled out of consideration, reading was assumed to be more effectively learned from books filled with sentences like "The fat cat sat on the mat" without the distractions that "uncontrolled" texts inevitably presented.

Any boredom that might have resulted from such instructional experiences was to be overcome by the steady dishing out of rewards in the form of right answers. By breaking down complexities into simple and carefully sequenced steps, each learner was expected to be able to proceed smoothly, and therefore with growing confidence and satisfaction, although these were rarely mentioned, from ignorance to knowledge, from incompetence to skillful performance. The security of such a scheme is that *every question has a right answer*, which is, of course, known by the teacher (or at least by the writers of the teacher's manual that accompanied the text or workbook). Learning right answers has become one of the foundations of the common sense of school learning, reinforcing the view that even though the process may be tedious, it is building a solid foundation of secure and unimpeachable knowledge and skill.

Carried to extremes in the form of programmed instruction, such approaches didn't prove very popular with either teachers or learners. Learners couldn't be counted on to keep their noses to the program's grindstone long enough to get its expected benefits, and teachers frequently resented being cut out of the learning transaction by a book or a machine which was even self-correcting. The most stultifying boring learning routine I remember being subjected to was trying to master behaviorist learning theory through Skinner's programmed text (Holland and Skinner 1961). The pace was so maddeningly slow that I kept losing the thread, and it was almost impossible to make any sense of the forest of the larger ideas as my fellow students and I wandered through the trees of subconcept after subconcept. It certainly didn't give *me* much satisfaction to be able to fill in blank after blank successfully, and little was retained, as that section of my final exam clearly showed! My painful memory of that experience, even though it was enlivened by a guest lecture by the great man himself and some terrific films of pigeons playing ping-pong, may help to account for some of my personal hostility to behaviorism, but my critique of its effects on schooling in general stems from other sources.

Programmed instruction in its fully developed form never had much success in schools, but it has returned in a new guise through the growing availability of computers and computer-aided instruction. The flexibility of the computer, as well as its capacity to repeat the same or similar exercises over and over again, has brought new life to the programmed instruction format. For one thing, the computer program has the apparent capacity to personalize its interaction with the learner. One of the first things such programs ask each user is to type in his or her name, which is then used to "encourage" the learner ("Congratulations, John, you got that one right!") or to put a velvet cover on the steel hammer of criticism ("Try again, John, that answer isn't the correct one"). Learners are then expected to keep plugging away at the drill. Because computer graphics make drills visually exciting—even the positive or negative comments are often accompanied by cutely drawn smiles or frowns—the boredom associated with the drill is, at least initially, often disguised.

But as Frank Smith (1987) has pointed out, boredom is not the worst problem with such computer programs in language education. The real difficulty is that like their workbook cousins, they are sending children the wrong message about reading and the skills it requires. By robbing them of a chance to understand whole texts and by putting all of the emphasis on bottom-up bits, children learn that reading is neither enjoyable nor a source of anything meaningful which could enrich their lives. They may or may not do the exercises, but the deeper meaning they make from the encounter is that reading really isn't anything much to get excited about, and, therefore, not really worth investing much mental energy in.

Commonsense Schooling and the Control of Learning

One of the controlling myths of commonsense schooling, as noted earlier, is that students learn what teachers teach. This has a corollary which suggests that whatever students learn, they must have been taught. These two myths seem to derive from an even less conscious construct: that it is possible to determine in advance not only what children need to learn but also the optimum sequence and means through which they should learn it. In some ways this is a natural consequence of behaviorism, but more deeply it may derive from the assumption that adults know best what is good for children whether or not the children believe it. The educational consequences of this belief are powerful, for they sustain both the idea that schools can and should completely preplan and prestructure all student learning experiences, and that whatever children know on the basis of what they have learned outside school has no significant consequences for the curriculum or the classroom.

Prestructuring is the hallmark of skills instruction whether it takes the form of programmed instruction, the controlled lesson structures recently advocated by mastery learning programs, or the "scientific teaching" promoted by Madeline Hunter. This total control illusion assumes that all children learn the same way, differing only in their rate of learning. Even instruction programs sold as individualized—as most computer programs are—are only individualized significantly for rate of progress, not for means of learning.

Another aspect of the control of learning that impacts on learners is the implication that learning is a completely individual process. Learners are expected to master the content and skills of the curriculum privately and completely. Learning in a commonsense classroom frequently seems to be played as a zero-sum game in which if Anne gets a high grade, then George will have less chance for one; in which for every winner there must be a loser. (Grading on a curve is built on this assumption as well.) Nor is this problem limited only to commonsense classrooms. Indeed some of the early implementations of the personal growth model have been criticized for ignoring the social context of children's learning.

While it is undoubtedly the case that all of us do learn as individuals, we usually do our best learning in a community of learners which features collaboration. If competition exists, it is not competition against other individuals for a finite number of rewards, but competition against agreed upon standards of performance. In such a situation, it is possible for everyone (or no one) to achieve these standards, and so working together can have the potential benefit of increasing each individual's level of success without necessitating that some will succeed and others will fail. Perhaps most significant of all, restricting learning environments to individuals working alone robs learners of the opportunity to learn to function in the kinds of team and collaborative environments which are much more typical of the workplace than solo performances.

Some commonsense schools have recently begun to respond to the problems of such approaches by trying to base their instruction on supposed differences in learning styles among children. Unfortunately, such differences have been too facilely assumed to be identified with racial and/or ethnic differences, so that for the most part they continue to ignore intra-group differences. Further, the instructional options are still based on the myth that instruction can be controlled and structured in advance, so little gain results from the attempt except that some children may be lucky enough to meet an approach that helps rather than impedes learning.

Commonsense Discrimination:
Grouping, Tracking, and IQ

The relatively narrow range of individual differences which schools take into account in their curriculum structures stems from the related beliefs that there are identifiable, and essentially fixed, learning capacities each learner brings to school, and that cognitive growth proceeds through a fixed set of stages from childhood to maturity. Although there has been continual debate about the relative roles played by genetic inheritance and environmental influences in determining children's capacities for learning once they arrive in school, there is little doubt in the commonsensical mind that some kids have it and others don't. Further, this belief is strengthened by the apparent fact, supported by research as well as teacher experience, that whatever gaps are apparent when children arrive at kindergarten tend to widen steadily as they progress through school. In reading, for example, the children who are the slowest to learn to read seem to fall more and more behind their faster peers as the grades roll on.

Whether or not this really means that children's potentials are genetically or even culturally predetermined is open to question, however, since such failures to make progress may be an artifact of the instructional approaches used with children of all levels of ability. If school instruction is structured to respond to a relatively narrow range of student performances, for example, or if particular kinds of student behaviors are seen as signals of future success or failure and responded to in this way, then what seems like an appropriate school response to student differences in capacity may instead be actually a process of turning differences into deficiencies. In his study of the reading group structure of a kindergarten class, for example, Ray Rist (1970) found that children were assigned to three reading groups by the eighth day of their school experience. Two striking facts emerged from his observations: first, that the basis for table assignment had nothing to do with the children's reading ability (none could read) but everything to do with the teacher's perception of their socioeconomic status; and second, that in the three years he watched this class, *no child ever moved up a group*, although several children moved *down* either from the highest group to the middle, or from the middle to the bottom.

There is no disputing the probability that socioeconomic factors do influence children's capacities to profit from school instruction, but these may have less to do with the general deprivations of poverty or a split-up family than with other related conditions such as how much children are read to before they come to school, or the school's attitudes toward such differences and its instructional responses to them. In Rist's study, all of the children were black, as was their teacher, and, relative to the rest of American society, they were all poor. But some were on welfare and others were not, some had both parents living at home and others did not, and some had neater and cleaner clothes than the others. The teacher apparently used these criteria to place the single-parent, welfare, least well-dressed children in the bottom group, where they stayed. Rist also showed some clear differences in the ways they were treated by their teacher including the fact that, except as objects of discipline, the bottom group received less of her attention, and when they did get instruction there seemed to be a clear expectation that they would do poorly.

One class of children in St. Louis, Missouri, does not a general case make, but Gordon Wells and his colleagues' longitudinal study of children in Bristol, England (1986), and Walter Loban's of children in Oakland, California (1976) showed similar results of differential attention and lack of upward mobility. Wells's study began before the children were in school and discovered some striking differences in the ways they interacted linguistically in their homes and, in particular, some almost astonishing differences in the amount they were read to. The most extreme difference of the latter sort was between a boy who had been read over 6,000 stories by the time he went to school (including, of course, many repetitions of the same story) and a girl who had never been read to at all!

The differences that Wells found in family language and reading patterns did not conform simply to socioeconomic differences of the sort that Rist's teacher had used to group the children, but once the children got to school they were treated as though they did. The effect of this treatment in the schools that Wells and his associates observed was similar to Rist's in that the schools' efforts to help children with perceived linguistic deficiencies did not actually improve their chances of school success. By not building on what was actually a considerable level of oral competency in even the child who had never been read to, and by not recognizing what a difference that might have made in her initial ability to cope with print, the school's program of special help in language instruction actually exacerbated her problems and seemed to diminish her capacities.

We do not fully understand the relative contributions of nature and nurture and the role of the child's home environment in shaping her capacities for school learning (which may not be the same at all as her capacities for learning in general). Nor do we know what instructional programs are appropriate for children who, for example, have or have not been read to extensively before they get to school. Even in my brief treatment of these issues here, however, I hope I have at least raised questions about the commonsense assumption that children's capacities are somehow given, if not at birth, then relatively shortly thereafter.

One of the reasons this belief has persisted, of course, has been that such judgments have been institutionalized in the structure of schools, whether in reading groups, separate tracks or curricula, or even in separate schools. (For a thorough discussion of the impact of tracking on schools and students, see Oakes [1985].) It has been further supported by the apparent scientific validity accorded to the process of intelligence (or IQ) testing, which has played a prominent role in forming our commonsense constructs of human learning potential throughout this century. Proponents of IQ testing have been firmly on the side of nature or genetic inheritance in the nature/nurture disputes, and their supposed capacity to measure an unchanging and unchangeable general intelligence factor has become a firm part of our commonsense constructs of individual differences.

Like the consistent failure of contrary research findings to shake the commonsense belief in the instrumental effectiveness of grammar teaching, the commonsense belief that some people are more intelligent than others, and that this difference can be measured by IQ tests, has survived a variety of research findings which call the whole enterprise into question. Unlike grammar teaching research, IQ studies have been found to have employed outright fraud, for example, the case of the now notorious "studies" of identical twins separated at birth conducted by Cyril Burtt. Burtt was knighted for his contribution to science for this work, which purported to show that such children had virtually identical IQs even when they were raised in very diverse circumstances; but he was found after his death to have made up most of his data, having invented numbers of cases of twins who never existed and used them to "prove" the power of the inherited factors which determine intelligence.

While fraud has been the exception even in the IQ research tradition, Stephen Jay Gould's powerful *The Mismeasure of Man* (1981) has made a convincing case that the whole tradition of trying to identify a single intelligence factor has been fraught with class and racial bias, with methodological errors in population selection, in statistical treatment, and in ways that results have been both interpreted and reported. Indeed, recent theory and research has begun to develop a notion of what Howard Gardner (1983) calls multiple intelligences, emphasizing that each of us has very different capacities in symbolic, linguistic, musical, spatial, and other abilities. This theory makes even more ludicrous the notion that there is one unified factor which can be used to classify us all as quick or slow. It remains true, to be sure, that school success probably depends more on some than on other aspects of our human capacities, but this fact should make us question the appropriateness of the current structures of schools, not cling to an unchanging, unifactor account of human potential.

It should also cause us to question the nature and role of learning in school and out. Although the best common- and uncommonsense teachers have always tried to take account of children's interests and backgrounds in class activities, the idea that children are and always have been powerful learners out of school rarely figures in commonsense curricula or teaching approaches. Children's acquisition of language, and with it the fundamental structures of their culture, their capacity to play games including, significantly, fantasy and imaginative dramatic play of the sort that Vivian Paley (1988) illustrates, and their emerging understanding of the workings of both the physical and social worlds they live in are rarely exploited in the commonsense curriculum. This systematic separation has the effect not only of devaluing the competence that children have already achieved, but of acting as though in-school and out-of-school learning involve different processes.

The major drawback to that separation is that it robs both pupils and teachers of a potentially powerful set of learning resources to draw on. And it further gives kids the idea that school is for the boring and meaningless stuff, and real life is where the excitement and action are. This distinction is obvious enough to anyone who has observed the differences in energy levels children and adolescents manifest in the corridor or the playground compared to the classroom, but its potential curriculum implications are rarely acted upon in commonsense schools. The continuing power of this separation is usually maintained into adulthood by people who recognize, when they are asked to do so, that much of their adult expertise has been derived from experience-based, self-directed, out-of-school learning, but who still insist that schooling must be devoted to the context-free, the teacher-directed, and the routine.

In the pervasive belief that adults know best, schools continue to be controlled by externally derived sequences of knowledge and skills, and student purposes and initiatives are limited to either learning to play the school game or not. The sequence of development is otherwise fixed. Although advocates of developmental stages as a way of accounting for human growth have not generally been sympathetic to looking at genetic or environmentally based limits on some individuals' learning capacities, they have provided an inadvertent rationale for the notion of skills sequences. Indeed Jean Piaget, the psychologist most influential in formulating the developmental stage account of human learning, was a strong believer in the common, species-specific properties of human intelligence and a firm antibehaviorist. His basic theory was that all human beings developed a common set of intellectual abilities in an invariant sequence, beginning with sensorimotor skills and developing through concrete to formal, logical operations. (For a useful introduction to his work see Piaget [1967].) Children developed these competencies by using their internally evolving construction of the nature of reality as a basis for interpreting the phenomena they observed and interacted with. One of Piaget's great strengths was his insistence that children brought these developing internal mental structures to bear on all learning tasks. Taking a very uncommonsense position, he insisted on stressing learning from the inside out as well as from the outside in.

His major contribution to educational common sense, however, was to provide an apparent rationale for the belief that there were conceptual tasks which were appropriate for children at different ages, that some skills had to be acquired before others, and that there were, consequently, some tasks or problems which were "beyond" the capacity of younger children. Although some educators interpreted his notion of stages as a prod to speed up children's progression through them—asking how to do so was so commonly done by American educators that, toward the end of his life, Piaget began to refer to this as "the American question"—a more common effect was to reify the bottom-up skills sequence approaches which were already the normal currency of curriculum planning. Ironically, the kinds of experiences thought of as teaching the "basic" skills/drills—workbooks, rules, and so on—were not likely to fulfill Piaget's understanding of the ways children achieved progression through his stages, but the idea of stages itself was taken to support conventional wisdom, even though Piaget was often horrified by the ways they were used.

Commonsense Knowledge: External, Objective, Conscious

Another keystone of educational common sense is its largely unconscious but nonetheless pervasive conception of the nature of knowledge. The externally controlled and sequenced emphasis of commonsense schooling is buttressed by a conception of knowledge as external to knowers. It is this construct that underlies such metaphors as the knowledge explosion and the view that libraries and the books they contain are repositories of knowledge. The metaphor of a knowledge explosion is based on the view that the recent proliferation of scientific discoveries, of new and complex technologies, and of new understandings of the complexities of nature and of human societies has increased the demand for specialization and reduced the possibility of any single individual having a broadly adequate understanding of more than one narrow field of inquiry. The enormous increase in the number of books, learned journals, data banks, and other material which can be known that has accompanied this explosion has made the difficulties involved concrete.

One effect of this proliferation has been to increase pressure on the curriculum at all levels to include more and more factual content. The pressure has not only been for increased specialization, but for specializing earlier and earlier in a child's schooling. Primary schools are frequently either becoming departmentalized or compartmentalized with each separate "subject" being assigned a specific time slot. The restriction of learning to specific content in a specific block of time is an additional consequence of the commonsense notions of knowledge as external, separable, and capable of being taught and learned in sequenced, bottom-up, patterns of instruction. In most cases such scheduling and sequencing have destroyed the natural rhythms characteristic of out-of-school learning, instead placing additional emphasis on children's capacity to master bits and snippets of content rapidly and out of context.

The curriculum itself has become more and more stuffed with content and skills which are presumed to be essential for living in a knowledge-exploded world. The recent calls for including computer literacy, an unsettling label at best, are only the most recent example of a trend which has been steady throughout our century. And the call for more and more content in the curriculum has made teachers extremely skeptical of any demands to change what they do in their classrooms because they just don't see when they will be able to find the time to "cover" it. Teachers attempting to move toward an uncommonsense approach to learning and teaching must recognize these pressures and find ways of showing how integration can help to relieve them. When the content and processes of learning are treated in an integrated fashion rather than in an atomic-bits and separate-skills approach, there actually can be more time available for learning. But to build toward that integration requires a thorough reconceptualization of the processes of schooling, not merely adding on, say, "the writing process" to an already over-stuffed curriculum.

Correlated with the view that knowledge is external is a belief in the importance of objective knowledge and of conscious knowledge. Objective knowledge contrasts with subjective knowledge in the commonsense view, and is based on the idea that what really counts in education is the student's mastery of information. One of the most common critiques of contemporary schooling is based on the view that ironically, and even dangerously in light of the knowledge explosion, students don't know as much as they used to. This was the main thrust of Ravitch and Finn (1987), and it is the main motive behind Hirsch's (1987) concern with decreasing levels of cultural literacy. The press periodically reports stories of tests given to students which show that they can't name the capitals of the fifty states or even locate and identify the states on a map, that even teachers can't correctly label the subject and predicate of sentences, or that children cannot multiply and divide. In my semester as an intern teacher I did my bit to rectify this situation by spending endless weeks teaching my seventh graders to identify the fifty states on a blank map. I wonder how many of them remember them?

Commonsense Transmissions

Underlying these commonsense views of knowledge is the belief that there is an external, objective world which can be, and largely is, known and understood. The rapidly increasing complexity of our understanding of that world may have put more pressures on schools, but it has made them seem more vital than ever in transmitting knowledge of the world to the young. Such transmissions must be done explicitly and deliberately so that students can achieve conscious mastery of the required information.

The belief that this external knowledge can and must be transmitted from teacher to pupil helps to rationalize the frequent observation that teacher talk dominates commonsense classrooms. (For discussion see Bellack et al. [1966] and the observations made by Goodlad and his team in over 7,000 classrooms [1984].) Whether in the form of lectures (the most common form of instruction in both higher education and secondary schools), or whole-class "discussions" in which the teacher asks all the questions and students are expected to give only minimal answers (a common pattern throughout schooling which my colleague Rita Brause and I characterized as an "oral workbook" in our classroom research (Brause and Mayher 1983), teachers talk and children mostly listen. Both silence and its antithesis, student talk with each other, are anathema in commonsense classrooms.

The metaphors of transmission and its conceptual cousin, covering the content, have rarely been examined within the commonsense framework, since it is assumed that they capture the primary functions of schooling. What is often forgotten about transmission is that to be successful it requires a receiver who is not only tuned to the right frequency (and whose set is on!), but who is capable of interpreting what he receives. We will see later how inadequate such a conception is for the normal processes of language use, and in terms of a metaphor for learning its inadequacy is revealed in the failure of such transmissions as the following taken from Douglas Barnes (1969/1986). The course is chemistry, and the students are beginning their secondary schooling. The teacher is explaining (transmitting?) the fact that milk is an example of the suspension of solids in a liquid.

TEACHER: You get the white . . . what we call casein . . . that's . . . er
. . . protein . . . which is good for you . . . it'll help build bones
. . . and the white is mainly the casein and it's not actually a
solution . . . it's a suspension of very fine particles together
with water and various other things which are dissolved in
water . . .

PUPIL 1: Sir, at my old school I shook my milk up and when I looked
at it again the side was covered with . . . er . . . like particles
and . . . er . . . could they be the white particles in the milk?

PUPIL 2: Yes, and gradually they would sediment out, wouldn't
they, to the bottom?

PUPIL 3: When milk goes very sour it smells like cheese, doesn't it?

PUPIL 4: Well it is cheese, isn't it, if you leave it long enough?

TEACHER: Anyway can we get on? We'll leave a few questions for
later. (p. 29)

Even though this teacher has made some attempts at ensuring
that his transmission will be connected to the students' receiving
capabilities (protein is good for you, helps build bones), their responses make it clear that his language and their experience are not
really on the same wave-length at all. They are trying to be good
receivers, trying to attend, but they can't bridge the abstraction gap,
and, as Barnes comments, "The teacher, frightened by his sudden glimpse of the gulf between them, hastily continues with the
lesson he has planned" (p. 29). Doing so may help him "cover" the
content of the course, but the students are more likely to remain
covered in ignorance than they are to have learned anything meaningful to their own frame of reference.

The metaphor of coverage is itself an interesting one, since it
provides another way of understanding the externally controlled
nature of commonsense schooling. The teacher, or more accurately
whatever collective powers have determined the curriculum—
including the textbook writers and editors, the experts in the "subject," the curriculum supervisors and administrators, and even the
parents and the school board—have usually decided what is to be
learned with virtually no reference to the particular learners in any
specific classroom. In the most extreme cases these decisions are
made so comprehensively that the school system's illusion, at least,
can be that each individual teacher need only march through the
specified lessons without any additional planning or adjustment.
In practice this rarely happens, but the impression that it *can* provides powerful pressures on teachers to ignore their own students'
needs and abilities, and to plow ahead regardless of how well they
are learning.

In such a context, covering the curriculum induces guilt in those teachers who aren't keeping up or who take too many unscheduled detours and causes resistance to change in those who have either willingly accepted the coverage mandate or who believe they are forced to do so by the pressures of external examinations. Both the control of curricula by people remote from the classroom and the use of external examinations, a trend which is rapidly growing throughout the country, are important aspects of the control of teachers by the commonsense system.

The deliberate transmitting of information has been somewhat less of a concern in language education because unlike the sciences, math, or even social studies, transmitting content as such has never been as central a focus in language education as has been developing the skills involved in learning to read and write. One effect of the overall belief that schooling = the transmission of knowledge has been to increase the use of the literary canon and information about literature as the content to be transmitted in secondary and tertiary English. In primary schools, the content became how to spell and punctuate, extending throughout the school experience to learning how to identify and label parts of speech. And once the subject had a content, it could then be transmitted and, most importantly, tested.

Another crucial ingredient of the commonsense view of knowledge as external to the knowers, which therefore must be transmitted to them by adult experts, has been the assumption that their processes of knowledge acquisition needed to be monitored and learning could be assessed by means of frequent tests. It is hard to overstate the controlling effects that testing has on schooling, but in this context we must explore their effect on learning. One primary effect is that they give students the idea that that is what learning is for. One of the most frequent, and, to the uncommonsense teacher, most frustrating, of student questions is: "Will it be on the test?" The ironic reality of a behavioristically patterned learning process has been to make the reward (a good mark for the right answer) the only currency of value in schools. We shouldn't be surprised that our maze runners don't find value in the path of learning itself, of either learning how to learn or of coming to value the knowledge and skills being acquired. We've succeeded all too well in making grades determined by teachers and tests the only motive for schooling, at least with those students who continue to buy into the system and still work for such rewards.

Students don't come to school asking "Will it be on the test?" The value of short-term testing and immediate feedback in the form of grades is one that we have carefully taught them. Not only has this had the effect of distorting the reason for doing school work in the first place, it has distorted all of our commonsense conceptions about how schools should work and teachers should teach. For language education, particularly, the focus should not be on the short term and the immediate test result, but on the long-term effects of our teaching on the students' ability to use language. It really doesn't matter whether or not kids can pass our test on *Silas Marner* or *A Tale of Two Cities* if they never choose to read another complex novel after they leave school. Similarly, no matter how well they can perform on spelling tests and punctuation drills, if they learn to fear writing and to avoid it whenever possible, we are not achieving our goals.

Short vs. Long Term Teaching: Learning to Forget

The combination of the overstuffed curriculum and the constant pressure of testing has also placed a high premium on learning to forget as well as to remember. Since the bits and snippets sequences of commonsense learning rarely require much carryover from this week's test to the next one, the system seems to be telling students to rapidly forget this week's material in order to prepare to receive the next set of transmissions. This week's vocabulary or spelling quiz can be passed by a process of short-term memory, but then that set of words must be washed away to prepare for next week's list. This subverts whatever long-term purpose there may have been in such learning, but it will keep each runner fresh for the new maze.

Another important effect of this process in language education has been to accelerate the process of treating things that are actually doing, or *knowing how*—like reading and writing—as things that are *knowing that*, or presumed to be externally transmittable in the commonsense framework. So students are taught and later tested on the rule telling them that a vowel is long in words with a final "silent e" (like rule), or the principles for recognizing nouns, or the rule for how to contrast the spellings of neither and achieve, or the formal features of an outline to be used before writing. Such things seem "objective," can be tested with "right answer" tests, can be sequenced and transmitted in deliberate fashion, and can be confidently pointed to as the knowledge that students of language need to acquire.

Such things are *not*, in fact, what students need to know in order to perform proficiently with language, but it is important here to notice that they are consistent with the commonsense approach to learning and therefore supported by the framework of accountability which sustains it. Teachers who attempt to change their approach to an uncommonsense one frequently find themselves confronting the reality that their professional performance is evaluated not by how much uncommonsense learning their pupils actually attain, but by how well they perform on standardized tests. The basic view of common sense that direct teaching is necessary to successful performance on such tests is so powerful that teachers are understandably fearful that they may be threatening both their own careers and their students' future success in the commonsense school system if they don't go along with the system. By direct teaching in this context I mean devoting time in class to drills which are, in effect, practice versions of the test, thereby both robbing students of the chance to experience the broader context of learning which the test is supposed to be sampling, and further emphasizing test passing as the central goal of schooling.

One of the classic examples of the failure of short-term teaching and testing can be seen in teachers' attempts to teach vocabulary. Possession of a large vocabulary seems to be one of the goals of education agreed upon by progressives and traditionalists, by both common and uncommon sense. The distinction between common- and uncommonsense views of the value of having a large vocabulary seems to be more one of how it is acquired than of whether it is a valuable thing to possess, but there may also be some distinctions as to whether it is to be valued as an end in itself, as implied in the commonsense attempts to teach it directly, or whether it is merely a means to other desirable ends—more competent language use and, especially, more powerful reading and writing—which is the uncommonsense position.

One factor that seems to give vocabulary independent status results from the use of vocabulary testing to predict future academic success and, in the case of college admissions tests like the Scholastic Aptitude Test (SAT), its use as a means of discriminating the able from the less able. This has led schools to routinely include direct vocabulary teaching in their curricula, and such direct vocabulary teaching forms the core of the growing number of SAT preparatory courses taught by profit-making tutoring schools. While there is some evidence that such direct teaching does help give highly motivated students some additional points on their college entrance tests, it is less clear that such teaching really results in the useful possession of a larger vocabulary. While students who have had such coaching may be more likely to recognize a number of out-of-context words in the test, it does not seem to have a corresponding impact on their ability to read with insight and write with power.

My own experience with trying to directly teach (or consciously learn) vocabulary words out of context is that it just doesn't work. When I was a junior and senior high school teacher, vocabulary building was part of the curriculum, and I dutifully tried to do it. The commonsense method I used was to select fifteen or twenty words a week for my classes to learn. Sometimes they were chosen from the literature we were reading, but more often from a text on vocabulary building. (In elementary and junior high school the emphasis was usually as much on spelling as on meaning, but by high school spelling had taken a back seat to learning definitions.) Students were expected to look the words up in a dictionary, write out a definition for them, use them appropriately in a sentence, and then "learn" them for the Friday quiz. This was how it had been done to me, so. . . . (That this procedure is still the norm was one of the depressing findings of Goodlad [1984].)

The first clue I should have responded to that this wasn't really efficacious came when I looked at the definitions and sample sentences. Kids being kids, and unwilling to invest their precious time in what they knew to be dummy-run busywork, almost invariably chose the shortest definition to write out when a word had more than one, even if it was the most obscure meaning available. Further, when it came time to use them in a sentence, it was rare for the sentence to really capture the appropriate frame for using the word, and even rarer for it to express the particular sense of the word that they had written as its definition. Actually these activities were probably confusing the students, so that if they actually did want or need to use the word, they'd either not know it, or get its conditions for use confused. (A similar phenomenon frequently characterizes inexperienced writers when they use a thesaurus to give variety and intellectual heft to their papers; the synonym they choose frequently does not work appropriately in the sentence into which they insert it.)

The second and most important clue, however, was provided by the fact that words "mastered" for the Friday quiz were already self-destructing in the students' memory by the time of Friday's final bell, and they were almost always completely forgotten by Monday. In one sense, of course, this too was an efficient school survival strategy, since erasing this week's words left more memory space available for next week's. And since few, if any, of the words were ever deeply connected to the student's conceptual frameworks, there seemed little or no point in saving them for the long term. Vocabulary teaching of this sort seemed to promote only the most vivid example of nonpermanent learning.

But why didn't it work? What does work? Clearly some people do seem to have larger and more versatile working vocabularies than others. How does this come about? And what can schools and teachers do to promote such useful growth?

The precise nature of our mental dictionaries is still by no means fully understood, but some vital factors are known. The first, and most important, is based on the general principles of language development which form the core of the uncommonsense theory being developed here: Vocabulary, like the rest of the language system, develops unconsciously and implicitly through the processes of purposeful and meaningful language use. More simply put, it means that we learn words in context. The source of new words, naturally enough, comes when we are receiving language as listeners or readers, but we receive them effectively only when we understand enough of the context to build a preliminary interpretation of what the words mean. And, what is less obvious, the words that become part of our useful vocabularies are those which we produce as well as receive.

It is often the case that we seem to have words which we can understand in the context of someone else's use of them, but which we have not yet included in our productive repertoire. This is a particularly familiar experience when we are reading (or listening to, say, a lecture) in a field or area that is relatively new and, therefore, unfamiliar to us. I can read and get some understanding of what *quarks* are from the context in which they are used, for example, but I'm not really confident of my understanding of their conditions of use to use the term productively. To do so I would need to be in an interactive situation where I could try out my understanding and see how well it fits with the larger conceptual framework. It seems likely that most of us have some asymmetries in our mental dictionaries, so that the number of words we can grasp and at least partially understand while reading or listening is greater than those we can use in speaking or writing.

When we are beginning to read or listen in a new area, the relative percentage of unfamiliar words can make a whole passage opaque because the context does not provide sufficient scaffolding to allow us to interpret them. This is particularly true if the author of the text or lecture has assumed the readers or auditors will be more expert than they are. When students are reading in an unfamiliar domain and when they are not allowed to check their interpretation with anyone else, they are in trouble. But when they are allowed to do so, when they can try out their tentative interpretations, ask questions about what they didn't understand, and thereby clarify what sense they made of the passage, then the words begin to become clear in the context.

It should be emphasized, however, that although the *result* of reading and writing and talking about these ideas may add some terms to the participants' vocabularies, that should not be thought of as its direct intent. We shouldn't think of having students read in new areas explicitly as a vocabulary lesson; we should, instead, want the participants to explore and think about the ideas of the passage. Nor would it be efficacious to try to preteach the technical terms before students read the passage, another frequently used commonsense technique, because until they have a context for using the terms—in this case in the attempt to build an interpretation of the text—the connection would be difficult to make.

This is the general problem with direct attempts to teach content without a meaningful context within which the learners can see some reason for learning it. The context of teaching and testing alone provides only the motivation to learn the material for the test, not a reason for making it a working part of one's permanently available knowledge structure. By emphasizing the short-term and bottom-up methods, the outside-in approaches of transmission and coverage actually short-circuit long-term and more usable knowing.

Changing the superstructure of coverage, of testing, and of other commonsense accountability systems will be a difficult task. The forces arrayed on the side of the educational status quo are many and varied. It must be remembered, however, that the larger commonsense context of schooling does have direct impact on everything that happens in the language education classroom, and that substantial change cannot happen if the only changes being made are within the separate classroom contexts of individual teachers and students.

Commonsense Learning: A Brief Summary

Based on behaviorism, the commonsense approaches feature a conception of learning which is essentially reactive to external stimuli and passive in its role for the learner, who is expected to function as a kind of recording and playback device receiving the transmissions of the expert teacher and texts and then feeding them back essentially unchanged in essays and on tests. The authority for these transmissions derives from an external view of knowledge as objective, independent of the knower, and that which needs to be consciously and deliberately taught and learned. Skills and knowledge will both be acquired most efficiently by breaking them into separate bits, which can then be mastered in small steps. Each step along the way features tests of achievement. This externally determined sequence helps to justify the standard school practices of dividing subjects into small blocks of time and content, and having classrooms where teachers do most of the talking and ask most of the questions.

This organization of content and skills into bottom-up sequences which move from simple to complex takes no account of the students' background or interests except insofar as they are directly concerned with the skills or knowledge being transmitted. The knowledge itself is disembedded from its human context, and its acontextual quality is regarded as a virtue not a defect because it allows for building a coherent sequence entirely on the basis of expert analyses of the structure of the tasks to be mastered or the content to be remembered. The only legitimate student purpose that is recognized is that of the need to learn the material, and this is to be ensured by frequent assessments and the accompanying rewards of good grades on the test.

Although commonsense learning theory says little about the nature of the human mind, since consideration of it had been, in effect, ruled out by positivist/behaviorist methodology, its implicit metaphors for the mental are all mechanical. Whether building solid foundations, making good recordings, acquiring networks of stimulus-response connections or, as one of my students, Lisa Bobst, put it, responding as a vacuum cleaner waiting to sweep up all school knowledge indiscriminately, the mental activities involved in learning are seen to be those of linear associations, amassing strings of facts and sequences of skills to allow the assembly of whole complex processes from disembedded bits and pieces. That such processes describe only a small fraction of the powers of the human mind, however well they may account for the learning processes of rats and pigeons, has not been allowed to trouble the common sense of learning.

These basic belief structures about human learning determine curricula, activities, and, perhaps most crucially, tests in schools. Teachers may, in actual practice, treat students more individually and with more human concern than these precepts seem to suggest. But doing so always brings some concern and may even make trouble for teachers in schools where the accountability systems have become rigid and controlling. As a result, teachers who deviate from the system sometimes feel guilty about wasting the students' time, and in some instances may actually be criticized by supervisors for doing so. If such precepts provided either an accurate or an effective basis for promoting student learning, I would have little quarrel with them, but however one looks at the quality and quantity of student learning in schools awakens serious criticisms and raises fundamental questions.

Some critics who have observed these deficiencies have called, in effect, for even more drastic adherence to commonsense approaches. This has been the thrust of the back-to-basics movement, of the proposals for longer school days or school years, and of much of the increased concern with academic excellence. Indeed one of the great ironies of commonsense schooling is that remedial programs for children who have failed to respond to commonsense approaches are often themselves based on the commonsense approach at its most extreme. The failures of such programs are legendary, and yet it is not infrequent for all concerned—teachers, students, administrators—to believe that somehow this time the commonsense approach will work because it will be accompanied by sufficient determination to pay off.

I think the cause of the problem lies in the commonsense approaches themselves, however, and no amount of "improving" them will yield better results. What is needed is an uncommon-sense reconceptualization of the problem and its solutions.

CHAPTER 4

Uncommonsense
Learning

Learning in Context

Despite my somewhat critical remarks about the use of Piaget's work to support preordered curricula, Piaget's great contribution to understanding human development was his capacity to look behind what children were doing and to attempt to explain the underlying mental strategies they were using. He looked more seriously than anyone ever had at what children were doing in an attempt to determine *why* they were doing it. Recent critics have found a variety of difficulties with his stages, and even with the notion of stages itself, but whatever the final verdict on his theoretical system, his recognition that descriptions of behavior alone were not sufficient to account for what people were doing, and his insistence that we must look deeper in order to explain it, will be a lasting and crucial contribution to the uncommonsense tradition.

Eleanor Duckworth, one of Piaget's former colleagues, has built on his insights by showing that the power of observing learning in action and asking why it happens can be a powerful means of helping adults, particularly teachers, examine and reformulate their constructs of learning and teaching. In one of her inservice courses, for example, teacher/students are asked to observe the phases of the moon and to account for the shape of the moon's crescent and its position in the sky at each phase. By having the students both do the learning and observe themselves and the strategies they use to figure out (or continue to be puzzled by) the problem, she has found that teachers can understand their own learning processes better and also become much more sensitive and insightful observers of what their pupils are doing as a result (Duckworth 1987). This combination of experience and reflection (called immersion and distancing and as further discussed in Lester and Onore [1985]) is not only a crucial part of professional education, the key to making what Donald Schön (1983) calls "reflective practitioners," but undoubtedly has broader implications for learning and teaching at all ages.

If commonsense approaches feature context-free learning, then for our purposes one of the most telling of the criticisms of Piaget has been made by Margaret Donaldson (1978) and her colleagues. They have shown that *children's capacities to perform particular intellectual tasks depend crucially upon the context in which the task is embedded and, particularly, on the child's understanding of what the requirements of the tasks really were.* They found that children who could not perform particular problems when presented with them in the traditional Piagetian approach could perform equivalent tasks when they were embedded in a context which was sufficiently meaningful to the child to enable him to fully comprehend what was required. For example, children who apparently didn't understand class inclusion when asked questions like, "Are there more black cows or more cows?" (the standard Piagetian question) could succeed when asked if there were more black cows or more sleeping cows (about an array of models where all were lying down sleeping but only three of the four were black). Apparently the addition of a second adjective allowed children to focus on the fact that the question was being asked about the whole class (p. 44). Similar experiments using other kinds of contexts which made the tasks comprehensible to the children enabled them to go far beyond the level of achievement which Piaget's stages would have predicted.

The idea that *learner's capacities to solve problems and to perform intellectual tasks are powerfully influenced by the way the problems are posed and by the learner's interpretation of what the task entails* is one of the first tenets I'd like to assert as part of the uncommonsense view of learning. Like much else in the uncommonsense view, it may not seem very surprising or even very novel. Many teachers and parents have long understood, at least implicitly, that the context in which a problem is embedded can either help it make sense to a child or make it more confusing. As young children struggle to understand their world, we know that we can help them most effectively as parents and teachers by listening empathetically to them, taking their point of view, and responding to the questions which emerge from their own current construal of their context.

Here's one of many examples of this process in action from Wells (1986, p. 59).

[Elizabeth, age 4, is watching her mother shovel wood ash from the grate and put it into a bucket.]

ELIZABETH: What are you doing that for?

MOTHER: I'm gathering it up and putting it outside so that Daddy can put it on the garden.

ELIZABETH: Why does it have to be put on the garden?

MOTHER: To make the compost right.

ELIZABETH: Does that make the grass grow?

MOTHER: Yes.

ELIZABETH: Why does it?

MOTHER: You know how I tell you that you need to eat different things like eggs and cabbage and rice pudding to make you grow into a big girl?

ELIZABETH: Yes.

MOTHER: Well, plants need different foods, too. And ash is one of the things that's good for them.

Wells goes on to point out that parents do not in all instances respond to questions as helpfully as this, because they may not know the answer, they may misunderstand the question, or they may be too busy to give the question the attention it deserves. In this case, actually, the mother's answer "to make the compost right" seems quite unhelpful, because it demands a conceptual understanding of the term *compost* which Elizabeth doesn't have yet and illustrates the common problem of a knowledge and experience gap between parent and child, as a result of which the adult is hard pressed to know where to start to fill in the relevant background.

More important, however, are both the overall success of this transaction and the active role of the child as initiator and questioner. Elizabeth asks four questions in this brief sequence, and together mother and child negotiate an interpretation of the event to make it possible for Elizabeth to use it to enrich her understanding of the world. It is a collaborative process of meaning making which succeeds because her mother takes her questions seriously and struggles to find an appropriate explanation. Throughout the process Elizabeth is tacitly but clearly encouraged to keep on asking questions until *she* is satisfied with the explanation.

While instances of this kind of learning (and teaching) are familiar enough to most of us in out-of-school contexts, they are rarely characteristic of in-school contexts, as Douglas Barnes and others have shown, and as we saw in the earlier example of the teacher trying to explain the nature of milk. One can easily imagine the same content being part of a science curriculum about how plants grow, but the pattern of instruction would be likely to be quite different. In commonsense schools the teachers typically ask the questions, not the students, and the answers they are looking for more often than not involve the acquisition of technical terms (like *compost* in the example above). Pupil-initiated question sequences are rare, and a situation where the same pupil could ask four questions in a row would be extremely unusual, even daring, for the pupil would be either displaying a dangerous degree of ignorance, or demanding an inordinate amount of attention.

Since teachers in commonsense schools determine the context and the content of instruction, the meaning that is to be made may be quite remote from and never really connected to the students' already developed set of understandings. They may, or may not, be able to pass the test on the nutritional requirements of plants, but in either case they are frequently unable to connect the school terminology to the real world of their own gardens, or, in the earlier example, to their experience with milk. And the incompetence that children frequently seem to show in school may not be the result of an actual incapacity to solve the problem or understand the concept, but an inability to understand the problem in what Donaldson calls a "disembedded situation." The verbal labels which for adults carry a rich constellation of conceptual and experiential connections may not do so for the child, and even if they "learn" the labels, they may not really understand, in an experiential way, what they stand for.

When that happens, the child's interpretations of her own experiences are likely to be unchanged and, perhaps even more significant for later school learning, the verbal labels quickly vanish from memory because they have no experiential roots. It is not likely that Elizabeth learned the term *compost* from this conversation, although she might have, but it seems very likely that she will never forget the potential role of ash as a plant food. The clear difference here is that she sees the ash, and can remember both her father's fertilizing the garden and her mother's previous discussions with her about her own nutrition. This combination allows her both to understand the new concept and to relate it to her previous concepts. Since both the common- and uncommonsense approaches to learning are based on the notion that *learning means a permanent change in our ways of understanding and acting upon the world*, the roles of context, of the learner's active participation, and of the opportunity for student and teacher together to collaboratively build a shared set of meanings have powerful implications for school practice.

Personal Knowledge

As Barnes (1969/1986, 1976), Britton (1970), Hull (1985), Wells (1986), and many others have shown, the "language gap," in Hull's words, between teachers and pupils is often an important factor in determining whether or not pupils comprehend actively, and therefore more permanently, the relations between what they know when they come to school and what the school is trying to teach them. When school knowledge remains disembedded and unconnected to the learner's experience, and, worse, when neither teacher nor student recognizes or tries to deal with the gap between the label and the experience, the only "learning" that is possible is what I have sometimes called verbal short-circuiting, in which the concept comes in the ear or the eye and goes out the pen but never gets sufficiently acted upon in the brain to find a permanent home.

The uncommonsense theory of knowledge contrasts sharply with the commonsense view of knowledge as external to knowers. For the uncommonsense view, *there is no knowledge without a knower.* It may, at times, be useful to distinguish different sources of verification of what we know, but those concepts which can be verified by appeal to publicly observable phenomena (the objective knowledge of positivist common sense) are no more real or valid than such publicly unverifiable knowledge as the fact that I have a pain in my foot or my interpretation of *Hamlet.* These subjective knowings can be shared, and we can come to some consensual agreement about them. The uncommonsense position does not impute an inferior status to them, since it recognizes that even such apparently "objective" truths as scientific theories have a strong subjectively relative component to them in terms of what questions they are trying to answer, what methods they employ, and what counts as data. (For further discussion see Kuhn [1961] and Rorty [1979].)

To fully explore the epistemology of this position would take us too far afield; here it is enough to contrast the external domination and passive character of the kind of knowing characterized by verbal short-circuiting and the purposeful, learner-driven active process we saw Elizabeth engaged in. The uncommonsense theory of learning has as one of its core constructs the idea that *human beings are active meaning makers who are continually learning—making personal knowledge—when they can act according to their own purposes.* This idea of personal knowledge, which derives as well from the work of Michael Polanyi (1958, 1966), provides a radical challenge to the commonsense approach because it insists on the importance of the student's personal connections to the material being learned, and of his individual reasons to be learning it.

For George Kelly (1955), in fact, the processes of human life are so permeated by learning that he finds it unnecessary to distinguish learning as a separate activity from living, since to live is to learn. For him the basic metaphor for the human being is the scientist, by which he means not that we should all wear lab coats and peer through microscopes but that in every life transaction we operate on the basis of predictions, like hypotheses, about how the world works, and that as we interpret the results of our actions we are constantly modifying what he calls the tacit mental constructs upon which our predictions were based. For him, this basic human pattern of construct building, prediction making, and construct modification is what scientists do, and therefore we are all scientists when we operate this way. Others, like Ann Berthoff (1978), take a similar position but characterize us as philosophers rather than scientists. The key point is the stance toward living and learning, not the label.

The pressure to build a world interpretation which will enable us to make successful predictions is clearest in young children and is one of the factors that leads them to be continual questioners, like Elizabeth in the example cited previously. Both Piaget and Kelly recognize that *the world does not come to us in preinterpreted form, but rather is constructed by our interpretation of our experiences.* This process of internal world building is socially constrained and mediated, of course, since we build our world theory through collaborative transactions with others, as well as through our own internal processes, as we saw Elizabeth and her mother doing together. But the crucial point here is that this combination of personal and social processes is consistently meaning-driven as we try to make sense of the way things work, the way people behave, and all other aspects of our experience of the world we live in.

It is also, in the sense most clearly articulated by John Dewey (1933), a process of problem finding or problem posing as much as it is of problem solving. In the context of our daily lives, problems do not come clearly labeled as such; part of the competence that we need to develop is the ability to recognize the problematic and then to bring to bear appropriate problem-solving strategies. The commonsense processes of school learning, in contrast, involve solving problems which have been externally determined and preset by the teacher or the text. The goal, of course, is to help students learn to solve such problems so that they will have an appropriate repertoire of techniques available when needed. Dewey pointed out, however, that this may never happen unless students also learn how to find appropriate problems to use the techniques on, since problems in life, unlike those in commonsense schools, have the disconcerting property of not being very neatly packaged and tagged with the appropriate strategy.

Even such an apparently uncontroversial and routine practice as giving students teacher-written or textbook-authored questions about a story or chapter may therefore have counterproductive effects. What is intended as a help to students in their meaning-making and problem-solving processes may actually *limit* the students' problem solving to those which the experts think they will face. Such limits don't help students either to determine their own actual difficulties with the text or to develop appropriate strategies to solve the real problems that they confront. By externally controlling the processes of problem finding and problem posing, we may be robbing students of precisely the experiences they need to develop their own capacities for interpretation and to build their own construct systems, using both problem-posing and problem-solving strategies.

Another way of looking at the problem-finding or problem-setting process is to recognize that it often requires a familiar context. Although such an analogical process may be quite literal, as in the case of Elizabeth's mother's connecting the nutritional requirements of plants to those of a child, frequently they require more imaginative or metaphoric thinking. Metaphor sometimes has been relegated to the periphery of human thinking, as a kind of textual decoration employed by poets for artistic effect, but recent studies have shown that it is fundamental to creative thought and both problem finding and problem solving (see Ortony 1979 and Schön 1983). In that sense it is also central to learning, since we can only learn new things in the context of what we already know. Metaphor can provide us with a new way of seeing a problem by construing it in terms of something we are familiar with, and thereby making either a new solution possible or revealing flaws in our conception of the situation. Lisa Bobst's view of the student as vacuum cleaner helped her understand the commonsense practices of schooling in a new way and enabled her to clarify her own position on teaching and learning in opposition to it.

By the time we are adults, we have developed a more or less adequate world theory, or set of constructs in Kelly's terms, which enables us to make generally accurate predictions about our lives, the other people we interact with, and the physical world. We are still learners, still capable of modifying our constructs in the light of new experiences, but Kelly recognizes that some of our constructs are more difficult to modify than others, and we sometimes persist in acting in unproductive ways even in the face of potentially disconfirming experiences. The impermeability of some of our constructs is made possible by the fact that we can only interpret the world on the basis of the constructs we already have, and nothing in experience itself inevitably provides disconfirmation.

Uncommonsense Metaphors for Learning

Sometimes a new metaphor can help us modify our prior constructs as Salmon (1985) shows when she explores three metaphors for living and development: life as a game of cards where we are dealt a hand and must play it (with some winners and some losers since there are only a fixed number of rewards); life as a natural process which unfolds inevitably through growth and decay; and life as a story where we have the possibility of changing its plot and therefore changing our lives in the context, of course, of those whose personal stories are entwined with ours.

The first metaphor, the game of cards, is the most consistent with commonsense beliefs about schooling, and as we've seen, it is embodied in schools both in the tracking systems based on innate and unchangeable views of individual human potential, and in the competitive individualism of school success as a zero-sum game. The second, organic, metaphor conforms more closely to the more progressive notion of personal growth and sees the responsibility of the school as being primarily to enhance individual potential. The third, development as story, gives the broadest scope both for individuals' control of their own destiny (plot) and for giving teachers a potentially large role helping learners to reinterpret, and therefore change, the meaning of the story of their life. Choosing metaphors which best capture our sense of the cycle of life may change our behavior and our understanding of teaching and learning. And changing our metaphors can help us reinterpret what we may have believed was given or fixed about our experience, while reinterpreting our past may provide new hypotheses to test in future action.

Similarly, George Lakoff and Mark Johnson (1980) have been developing a theory of language and learning which postulates that complex and interrelated metaphoric schemas govern our category systems, our interpretation of events, and all other aspects of our world view. One example of such a schema is what Michael Reddy (1979) called the "conduit metaphor of communication." In his discussion of our "language about language" he showed that virtually all of it treats language use as the sending of meaning from person A to person B by means of some kind of channel or conduit. He found this inchoate theory so built into our vocabulary and concept systems as to make it almost impossible to construe communication in any other ways. Given the centrality of transmission (one of the versions of the conduit metaphor) to the common sense of schooling, it seems clear that trying to explore and examine its adequacy will be a crucial part of trying to deconstruct the commonsense vision of learning and to reconstruct an uncommonsense one.

The pervasiveness and unconscious qualities of these metaphoric schemas make it all the more important to try to explore the commonsense ideas they express, since these are frequently more or less public versions of our private constructs. And they persist both individually and collectively because they seem to work, that is they do make sufficiently accurate predictions within the social context we live in to cover most contingencies. The sun really does seem to rise in the east and set in the west as our common sense— and, crucially, our language—still maintains; and it frequently takes as much of a personal construct revolution as the scientific revolution spearheaded by Copernicus to modify our world theory. Metaphor—asking what if we think of this as X rather than as Y—can be one of the tools we employ in reshaping our world.

Learning Is Learning: In School and Out

As implied earlier, one reason we don't often use our personal experience of encounters with children like Elizabeth to question and modify our commonsense view of school learning is that we frequently make a substantial distinction between learning in life and learning in school. We expect school learning to be the acquisition of disembedded knowledge and skills. Therefore we consistently believe that it requires a set of learning principles and activities quite different from learning how to ride a bicycle or bake a roast or order a beer or court a mate. If we believe that in-school and out-of-school learning involve different processes, then we will see little need to modify our constructs of the former in light of our experiences of the latter. Since this distinction itself has become part of educational common sense reinforced by our normal curriculum and, most crucially, our testing and assessment systems, questioning the reality of the distinction or wondering whether disembedded knowledge and skills need be the substance of school learning is both infrequent and, when attempted, very difficult.

Another crucial tenet of the uncommonsense theory of learning, therefore, is to assert that *learning is learning—both in school and out.* That is, there may be different modes of learning which may be more or less effective for particular problems, tasks, and concepts, but they share certain properties when they are effective, among them the active, personally meaningful, socially transactional qualities we have discussed so far. Further, it means that examples of effective learning not only need not be restricted to school-based instances but in fact are far more likely to be found in our out-of-school experiences. One of the overriding pedagogical premises of the uncommonsense theory has been to try to make learning in

school more like learning out of school. The content to be learned
will often be different, of course, but the processes of doing so
should be the same.

Tacit Learning

One reason out-of-school learning is effective is that it is frequently both implicit (or tacit, in Polanyi's terms) and acquired not
as an end in itself, but as part of the process of trying to achieve
some other end. Language itself is probably the best example of a
system acquired without conscious awareness of explicit teaching
and developed most effectively through meaningful use. We will
discuss those learning processes more fully in subsequent chapters. But for the moment think of something you, yourself, happen
to do well that you learned exclusively or almost exclusively in an
out-of-school context. Whether it is a physical activity like playing
tennis or just running, or a mental process like how to order food
in a restaurant or ask a person for a date, most of us can't verbally
describe the skills required to do the task. This is natural enough,
since they are almost entirely unconscious and we developed them
largely through trial and error. We may have been aided by tips
from expert performers, but these are frequently not very helpful
because even experts may not consciously know how they do what
they do, or may give advice in a form useless to anyone without the
same experiential background. I remember being given lots of un-
usable advice on how to use the clutch as I learned to drive, and
then, ironically, largely repeating the process when teaching my
son and daughter the same thing.

Above all, we succeeded when we did because we wanted to
badly enough to pick ourselves up and start over whenever we
stumbled during the learning process. The goal was sufficiently at-
tractive to be worth the investment of energy and time and to overcome whatever risks there were of looking foolish. We probably did
learn some by watching expert practitioners, and some from trying
to imitate them, but even there it was probably not the detailed
steps or skills that were most helpful but the picture of the whole
activity we were able to build by observing how it is supposed to be
done. This is vital because learners must have the big picture of
the whole building if they are to grasp the meaningfulness of the
foundational activities required for eventual mastery.

In addition to purposefulness, another of the characteristics of
such learning is its holistic quality. That is, the unit of learning has
a kind of integrity of meaningfulness which can provide the learner
with a clear overview of the connections between the subroutines

to be mastered and the whole activity. There may be times when particular subroutines need to be practiced independently, although even there I would tend to question the commonsense assumption that such practice is more useful than attempting whole tasks over and over again, but unless the *learner* can clearly see the connection between the part and the whole, practicing the part is likely to be either useless, in that it won't transfer to the whole, or even counterproductive, in that it may give the learner a distorted picture of what the whole is.

Top-Down/Holistic Learning

One of the clearest examples of the conflict between common- and uncommonsense views of learning can be seen in this contrast between the commonsense view of bottom-up, part-to-whole learning and the uncommonsense advocacy of top-down, holistic learning. For the uncommonsense position, *the basics are not the set of separate skills that can be analytically identified as parts of a larger whole, but a sense of the whole itself.* So when a child begins to read or to write, for example, the child's view of the task is—and should be—a holistic one: to make meaning from the text being read or to create a meaningful text by writing it. Children will not be fully successful in their first attempts, of course, at least from an adult perspective and probably from their own, but these attempts are nevertheless holistic right from the start.

Frank Smith's famous list of "12 ways to make learning to read difficult and one difficult way to make it easy" (1973) expresses this conflict clearly, since his ways to make beginning reading difficult are all based on the bottom-up, analytical approach so common in schools and supported by the commonsense view of learning. His easy way, to attend to what learners are doing when they read meaningful texts from the very start, perfectly expresses the holistic view. In her dissertation, Martha Bell (1977) provided support for his view by showing that beginning readers who had not had any reading instruction (of the commonsense sort) began to succeed as readers once they realized that the written text didn't vary from one reading to the next (unlike oral stories which can and do vary even though they are still the "same" story), and once they began by reading the texts in meaningful units—phrases or sentences—only attempting to decode particular words or letters when they couldn't make sense of the more holistic attempt. Children who started with individual letters or words, by contrast, had great difficulty putting the larger pieces together and rarely, if ever, were able to make sense of the text.

The same has been shown to be true of children's first attempts at writing, where children intend their texts to be meaningful from the very start. They may not, initially, be able to read their own texts, but even then they often believe they are meaningful. In the case of Vivi, studied by Anne Dyson (1983), her scribbles were incomprehensible to her (since she knew she didn't know how to read), but she was sure they could be read by her mother who did know how to read. Such texts probably will not employ conventional spelling, but as Charles Read (1971), Carol Chomsky (1974), and Glenda Bissex (1980) have shown, that does not mean they are completely randomly spelled. (Indeed, children's invented spellings are remarkably systematic, consistent both within and across children, and display considerable phonetic acuity.) And the texts they produce using such spellings are always intended to be meaningful even if, as adults, we may have some trouble in reading them as such until we learn the code being employed.

The first written text composed by Glenda Bissex's five-year-old son Paul, for example, was a note to his mother which asked,

RUDF [Are you deaf?]

This brief note called upon:

• His sense of purpose: to get his mother's attention away from the book she was reading.
• His sense of audience: his mother, the reader.
• His communicative competence: questions must be answered in such a social context.
• His linguistic competence: correct vocabulary and syntax, albeit still a bit unconventional on the spelling front.
• His knowledge of the world: there are deaf people in the world who cannot hear, but his mother is not one of them even though she was temporarily acting as though she were, so there is an ironic quality about this note as well.
• His rhetorical skills: a personal appeal to his mother's sense of guilt was likely to be an effective attention-getting device.

The point I want to emphasize, however, is that even though we can analyze the competencies required to produce such a note, the striking thing about it is that it works as a whole and was so intended. In fact it did the trick, his mother reports, and she did stop reading and attend to him. Paul couldn't have made that analysis, nor was he consciously aware of using such systems. They are not "skills" which can be or should be separately taught. Conversely, "diagnosing" Paul's "problems" as an inability to spell or use lower-case letters or appropriate punctuation, and then pre-scribing a set of drills before he tries to write again, which might be the commonsense response, would ignore the level of sophistica-tion he has already achieved. Even more important, it would deny the centrality of his intentional use of the written language, which had driven him to write in the first place and which would be the most likely motivation for him to continue to do so to improve all aspects of his emerging competence.

The bottom-up view based on the analysis of such "skills" into a sequence of subparts assumes that such parts will eventually coalesce into wholes. The uncommonsense position, by contrast, is that the multilayered quality of textual meanings that we've seen even in the relatively simple text produced by Paul, *means that the whole is greater than the sum of its parts because it involves the simulta-neous interaction of all these aspects of meaning.* So, unlike the com-monsense position, here the "basics" are not separable atomic skills but are integral to and inseparable from the overall meanings being constructed. Every reader or writer is making a whole construction, and any examination of how successfully it achieves its purpose depends on first looking at the whole and then later, on reflection, looking to see where and how it could be strengthened or enriched. In Paul's case, therefore, an uncommonsense teacher would not first teach him to spell so that he could later use the words in written texts, but would instead encourage him to write and then work with him to see how his texts could be made more readable by others, for example by making his spelling more conventional, but only gradually and unobtrusively.

This corresponds directly to Frank Smith's *"one difficult rule for making learning to read easy: respond to what the child is trying to do"* (1973, p. 195, his italics). He calls it difficult in part because it demands teacher attention to each individual child and a high level of "insight, tolerance, sensitivity and patience" (p. 195), not easy things to achieve in a commonsensically ordered school or class-room. And, as I have tried to make clear, it violates the common sense of learning which underlies conventional instruction in read-ing and writing. But, as he argues, "there is no alternative. The rule recognizes that the motivation and direction for learning to read [or, I would add, learning to write or learning anything else] must come from the child, and that he must look for the knowledge and skills he needs only in the process of reading" (p. 195).

One reason that it is so important to explore our common-sense theories of learning, in fact, is that the assessments we make of student abilities and deficiencies stem directly from our implicit or explicit theories of the ways such abilities develop. In part what is involved here is a contrast between those who view the glass as half empty and those who see it as half full. The bottom-up commonsense approach has tended to look at what children cannot do, while the top-down uncommonsense perspective is much more likely to stress what they can do. In the commonsense view, errors are seen as proof of deficiency; *the uncommonsense view, in contrast, regards errors as evidence of learning,* the challenge being to determine what has been learned in order to help the child go on to new and more appropriate learning. The adult response is also likely to differ from each perspective with the half-empty view leading to an emphasis on how much still has to be learned, while the half-full response would stress the power already achieved. Which response would you rather receive? Which is likely to make you want to try again?

This positive emphasis does not mean that the uncommonsense view is endorsing an "anything goes" position. Children still must learn how to spell and punctuate, to read texts attentively and not as Rorschach blots, and to develop the capacity to express themselves with both power and clarity. Mastering the conventions of the standard written language is essential for school success from both points of view. The difference being stressed here is one of means, not ends; the uncommonsense position is based on the notion that more children can learn to achieve powerful command of the written language in this way than has ever been the case using commonsense approaches. The uncommonsense position is not, as it has sometimes been accused of being, a path to lower standards; it is an approach which can lead to the achievement of even higher levels of performance by a wider segment of the population.

The contrast between top-down and bottom-up learning is also built on the recognition that most of the abilities we are trying to have children develop are not achieved on a once-only basis. That is, we don't learn to read or to write, for example, once and for all at first grade or tenth grade or whenever. Each text we try to make meaning from as readers or construct meaning in as writers presents new problems of interpretation and construction. There are, of course, things which we carry over from earlier texts as we confront the new one, but they are not separable, conscious skills like the sound-letter correspondence of "K" or the rule for placement of topic sentences in paragraphs. Some of those "skills" may be determined by analysis to be part of the student's repertoire, but in the actual processes of reading and writing, they are functioning completely without awareness and are attended to consciously only when problems develop and the pupil is reflecting on the meaning he has made either to clear up a difficult passage or to prepare for revision of his text.

Further, they are acquired not through deliberate attention to each bit but as part of the unconscious process of meaning making. As we will see when we look more closely at the processes of language acquisition and use, the processes of using language function unconsciously while we are using them. What we are conscious of, and therefore can control deliberately, are the intentions we have in using the language and the products we produce— meanings—as we do so. What this suggests, therefore, is that learning must be seen as a cyclical, constructive, and intention-driven process in which the learner pays attention to what he or she is trying to accomplish during the process of language use and considers the means of doing so only in moments of reflection on what has been accomplished.

Competent Children

Another aspect of my interpretation of the underlying competencies revealed by Paul's "RUDF" text is to see that the level of thinking he has already achieved calls into further question the conventional view of stages of intellectual development. Phillida Salmon's *Living in Time: A New Look at Personal Development* (1985) emphasizes that the conventional development view of moving from childhood incompetence to adult competence and power followed by a decline of abilities as we reach old age at best oversimplifies and at worst actually distorts both our understanding and our actions. She emphasizes how much children at five have already mastered.

By the time they reach school, all children possess rich resources of human understanding. If only through tagging along with Mum in her daily routine, young children have learned much about the way people live, the way people relate to each other, the way matters are organized. What kinds of things happen to people in buses, shops, post office, clinic—what transactions are done, how people behave, what is possible and not possible—all this is familiar territory. The domestic scene, the domain of women with young children, is, of course, intimately known by five-year-olds, most of whom will, too, have visited homes other than their own. Many children have, by this age, acquired a specialized knowledge of their own. The experience of play school, nursery groups or being "minded," bring their own insiders' understandings, as does that of being taken into care, or living with parents who are breaking up. A few children, through the circumstances of their family housing, spend much of their preschool lives outside the house and become "streetwise." Others have, by the time they start school, become aware of their own ethnic minority status—they know how to be inconspicuous in public, what places to avoid and what kinds of trouble they and their families may meet. And children of five have not acquired all these kinds of understanding by being merely spectators on life; in one way or another, they are already active participants in living. (p. 24–5.)

She goes on to point out that despite these achievements, both the common sense of our own adult perspective on childhood and much of developmental psychology goes on emphasizing the incompetence of childhood. Indeed it is this perspective of the child as helpless and in need of guidance that has created the institution of the school and the legal compulsion which requires children to be there from six to sixteen.

Neither she nor I would question the *potential* benefits for children of going to school, but the reality is often less than positive as long as schools systematically ignore the competence that children bring with them when they arrive and the modes of learning that they have developed in their out-of-school life. The crucial thing about all of the learning Salmon lists in the quoted passage is the evidence of how much "children are able to learn what they have not been explicitly taught—to assimilate, through a kind of osmosis, what is happening around them, *if they can directly participate in it*" (p. 27, my italics). The commonsense views of learning have tended to ignore or minimize the significance of such osmotic learning, and yet it is clear that most of the competencies we need to function in life are learned just that way. (Ironically, in view of my concerns here, common sense itself is a set of those competencies acquired by osmosis. But like any predictive set of constructs, common sense can become ossified and impermeable if it is not the subject of reflection.)

Spontaneous and Scientific Learning

Given the power of such learning in context, how can it be related to the more systematic and disembedded kinds of learning which are the hallmarks of schooling? In some cases we need to abandon many of the disembedded attempts to teach rules and drill on out-of-context skills. While such "direct teaching" does not seem very useful, there are instances when children can benefit from adult guidance and instruction. In order to be able to identify such cases, we need to explore what sorts of learning principles and processes are involved.

The key thinker in helping us do so is the Russian psychologist, L. S. Vygotsky, whose two major works have been translated into English as *Thought and Language* (1962) and *Mind in Society* (1978). They were written in the twenties and thirties in the U.S.S.R. prior to his death from tuberculosis at the age of thirty-eight in 1934. Of particular relevance in this context are his emphasis on the role of language and the culture from which it springs as driving forces in the development of thought, his concern for the relationship between concepts developed through experience (spontaneous concepts) and those acquired through the mediation of others (scientific concepts), and his exploration of a framework and a mechanism for fusing the two, his now famous "Zone of Proximal Development."

The kinds of learning outlined by Salmon in the passage quoted above would have been, for Vygotsky, excellent examples of acquiring spontaneous concepts. Essentially such concepts are derived from our experiences in and observations of the world we live in. This aspect of learning is quite similar to the ideas of Piaget, and Vygotsky acknowledges his debt to Piaget's early work. What Vygotsky adds, however, and what is crucial for understanding the dynamics of school learning, is that once such concepts have been acquired spontaneously, they can then be reflected upon consciously, and when they are, in particular through transactions with others, they can be generalized, extended, and, in effect, remade into scientific concepts.

Unlike the commonsense approach which stressed being conscious and in control from the start of a learning sequence, for Vygotsky "Consciousness and control appear only at the late stages of the development of a function, after it has been used and practiced unconsciously and spontaneously. In order to subject a function to intellectual control, we must first possess it" (1962, p. 90). He is clear that the process of conscious reflection is necessary to give us intellectual control, but until we have some experience to reflect upon, some possession of the concept derived from our experience of it, then there is no possibility of reflecting, since the experiential well is dry.

What has gone wrong with many of the commonsense approaches to schooling is that the reflection and analysis of, say, the skills involved in reading have been done by adults who have had the experiential background. This would not be dangerous, and might even be helpful, if the result of that analysis and reflection had not been made the basis of reading instruction for children who have not had the experiential background to develop sponta-

neous concepts on which to reflect. It is this step, taken by educators in an honest attempt to make the processes of learning more
effective, which has turned out to be a recipe for failure for those
children who are asked to learn things consciously before they have
experienced them holistically and spontaneously.

In the case of reading, Vygotsky's theory provides an explanation for the often observed phenomenon that *those children who learn
to read best in school are those who have been read to frequently before they
get there*. In Vygotskyan terms, the process of reading to children has
enabled them to develop a variety of spontaneous concepts about
the nature of the processes involved, including such things as how
to distinguish the first and last pages of a book, how to tell whether
the book is upside down, the direction of text (left to right, right to
left, top to bottom, etc.), the fact that the squiggles on the page
correspond to the language the child is acquiring simultaneously,
and so on. None of these things is "taught" to children as they sit
on their parent's lap, any more than they are taught that stories
contain worlds of pleasure and mystery and surprise, but without
such experiences through which children can build such spontaneous concepts, there is not the foundation necessary to build a
more intellectually controlled approach to reading.

Therefore *the first step in an uncommonsense approach to school
learning will be to build on young people's spontaneous concepts where
they are available, and to provide experiences which will help develop them
when they are not*.

But it also should be emphasized that Vygotsky is not suggesting that spontaneous concept development is the end of the
developmental process. For him "Human learning presupposes a
specific social nature and a process by which children grow into the
intellectual life of those around them" (1978, p. 88). His emphasis
on the social nature of learning derives from his observation that
children do not learn and grow completely from the inside out by
acting alone on their environment, as Piaget had seemed to suggest, but do so in a sociocultural context centrally involving other
people. The process involved is that of teaching and learning
within the "Zone of Proximal Development [which is defined as]
the distance between the actual developmental level [of the learner]
as determined by independent problem solving and the [learner's
current] level of potential development as determined through
problem solving under adult guidance or in collaboration with more
capable peers" (1978, p. 86). What the adult or more capable peer
provides is a kind of scaffolding which enables the learner to develop further through reflecting on experience, making connections
between prior and new knowledge, and learning from the more
able performance of teachers and/or more knowledgeable peers.

We've already seen one example of this process at work in Elizabeth's conversation with her mother about the fireplace ashes. But in the interests of freshness let's look at another, this time from a group of older children working together in school. The example is taken from Mike Torbe and Peter Medway's *The Climate for Learning* (1981). The children are thirteen, the course is science, and the lesson is about the food chain. Mary plays the role of the more competent peer; Barney is working through his own zone of proximal development. Their problem is to comprehend a worksheet with a diagram of a food chain involving insects, small animals and birds, and a cat. The children spontaneously know something about who eats whom in the natural world; the goal of this lesson is to turn those spontaneous concepts into a more scientific one.

BARNEY: (*reading from sheet*) Could you say something about the number of greenfly compared to the number of cats—the number of cats compared to the number of owls?

MARY: Hmmm, well, there are more greenflies than cats, actually—hang on a minute, let's have a look. Yeah, because a cat, right, the cat has only got one thing to feed on, hasn't it?

BARNEY: What's that? Sparrows?

MARY: Look, mouse

BARNEY: And sparrows

MARY: Well, you know, but—

BARNEY: The cat can feed on the sparrows and . . . on the mouse.

MARY: Yeah, but there are more greenflies because it's got lettuce, wheat, and grass, and really there are more greenflies than cats.

BARNEY: Well, if . . . the cats die, the sparrows will increase more, 'cos the cat eat more sparrows than mouse, 'cos the cats can't find mouse 'cos they hide. . . . (p. 13.)

Barney is using his spontaneous knowledge of cats (they kill both mice and sparrows) but mice are harder because they hide (he's apparently forgotten that sparrows can fly) to wrestle with understanding the larger picture of the whole food chain. Mary, who understands it somewhat better, provides some learning strategies ("Hang on a minute, let's have a look"), and also some richer interpretive knowledge ("There are more greenflies because it's got lettuce, wheat, and grass [to eat]"), as scaffolds to facilitate Barney's forming tentative conclusions as well as to make him feel safe in doing so.

In some ways peers are better able to do this than adults because there is no gap between them as there usually is between child and expert and which we saw earlier in the milk example.

Further, there are far fewer threats of embarrassment or assessment from peers. There are some, of course, and Torbe and Medway introduce this section by saying that this peer interchange was
slow to get started because Barney and Alan, the other boy at the
table, were hesitant to work with a girl (these are thirteen-year-
olds, after all), but her competence eventually won them over in
what was, also, a positively collaborative classroom atmosphere.
Children (and teachers) have to learn how to function in and structure such a collaborative atmosphere, but once created it can, in the
title of Torbe and Medway's book, provide a powerful *Climate for
Learning*.

One of the concerns that is sometimes broached about such
peer interchanges is that they may be beneficial for the less able
pupils, but they have little to offer the more able. But it's a rare
situation where any one pupil is always more able in every learning
domain than her peers; in this case it's more crucial to remember
how much *all of us can and do learn from teaching*. What seems to
happen in Vygotskyan fashion is that the process of engaging in
such conversations requires us to clarify our own understandings
through the need to articulate them. Or we may use the encounter
to actually push and develop our understanding further.

Torbe and Medway show that this is exactly what happened
for Mary (and, happily, for Barney too, since he was sharing Mary's
consciousness at the moment) at the end of the discussion. In their
words, "something else happens. Barney reads the last question,
and Mary's answer takes them both clear away from the hot classroom, along a logical chain to an important generalization."

BARNEY: Can you think of any reason why people try to save
    endangered animals from being ex- . . . extinct?
MARY: Because if one of those animals dies, obviously the other
    animals will have less food to feed on, right? And that food-
    chain is getting more dangerous, and less and less, and we're
    one of those food-chains, we're in part of that food-chain, so
    we hope they'll be all right. (p. 13–14.)

They go on to point out that they still have more to learn
before the concept will be fully generalized and more secure, but
most important:

Once patterns like that are perceived, even dimly, then learning stops being a chore. On the tape, the quality of the voices
changes: the serious tone of voice of both speakers, the tenta-
tiveness, the note of recognition, indicate that the pupils have
now become active seekers after the understanding of these
difficult new ideas. (p. 14.)

Perhaps the crucial thing about the generalization is that for all its scientific validity, it feels like—and is—*their* construction: It is the meaning that they have made from this transaction between the school's knowledge and that which they brought with them. They can be confident about it because it unites both kinds of knowledge, and because through their reading and, above all, their collaborative talk, they have made it for themselves. It is this sense of confidence and satisfaction which produces the changes Torbe and Medway note, and which has the power to continue to animate their learning.

Since this process involves joining spontaneous and scientific concepts, it develops personal knowledge and acquires its sense of purposefulness from its connection to their continuing desire to understand their world. Like Elizabeth with her questions about ashes, Mary and Barney are building their Kellyan world picture, and the constructs they are acquiring here do help to modify their understanding of the way the world works. And unlike the earlier milk example, in this context their questions and concerns are directly connected to the school learning. Mary's sense that "we hope [the endangered species] will be all right" is not an empty or merely verbal construct, it is deeply felt and firmly connected to her growing understanding of how she fits in her world. Had these students not been allowed to use their own language and their own experiences as the basis on which to build their generalization, they might have been able to "learn" it (in the commonsense meaning of being able to feed it back correctly on the test), but it probably would not have modified their world theory because it would have lacked the essential ingredients of personal purpose, personal experience, and active participation in the process of building it.

Another feature of the disembedded concepts and context-free skills which have been the primary staple of commonsense schooling has been their almost relentless cognitive emphasis. That is, commonsense learning theory has been built almost entirely on how children acquire objective knowledge and transferable skills, with little or no attention to the affective or feeling side of the learning process or the content of school learning. Uncommonsense approaches have seriously questioned that dichotomy and it is clear that every construct includes both cognitive and affective elements. We can see this in the "hope" expressed by Mary, Elizabeth's intense involvement in finding out why her mother is shoveling the ashes, and even in the thwarted efforts of the chemistry students to relate their experiences with milk to the teacher's concern with particles in suspension. Part of the reason for the uncommonsense emphasis on the role of student purposes in learning springs from this recognition that personal involvement—and

hence affect—plays a crucial role in every aspect of the learning process. Indeed the uncommonsense approach deliberately re-
verses the commonsense equation of work with suffering, and
insists, instead, that *genuine learning should be personally rewarding
both for the sense of confidence which comes from building competence and
from the inherent fascination of the things themselves.*

A related difference between common- and uncommonsense
approaches stems from the fact that commonsense learning is conceived as a more individual, and hence actually or potentially competitive, process. It is clearly the case that, finally, each student
must develop a sense of individual achievement, but the processes
of learning in the uncommonsense view are much more likely to
be collaborative. Barney and Mary are clearly benefiting from their
collaboration, and, while it would be hard to prove, it seems likely
that they are learning more working together than either would
have done working alone. There are times when children must
work alone—reading or drafting a text are normally done most
effectively in private—but even in such cases both the reading and
the writing will be enriched if the meanings which are made privately are then shared for feedback and enrichment. Collaborative
learning is not a panacea for student success, but when understood, it can be seen as a powerful boost to individual learning
efforts.

Learning How to Learn

Neither Barney nor Mary is likely to have been conscious of
the process each was using to turn spontaneous into scientific
concepts, nor should they be at the moment of struggling to solve
the problem. One of the crucial aspects of the uncommonsense
approach to learning is that conscious reflection on what you've
learned and, crucially, on how you've learned it, should play a
central role in the learning process. Focusing on what has been
learned is important because it helps to solidify the accomplishment and build the kind of confidence that can only come from
genuine achievement. Focusing on how one learned it may, in the
long run, be even more significant because *the most significant learning that one can accomplish in schools is to learn how to learn.*

Even commonsense schools have often given at least lip service to the idea that their pupils should be learning how to learn,
but for the most part have done little or nothing to promote it
beyond such vague principles as study hard, do your work regularly rather than cramming for tests, and be well organized. Since
the commonsense curriculum has been based on adult analyses of

how subjects and skills should be most effectively presented to ensure their transmission, the processes of learning required to do such analysis and synthesis have been largely reserved to the teacher. Pupils have been expected only to work their way steadily and diligently through the predigested syllabus, and if they were never able to connect its scientific concepts to their own spontaneous ones, that was not viewed as a problem as long as they could meet the assessment demands of the commonsense-based testing system which have been, primarily, regurgitative of information and imitative of skills.

One thing far too many students have learned about school learning is that it doesn't really touch their real lives at all, and so they have increasingly welcomed the boring irrelevance of school since it made few demands on the kinds of energies they were devoting to finding and solving the real problems of life. The implicit negotiations between teacher and students revealed in the observations of Powell et al. (1985) and Sedlak et al. (1986) reveal how effective students can be in limiting the demands of the classroom and in making sure that it doesn't impinge on their time and energy once they have done their part by being minimally disruptive in class. The energy level students show in the playgrounds and corridors of most schools contrasts sharply with their torpor within the classroom. The uncommonsense approach to learning hopes to find some way of capturing those energy levels and devoting them to school learning as well as to life learning.

Further, as Robert Hull (1985, esp. Ch. 4) has pointed out, one of the ironies of the attempt to simplify and sequence the material being learned is that it is presented to students in a kind of intellectual shorthand whose apparent simplicity may actually make it more difficult for children to understand what is going on. The generalization that Mary and Barney come to about the food chain can only be fully comprehended by them after the processes of interpretation and construct building that have preceded it. Presented cold by the teacher it might be memorized and therefore recalled, but it would be unlikely either to be connected to their own experience or contextually understood. Hull's book is full of examples of discussions with children who have "learned" a concept, only to find when talking to them that they didn't really understand it. Quite similar findings were shown by Mary Barr (1983) in her discussion with physics students about the second law of thermodynamics after they had already passed the test. The "best" students, those who scored highest on the test, were the most surprised of all to find that they really hadn't "gotten it" to the point where they could explain the concept to someone who didn't understand it. They possessed only the verbal version of the scientific concept, not the experiential understanding which would have enabled them to discuss it with someone else.

In addition to a misguided notion of what will make content easier to learn, however, *commonsense schools often don't help students learn how to learn because they don't think students really can*. It seems to be tacitly assumed in commonsense schooling that only the elite few can really learn how to learn, and they will figure it out on their own. The rest of the student body is assumed to need both a carefully sequenced curriculum and lots of prodding and monitoring in the form of drills, homework exercises, and frequent quizzes or tests. Part of my own experience as a student has been that the amount of close supervision of this kind varies inversely with the institution's sense of the competence and talent of its students. If the school thinks the students are bright and capable, the busy-work and monitoring goes way down, while schools (or tracks within schools) that have less confidence in the ability of the pupils ride them continuously.

This is not an invariant feature, however, as I discovered in visiting schools in Australia where, in the state of Victoria, the last two years of high school consist of two optional types of courses. The first type, which prepares people for the university entrance exams, features conventional commonsense instruction with a high emphasis on "covering" the required content. Lots of work is required, but it is all set and closely monitored by the teacher. The second, which can lead to university entrance but is more commonly elected by students who don't intend further education, is a much more individualized set of courses, whose content and learning processes are negotiated between the teacher and the students. Here, too, there is a heavy workload, but the choice of what to do and, crucially, of how it will be assessed is much more significantly determined by the student. Also, self-assessment is a vital part of the process. Here, contrary to American practice, it is the less academically inclined who are encouraged to become independent problem setters and solvers responsible for their own learning, and they refer to their peers in the more conventional academic track as "spoonies" because they are still being spoon-fed.

The success of these students in learning how to learn gives the lie to the idea that it is somehow beyond their capacity to do so, but it must be emphasized that they need—and get—a lot of help in doing so. One of the crucial roles that teachers can play with students as they transact with them within the zone of proximal development is to help them reflect on their processes of learning and on their growing achievements. Once we have mastered a particular ability we don't need to be continually evaluated on it because we know we can do it. But while we are in the process of developing our ability we need to learn to reflect on our progress and to develop criteria for assessing how far we have come and how far we have still to go. None of this is automatic, but once begun it can provide learners with both the ability to function effectively within the school context, and, more important, to continue to do so in the context of the novel learning challenges which will confront them once they leave school.

Uncommonsense approaches to learning, therefore, depend on both tacit (spontaneous) and explicit (scientific) knowledge, with the caveat that both kinds of knowledge are personal, not external to the learner. Tacit knowledge is acquired primarily through doing, that is, trying to accomplish some purposeful task, which simultaneously calls for and develops the competency to achieve it. It doesn't happen all at once, or perfectly the first time, to be sure, and there is need for a kind of apprenticeship period in which the learner is working collaboratively with peers and adults who are competent and can provide models of successful performance as well as shared efforts at achieving success. This sharing of consciousness, which is the hallmark of learning within the zone of proximal development, makes possible the acquisition of the more explicit, generalized, and scientific knowledge which results from conscious reflection on prior experience.

Learning and Narrative

We cannot leave the uncommonsense approach to learning without considering the role of narrative in learning and memory. The uncommonsense theory, like all theories, is in the process of evolving, and many of its principles will undoubtedly need to be revised before the full story of human learning is understood—if indeed it ever is. But there is no doubt that our holistic ways of knowing are best exemplified by and rooted in our personal stories. They create the space with which we explore our own place in the world. They not only help us consolidate and frame our knowledge of the world, but our own stories and those we hear from others are particularly crucial in helping us understand human motives and actions.

In recent years there has been an explosion of interest in the study of narrative: Philosophers, psychologists, literary theorists, linguists, anthropologists, and teachers have all been struck by the role of the stories we tell and the stories we hear as one of the major ways that we organize our worlds and our individual lives. Although there are, as in any academic endeavor, differences of emphasis among these perspectives, the striking thing about them all is their conviction that *the processes of stories provide a powerful way to understand how we think and feel, how we develop and sustain our identities, how we come to understand others both as individuals and as part of our culture, and how we come to know the world.*

From the positivist perspective, narratives were highly suspect entities with no possible truth value to their statements and an unseemly emphasis on the world of "what if." The meanings of narratives could not be pinned down neatly in propositional formulae, and therefore they were dismissed as insubstantial and, while possibly entertaining, not sufficiently serious to be worthy of serious (i.e. philosophical) consideration. This way of thinking has been described by Jerome Bruner (1986) as paradigmatic thought, with its emphasis on logic and on general cases, and he contrasts it with narrative thought, which is focused heavily on the particular, the unique, the individual. He finds these two modes of thought distinct but complementary, and in his recent book is at pains to redress what he sees as a traditional overemphasis in Western culture on the virtues of the logico-scientific focus of paradigmatic thought.

I am not so sure that the two are, for the individual, as distinct as he seems to think, since for me much of the logic of a generalized paradigmatic argument is built first by individuals through their capacity to tell stories with a point—or, in Labov and Waletsky's (1967) terms, to evaluate the significance of the story incidents— but it is clear that the values of our culture have heavily emphasized the paradigmatic at the expense of the narrative. One of the reasons for the emphasis in schools on objective truth and external knowledge has stemmed from that bias. So, too, has the method of teaching children by means of generalized rules, maxims, and precepts based on an analysis of the general principles required for, say, reading and writing. The point is not to suggest that such modes of thought have no place in schools, but rather to argue that they are not the only ways that humans think and that restricting schooling to them risks distortion.

Further, it fails to capitalize on one of the primary roles of narrative: to make personal meaning of the experience of our lives. This is such a normal experience for us as human beings that we often fail to see how significant it can be as a mode of learning. It seems so natural to share our experience with others in the form of stories—whether the mundane events of the weekend or, as in Labov's research, a dramatic incident when our life was in danger—that we tend not to notice how pervasive it is. Nor do we think about how stories are the major organizing principle of our memories so that our childhoods, our work and social lives, and our experiences of family and culture are frequently stored not as strings of propositions or even sensations but as stories: the time I painted my brother red with leftover paint; the moment George Harrington told me my parents were divorced; the first class I tried to teach when I was so nervous I could barely talk; or the first time I flew in a helicopter.

Social interactions are so commonly exchanges of stories that their very normality makes them almost invisible. We do notice them, sometimes, when we hear them a second or a third time, as is common in many family gatherings—so much so, in fact, that it might be argued that a common store of stories is what makes a family a family—but even there, they are frequently welcomed as evidence of our common heritage and of group solidarity. Cultures without writing systems depend very heavily on oral stories as a means of initiating neophytes into the culture and continuing to develop feelings of togetherness among the in-group. But even in literate cultures, story continues to play a similar role whether through common texts—the most powerful, traditionally, in our culture being the Bible—or through stories for children, or even, in contemporary culture, through the stories of the mass media: television dramas, soap operas, and, perhaps most significant, commercials, most of which are, not surprisingly, mini-narratives. One of the reasons for Ronald Reagan's continuing hold on the American public was clearly his capacity as a storyteller. Even the revelation of his frequent conflation of stories from the movies with historical reality only serves to emphasize the centrality of narrative as a mode of understanding the world.

For Phillida Salmon (1985), the metaphor of life as a story is the most powerful way we have to envision human potential and to value each stage of life as a time of worth. One reason that I have been telling stories of my own experience as a teacher and a learner throughout has been that *in telling each story I have been able to reflect on the experience and to change the interpretation I made at the time.* This possibility for reinterpreting the meaning of our experience can be done most naturally through telling a different version of our life story, for although the incidents may remain the same, the value we attach to them and the interpretation we make of them can be quite dramatically altered. I was, for example, quite proud of my performance as a lecturer in junior English, and had I told the story of that year while I still had a commonsense perspective, it would have had a very different quality than the story of the "same" events told from an uncommonsense perspective. Just as the same book has different meanings for us at different stages of our lives, so the stories we tell about our own lives can be shifting in interpretation if we are still growing and changing.

Further, the intimate connection between the story of our lives and the lives of the others who play significant parts in it enables us to see dramatically the interdependence of human lives and human cultures, to see why and how we come to value the stories of others as we are composing our own, since the experience of others' stories enables us to try out alternative lives both as potential models and as patterns to avoid. Oliver Sacks (1985), in working with brain-damaged patients, has found that some forms of amnesia rob us of our identity, so that a patient with Korsakov's syndrome:

> *must literally make himself (and his world) up every moment.* We have, each of us, a life-story, an inner-narrative—whose continuity, whose sense, *is* our lives. It might be said that each of us constructs and lives a 'narrative,' and that this narrative *is* us, our identities.
>
> If we wish to know about a man, we ask, "what is his story—his real, inmost story?"—for each of us is a biography, a story. Each of us *is* a singular narrative, which is constructed, continually, unconsciously, by, through, and in us —through our perceptions, our feelings, our thoughts, our actions; and, not least, our discourse, our spoken narrations. Biologically, physiologically, we are not so different from each other; historically, as narratives—we are each of us unique.
>
> To be ourselves we must *have* ourselves—possess, if need be repossess, our life stories. (p. 105, his italics.)

Although rarely reflected upon or noticed, such a conception is not incompatible with common sense, at least the out-of-school common sense which we employ as parents and professionals, as partygoers and workers, as friends and lovers. What makes it uncommonsensical in this context is recognizing its potential role as a means of learning and knowing in school as well as out. This can happen by encouraging children to use personal narratives to understand their own worlds and those of others. Or it can happen as we experience and make our own meanings from the lives of others through fiction, biography, and even history. As Harold Rosen (1984) has pointed out, "We neglect it at our peril. We have to reinstate it to its proper place in the discourse of the classroom" (p. 24). He goes on to argue that to continue to ignore the central role of narrative in meaning making in school is to concede defeat to the technocratic test makers who value the general over the particular, the decontextualized over the personal, and the extant text over the processes of meaning making which are involved in creating and interpreting such texts.

The stories that Wally and the other children tell in Vivian Paley's classroom (1981) are both means of revealing what they know and, more important, of making new meanings as they grow in understanding of themselves, their classmates, and the larger world in which they live. For young children, especially, the general is always embedded in the particular, and narrative is the bridge between the two because its evaluative properties bring general meanings from particular events. As some of the persistent confusions (from an adult point of view) of *Wally's Stories* demonstrate, the process of learning through stories is not always linear or immediate, but if the point of observing the meaning-making process is to track the sense that children are making of the curriculum, then stories can function effectively both as a means of promoting such meaning making and as a way of revealing those understandings that have still not been mastered.

This kind of an uncommonsense approach to learning contrasts sharply with the commonsense approach, for it is centered on the child's achievements as a personal meaning maker, not on the capacity to reproduce in whole or in part the prestructured meanings that we are attempting to transmit. As teachers we often at least dimly understand that the meanings our students are making are different—sometimes even radically different—from those we intend them to be deriving from our texts and tests. Commonsense approaches to learning have usually responded to such "problems" by trying to restructure the way we are transmitting and testing for knowledge or by blaming the students for perverseness, stupidity, or lack of motivation. Uncommonsense approaches, in contrast, take the position that we must understand and value the learners' meanings, for they are what the whole game is about.

All learners finally must make whatever sense they can out of the experience of school just as they do of the other experiences of their lives. Uncommonsense theory celebrates that reality rather than trying to conceal or deny it, and finds in narrative modes of thinking and the experience of telling (or writing) and listening to (or reading) stories one of the primary modes of placing the student at the center of the learning process as a meaning maker, not only as a meaning receiver. And like Vygotsky's spontaneous concepts—which are closely related to the concepts we build through the stories we tell of our experience—the truths of narrative need not be the end of the process, since they can and should provide the basis upon which to build the more abstract, the more general, the more scientific, the more paradigmatic modes of thought as well as retaining their value as meaning-making processes throughout our lives. Indeed stories are the natural ways we begin to see scientific causation through narratives of the life cycle of insects, the seasonal cycle of agriculture, and the like. We do not lose our need for narrative, as Salmon and Sacks have made clear, but we can build on it toward more generalized knowing as well.

As we look further at the nature of language and its role in both meaning making and knowing we will see more clearly the intimate connections between learning and language, and, particularly, learning and narratives. Like much else in the uncommon-sense theory of learning, there is much more we need to know and understand about their interactions, especially how they can be fostered in uncommonsense classrooms. A lot of that further understanding will have to be developed by reflective teachers functioning as researchers and observers in their own classrooms in the way that Vivian Paley has already vividly demonstrated. The story of stories has only begun to be told.

Uncommonsense Learning: A Brief Summary

Uncommon sense is based on learning as the result of intentional or purposeful action. The learning itself may be tacit or unconscious, but the motivation for performing the tasks which will lead to the learning has to be a sense of personal meaningfulness for the learner. This can be seen both in the importance of contextualized as opposed to disembedded learning and in the recognition that learning in school and out of school involves fundamentally similar processes.

Tacit learning is holistic and top-down in the sense that whenever analytically independent bits of knowledge and skill are acquired they are mastered in the context of a meaning-making task rooted in experience. In that sense they are acquired in passing, on the way to doing something else which has a meaningful integrity for the learner. Learning is not something distinct from living but an integral part of all life processes. We learn by constructing our mental theory or our story of the way the world works; and we do this through a continual process of prediction/hypothesis testing based on the transaction between our interpretations of our prior experiences and the new ones we continually face. These processes engage all aspects of our minds: our feeling and perceptions as well as our constructs and conceptions. There can be, therefore, no meaningful separation into cognitive and affective learning, since every idea has a feeling component, and every feeling also involves an idea. Thus the basis of all learning is personal meaning making, which is an active process.

These learning processes are species-specific capacities of human beings, and although there are undoubtedly different talents and different experiential backgrounds which play a role in determining student learning potentials, the differences are greatly out-weighed by the similarities, and even the differences don't seem to be fixed or immutable. It seems likely that given the proper educational experiences, most children can achieve far more than they do in commonsense schools, and they can learn how to learn more effectively by mastering a variety of strategies, including those of reflecting on what they have achieved and assessing where they need to go. To do so they need help, of course, because learning is as much a collaborative social process as it is an individual one.

This help can come from both teachers and peers in school and from all sorts of people out of school. Learners are, finally, responsible for their own learning. They have to set and solve the problems and develop the skills, but they will do so most effectively in an environment which takes their meanings and purposes seriously and which allows them to act as well as to react. It will not be easy to achieve such climates for learning in conventional schools, and many aspects of those schools will have to change. But part of that change will occur only when teachers change our constructs and our stories of the nature of learning.

CHAPTER 5

Language I

Nature of the System and
How We Acquire It

One of the most striking features of commonsense views of language and language acquisition is how few there are. Language is so invisible, in the sense that it functions so automatically and unconsciously, that it is usually taken completely for granted until some sort of a problem presents itself, like being in a place where our language is not spoken, or trying to talk to very young children who have not yet acquired language. Our facility with language is so normal and apparently unremarkable that it is difficult to appreciate just how flexible and powerful the system of human language is. One of the tasks we face, therefore, is to try to make this familiar system strange, to see it as a source of wonder, so that we can more fully understand what its properties are and what they can tell us about the nature of the human mind and human learning.

My Path Toward Uncommon Sense

Although my experience of trying to make the transition from a commonsense education to uncommonsense theory and practice has been shared by many others, we have all had different critical incidents and different experiences which led us to the insights we now share. In my own educational and professional experience, the study of linguistics and, particularly, of how children acquire their first language was one of the major turning points. Part of the reason for this was timing: Not only did I come to the study of language at one of its most exciting periods, from 1966–1969, I also had the good fortune to be watching my two children developing their language systems and beginning to encounter the written language during the same period. Other factors which caused this field to have a great impact on me included both my dissatisfaction with the ways I had been expected to teach grammar as a junior and senior high school teacher, and my good fortune in studying with teachers and fellow students who were as excited about these developments as I was. These personal experiences have left me with a continuing fascination for the mysteries of the human mind which are so intriguingly hinted at by the properties of the language system, and also with a deep respect for the power of tacit learning, which is nowhere better illustrated than through the processes of first language acquisition.

In teaching linguistics and language acquisition to practicing and prospective teachers for many years, however, I have come to recognize that my path to uncommon sense is not a universal one, and that there are others which work equally well. In this chapter, therefore, I will try to show some of what has fascinated me about these topics and some of why I believe the theories and research in this area provide the most powerful scientific underpinning for the uncommonsense approach. It won't be possible here, however, to develop anything like a comprehensive account of these theories or the phenomena they explain. What I will try to do instead is to provide an account of the major implications of this area for language education.

The Study of Language

In order to accomplish the above task I have made a somewhat arbitrary decision to divide the exploration of language into two chapters. This one will focus on the nature of the system primarily from a linguistic and psycholinguistic point of view and will explore how the system is initially acquired, with particular attention to the ways in which producing language contributes to its acquisition and development; the next will look at how the system is used for communication and at how its use leads to further development of our capacities. It is important to acknowledge from the outset that this division may distort as well as reveal, since in many ways these aspects of the system are interdependent and interactive.

This division roughly corresponds to a distinction between the study of linguistic competence—what we *know* when we know a language—and linguistic performance—what we *know and do* when we use it. This distinction, originally proposed by Noam Chomsky, is far from universally accepted, particularly by those whose primary concern has been the study of language use. They have, following Dell Hymes, preferred the term "communicative competence" to performance theory as a more appropriate characterization of what people know as language users, since it emphasizes the primacy of communication as the chief function of language as well as recognizes the need to account for what we know as a basis for understanding what we can do.

I mention such theoretical disputes here because I have found that they confuse teachers or have made them decide that since the experts don't seem to be able to agree, then there is nothing of value in this area for teachers to learn. This has been particularly true for those of my teacher/students who have adopted the commonsense view that what gets transmitted to them in graduate school is "knowledge," which is then to be transmitted to their pupils. So they often think I'm proposing that they teach linguistics as a prescriptive discipline, replacing the "old" grammar with a newer, more scientific model, even though I *say* that is what I don't want them to do. My intention is, instead, to help them develop a new way of construing the language processes that their teaching involves. In fact, one way I learned to question the effectiveness of transmission teaching (preaching?) was by watching its lack of effect on my graduate students.

Part of the reason for this reaction, I think, stems from the misteaching of science—particularly to nonscientists, which language teachers generally are—as a body of consensual knowledge about which there are no fundamental disputes. When scientific knowledge is presented as an inert body of facts and laws, as it is in most secondary school and introductory level college science courses, then seeing scientists disagree does seem confusing and of doubtful value. A more accurate picture of what science is and what scientists do, however, would reveal that while there are areas which are quite well understood and about which there is broad agreement, the most interesting aspects of the discipline, and the reason scientists continue in it, are the areas where questions, problems, and mysteries remain. Such areas are frequently marked by conflict of theories and methods, but they are, all the same, the fields which are the most dynamic and most interesting.

The human mind in general and the language system in particular are areas of considerable contemporary scientific ferment and intellectual energy, containing many unanswered questions, unsolved problems, and as yet impenetrable mysteries. Language plays such a central role in human life and provides such an intriguing window on the hidden aspects of the human mind that it has become the focus of study not only for linguists but for anthropologists, philosophers, sociologists, neurologists, psychologists, and those of us concerned with language education. And from this ferment of enquiry have come remarkable discoveries and insights, despite the fact that many uncertainties remain. In any case the existence of disputes and controversies is not a sign of weakness, but rather demonstrates both how complex this field of study really is and how central it is to understanding the nature of human beings.

The Common Sense of Language

Although common sense takes language for granted—indeed, in one sense, common sense is itself couched in and acquired concurrently with language—it does so only in relation to oral language. Common sense may recognize that speaking and listening are automatic and unconscious and learned without formal instruction, but it believes reading and writing to be quite different. The commonsense view of the written language is that it cannot be learned without deliberate teaching and that its use is a much more conscious process. This belief rests partly on the commonsense approach to learning which we have already explored, partly on the common experience that *most of us believe we were taught to read and write in school,* and partly on the undeniable fact that all human communities have a spoken language system, but many do not have a written language system.

The commonsense view of the spoken language as an invisible system corresponds very well to the basis from which descriptive linguists start, since their most fundamental belief is that all of us possess a fully functioning language system which is acquired as a natural part of human development and which is functionally adequate for the purposes for which we employ it.

When we explore our commonsense beliefs about the nature of the oral language system, we frequently find them confounded by our experiences in school and, in particular, with the written language. This experience with learning the written language seems to be at least one source of the common belief that languages consist of sets of words (a complete dictionary would therefore contain the language), with perhaps a dimmer recognition that in order to be used properly these words must be combined according to a set of rules. When we hear people pronouncing words differently than we do, we may also become aware that there are rules for pronunciation as well as word order. Similarly, if we notice people using different patterns of, say, tense marking (he *be* going, not he *is* going), or pronoun case (*him and me* are going, not *he and*

I are going), we may understand more fully the nature of the patterning rules involved. Since in many cases these kinds of variations have been part of what we studied in school, we may be more sensitive to them than we might otherwise be, and specifically, may be convinced that learning such differences is a conscious process.

The common sense view of language acquisition, therefore, makes the process a relatively conscious one—consistent with commonsense learning theory—whereby children learn words and rules through parental (and, later, teacher) labeling and the explicit presentation and imitation of parental (and, again, teacher) models. Nothing much hangs on what parents believe in this case since, as we will see when we get to the uncommonsense theory, most of what they do proves to be remarkably helpful, to the extent that help is needed. What is important here is that this view has infected educational common sense and provides a continuing rationale for the kind of skills and drills approach which we have already seen characterizes commonsense learning theory in action. In particular, it continues to provide support for the complementary commonsense axioms that if something has been learned it must have been taught, and if it is to be learned it must be directly taught.

This attitude affects both the teaching of the written language—reading and writing—and the teaching either of a second language or of mainstream dialects to speakers who haven't learned them at home. The commonsense position on all of these three areas is that they must be deliberately taught and consciously learned. Although commonsense proponents may concede, in the face of the overwhelming reality of children coming to school speaking and listening to their native language, that acquiring such ability may be a natural process and not one that is deliberately taught and learned, the reality that some children do not learn to read and write and others fail to learn a mainstream dialect or a second language, in their view, justifies the need for direct instruction.

So commonsense schools provide it. We've already seen some examples of it in vocabulary and spelling lists, phonics rules, and prescriptive grammar drills. What they all have in common is their out-of-context quality, that is, they are not seen as part of the process of learning language in meaningful ways, but are presumed to be prerequisites of it. Further, someone else has done the real learning: the teacher or the textbook writer. *They* have had the experience of using the skill in context, and then, having analyzed what it requires, of providing drills intended to help develop that skill in others. Pupils are left to fill in someone else's blanks which often have no connection to their spontaneous concept-building experience to make them either meaningful or useful.

The combination of drills which look like tests and tests which echo the drills has made for a vicious instructional circle which has proven to be remarkably resistant to change. It pervades the early grades, and its manifestations echo upward in remedial programs ranging through the first year of college, all of which tend to be dominated by such dummy-run drills. And they are hard to eliminate because all parties to the process—test makers, textbook writers, teachers, students, administrators, and parents—really believe they are the key to learning. It seems so commonsensical to assume that if students are having difficulty with some aspect of writing or reading which we can identify analytically, then we can help them master it by teaching the appropriate rule and/or by drilling, whether the problem is how to use a comma before a coordinate conjunction, how to spell words with "e" and "i" combinations, or how to decode initial consonant blends. These shortcuts seem so sensible and so helpful that we can't imagine that they not only aren't helpful but are actually harmful.

Part of what makes them seem helpful is the fact that they are expressed in language that derives from the more prestigious field of medicine. Commonsense reading specialists *diagnose* problems and *prescribe* solutions. And parallel, if not so explicitly medical, terminology is used by writing teachers when they *mark* and *correct* errors. For those students who have had a sufficient amount of experience with actual reading and writing, such efforts are less likely to do harm, except by taking time away from the continuing experience they need to keep improving. What makes the exercises seriously harmful for many children and adolescents is the message they send about reading and writing: that each really consists of these out-of-context skills, even if there is never a reason or a need to use them.

Uncommonsense Language: Generative Grammar

A better model for developing the speaking and listening abilities of students, and for reading and writing instruction, can emerge from an uncommonsense look at the nature of the oral language system and how it is learned. The uncommonsense theory of the nature of language which forms the core of this chapter is based on the pioneering work of Noam Chomsky. Since the 1950s, Chomsky has been developing a linguistic theory called generative grammar, which is radically different from its predecessors and still the subject of considerable controversy both within and without linguistics.

My own introduction to Chomskyan linguistics illustrates how a new theory can function as a new set of lenses through which to view the world. As a high school teacher, I had become increasingly dissatisfied with the efficacy of the prescriptive grammar I was being required to teach by the commonsense curriculum. In part I remembered my own experience as an eighth-grade student sitting in Mrs. Norwood's room trying to come up with counter-examples to the "rules" propounded in Warriner's grammar. It didn't seem sensible to me, even at thirteen, that nouns were defined semantically (the name of a person, place, or thing) and yet identified functionally (the subject or object of a sentence, etc.). The fact that I was often successful in finding problems and exceptions raised my first questions about the validity of such rules, and my attempt to explain and justify them as a teacher—with the same book, ten years or so later—brought even more contradictions to the fore and made me even more skeptical.

Initially, therefore, my study of linguistics was an attempt to develop a more systematic basis for the kind of grammar we were teaching to children and adolescents. Indeed my first publication (Mayher 1968) can be read that way, although even then I was having a hard time fitting my emerging understanding of generative linguistics into the commonsense framework of prescriptive grammar teaching. This difficulty occurred not only because generative grammar is descriptive not prescriptive, but because it takes a radically different view of the notion of linguistic rules. The rules of language, for Chomsky, are not consciously developed maxims for proper usage but entirely unconscious constraints which, in effect, constitute or define the language itself. A generative grammar may attempt to describe the rules of our mental grammar, but in doing so it is modeling, in its representation, the properties of an individual's unconscious knowledge of the rules of the language, not laying down prescriptions to follow.

What would be the point, therefore, of teaching pupils rules which they already knew? The only sense one could make of such an attempt would be that it would somehow enable them to use the language better if the unconscious rules could be made conscious. But *there is no evidence that making rules of this sort conscious enhances language performance.* And the more I have studied language from this perspective, the more it has become clear that to attempt to have students make such rules conscious for the sake of improving the way they use language in writing or reading, speaking or listening, would be a serious distortion of the nature of both the process of language learning and the many processes involved in language use.

Generative linguistics attempts to understand more about the nature of the human mind. In that sense it does have things to tell us about language teaching and learning, but unless we want to teach some aspects of linguistics to students for the same sorts of reasons we might want to teach them other aspects of human biology and psychology—so that they will understand themselves and their world better—we must recognize that *there is no direct, instrumental connection between knowledge about language and language use.* I found the abandoning of this commonsense connection liberating, because I could now look first at the nature of the language system itself and then, separately, at its implications for language education.

I also found it fun, since, for me, it provided a fascinating lens through which to look underneath the appearances of what people do to the underlying structures and abilities that enable them to do so. I remember being fascinated, for example, by the fact that as children learn to speak, they go through three stages in mastering past tense forms of English irregular verbs. They start by getting them right, probably by more or less direct imitation, without understanding that they are composed of two parts: a stem and a tense marker. So initially they will say, *"He brought"* or *"She sang."* A bit later, as they are building their language to include a productive, albeit unconscious, rule of past-tense formation, they notice that most English verbs form the past tense with a regular *-ed* ending like *laughed.* At this stage they are likely to overgeneralize and overregularize all of the verbs, saying, *"He bringed"* or *"She singed."*

This phenomenon is particularly interesting because these are forms that they have never heard, which can therefore only be accounted for by something other than imitation or any kind of stimulus/response-based behaviorism. Finally children begin to sort verbs out, but the phenomenon lasts for quite a long time. Eventually, it becomes one of the things we can monitor on output, so that I remember my son Jack, when he was eight, saying, *"She teached us . . . ooops . . . she taught us."* He giggled a bit because he'd recognized his error, but both the error and his recognition of it tell us we must look beneath the surface of what he said in order to understand why he said it. I've taught linguistics long enough to know that not everyone shares my pleasure in the search, but I remain optimistic that teachers can come to see the significance of the results.

Language as a Creative System

The principal tenet of generative linguistics is that *language is not something we do with our voices or our ears, but something we know; a mental system which underlies our behavior.* For Chomsky the most interesting property of an individual's language system is its creativity. He does not mean creativity in the restricted sense we usually reserve for "creative" or imaginative writing of fiction or poetry but in the more extended sense which recognizes that each sentence we create, and each sentence we understand, is created or understood as though it were a wholly novel utterance. That is, in the normal, everyday ways we use language, we are making and interpreting new sentences which are in all relevant respects unique. There are, to be sure, some formulaic expressions which are repeated frequently in such activities as greetings and partings, but these are notable precisely because they are not the norm. When we reflect on our typical uses of language, including in this instance such activities as my writing or your reading this sentence, it is easy to see that the overwhelming number of utterances we produce and understand are completely new to us. That is what Chomsky means when he says the normal use of language is "creative" (1965, p. 6).

For language educators, the normality of the creative use of language has a variety of implications. One of them is that it is true of all human beings, not just a special few. When the telephone rings, for example, we may answer with a formulaic "Hello," but once we've gone beyond that, the rest of the conversation can potentially exploit our whole vocabulary, all of our rules of syntax, and so on. We almost never deliberately choose a particular word or syntactic construction for its own sake, but only to further the meaning we are making in the conversation. We may be funny or not, metaphoric or not, serious or not, but the unconscious creativity of the language system functions to support our intentions without our having to be aware of how it is working. In fact, trying to be aware of it makes the process cumbersome at best, and impossible at worst.

Commonsense teaching of first and second languages, with its stress on conscious control of vocabulary and syntactic rules, often functions, ironically, as an impediment to such creative use rather than as an enhancement of it. The first time I lived in France, long after my three years of high school and one year of college French instruction, I found myself so worried about getting the endings right or choosing *le mot juste* that I was unable to speak with any fluency, and I normally lost the thread of what the other person was saying. The experience of using French helped, and when I returned ten years later I was less inhibited by the prescriptions I'd been taught, so that I was less afraid to make a mistake and better able to concentrate on the meanings being made as both a listener and a speaker. I'm still very far from fluent, but I am much less self-conscious and more able to use the mental system I have to make meaning than I was.

The productivity of our individually creative language system also involves one other significant property for Chomsky: its capacity to produce sentences appropriate to, but not determined by, the context in which they are employed (1972, p. 100). The constraints which make a sentence contextually appropriate go beyond the constraints with make a sentence grammatical. Grammaticality is a property of the linguistic rule system which enables us to distinguish:

(1) The dog was chasing the cat

from its inverse counterpart:

(2) Cat the chasing was dog the

and yet permits:

(3) The cat was being chased by the dog

and:

(4) The cat was chasing the dog.

Appropriateness (in the sense of whether 1, 3, or 4 should be used in a particular context) is, in contrast, a property of the interaction between the competence system, which determines grammaticality, and the performance system, which governs appropriateness and all other aspects of language use.

Although I said that this normal creative use of language is not the same thing as the special sense of creativity usually reserved to describe what novelists, poets, and master essayists do, it is the basis for all language use, however creative or noncreative it may be labeled. While I would be willing to grant that there are some people who achieve extraordinary levels of language mastery, they are using a linguistic resource which shares the same properties as that possessed by the rest of us. What this suggests is that the capacity for even the special sense of creative language use is something that all of us can develop and, indeed, the results of attempting to teach children to write poetry and stories shows that everyone can do it. (For recent examples and discussion, see Hull [1988].) As noted in the discussion of narrative in Chapter IV, telling stories is a universal human trait because narrative is, in Barbara Hardy's (1975) terms, "a primary act of mind."

From a commonsense perspective the need to develop such capacities is often considered rather soft stuff, even an educational frill. This attitude partially derives from the common opinion that creative writers are effete and impractical people, whereas what all students need is not such self-indulgence but hard-headed mastery of spelling, punctuation, and the ability to write memos. The uncommonsense argument, in contrast, points out that telling an effective story or writing an arresting poem involves the mastery of a wide range of cognitive and affective abilities which may prove to be remarkably utilitarian as well as aesthetically powerful. The

powers of careful observation, of understanding why people behave as they do, of determining the meaning of our experiences, of
exploring and understanding our own and others' values, all of
which are needed to write such poems and stories, are all "skills"
required by even the most utilitarian of memo writers. Further, and
equally practical, such creative efforts can, when they are done
with genuine commitment, provide the best opportunity for learning to care about spelling, punctuation, and so on for young writers
who are much more likely to be interested in sharing a story or an
observation with their readers than in writing a business letter or
an expository essay.

Since all writing is creative if it is genuinely committed to
discovery and expression of the writer's meanings, the distinction
between creative and expository writing is probably a hollow one.
To help learners tap their creative writing powers teachers must
create situations where writers can focus on the specific effects of
particular choices of words and incidents. Writers also need a responsive context where they can collaborate with others by getting
feedback on the effects of their choices. There are no magic techniques for setting up such contexts, but an atmosphere of trust and
safety which encourages experimentation and risk taking seems a
natural prerequisite. Such an atmosphere is hard to create in a
commonsense classroom dominated by the search for the right
answer, where errors are regarded not as useful attempts at trying
something new but simply as mistakes to be corrected.

Nor should such creative projects be looked upon as entirely
devoid of cognitive utility, even the utility of learning an apparently nonpoetic subject like science. Robert Hull (1988), for example, discusses his use of poetry writing in conjunction with the
science teacher in his school; he found that the children were able
to use and develop their powers of observation through the opportunity to write poetically about what they saw and what it meant to
them. They included Dominic's, based on a videotape of a science
experiment which Hull had shot and shown to the class.

DISTILLATION

Mr Coldwell comes round
The bunsen is lit,
"Goulding you stupid . . . " Simon says

John takes a peep
Under the gauze
"Look up there!" he says to me,
"It's all yellow and blue."

The beaker flashes in the light,
George the giant sneezes,
And Simon looks up in disgust.

The owl seems to watch
Over the whole class,
But then its wing catches fire
What a brave owl

One-eyed Jack
Sits quietly
And a baked bean can
Drifts toward the sea.

Rory posing,
Jacqueline whistling,

John points at the camera
To tell me that its on
Then Mr Coldwell's voice gets higher,
"Look over here!" he says.

What an experiment!

Hull comments:

> "One-eyed Jack" and "the bean can" were part of the drawing
> the teacher put on the board to illustrate the idea of distilla-
> tion, and there was a stuffed owl in a glass case that reflected
> the bunsen flame, producing an eery image of wings in
> flames. Dominic used these details with assurance; his notion
> of the owl watching over the class was not one that had been
> mentioned in commentary on the video, nor had we noted the
> can "drifting out to sea." I read it aloud to the class, and it was
> enthusiastically received with "Brilliant," "Really good," and
> so on. (Hull 1988, pp. 204–205.)

While Hull was quite pleased with the poems as poems, he
was less secure about their utility in learning science. The science
teacher's views in this instance were reassuring. First he pointed
out that normal laboratory work in science is less experimental than
Hull had assumed:

> The word experiment is a misnomer. In fact time rarely allows
> genuine experimentation. During practical sessions, science
> teachers invariably lead their pupils to make specific observa-
> tions, whether consciously or unconsciously. This is not nec-
> essarily good "science."

When asked to write poems, based on the experiment, the children were liberated, and felt free to include any observation they had made. Being less constrained, they write on many aspects of the lesson, some of which would have been ignored in a formal write-up, yet were nonetheless important discoveries. (Hull 1988, p. 211.)

So the poems gave the class a chance to express their observation using creative language, and led to their recording a wider and deeper set of observations as well. Hence, they were, in fact, better science than would have been produced by a set of formal write-ups alone. Clearly there is value in learning how to do more formal laboratory reports, but they are neither the only way to learn science nor the only writing genre which can lead to cognitive learning.

The Psychology and Biology of Language

The normal creativity and infinite potential of the language system provided Chomsky with a new explanatory problem, a new set of questions. Among them were: What is the nature of the system which can be infinitely and creatively varied and yet is still contained in a powerful but nonetheless finite brain? And how can such a system be acquired by individual children? Attempting to answer them (and they are still far from completely answered) required not only a different theory, but a different type of theory, based on trying not only to accurately describe the properties of a language but also to explain them in a way which would account both for the system's creativity and the fact that it is learned by children. Trying to answer the first question showed that linguistics was a branch of cognitive psychology; trying to answer the second involved biology as well.

The biological aspect of language stems from the fact that the capacity to acquire language seems to be specific to the human species. In this view language is part of the same genetic endowment that gives us binocular vision and binaural hearing, and the capacity to walk upright and use our hands to grasp things. There are, to be sure, a few human beings with sufficiently damaged brains or, especially, damaged or absent aural capacities, who do not and cannot acquire a spoken language, but their very exceptionality is further evidence of the normality of the process for everyone else. Prelingually deaf children do acquire a visual or sign language in what seems to be identical ways to those used by children who can hear enough to discriminate speech sounds, and the visual languages so acquired have properties nearly identical to spoken languages in all relevant respects, including normal creativity and infinite potential (Klima and Bellugi 1979). In contrast, despite intensive efforts to teach sign language and a variety of other visual symbolic languages to chimpanzees and gorillas, the consensus of the evidence is that no other species has the capacity to acquire languages which are humanlike in nature or use (Terrace 1979).

That language has a biological, genetic basis is broadly agreed to by linguists and pyschologists, with the exception of some diehard behaviorists, but the nature and role of the biological foundations involved is a matter of considerable and often heated controversy. The disagreements center on the contribution of innate factors to language acquisition, but they also include issues of the nature of language itself. Piaget and his students and colleagues, for example, have argued that language and its acquisition are only one aspect of the more generalized human cognitive capacities. Children develop these through the processes of acting on and interpreting their world as they learn such things as the properties of space and time, the nature of classes and class inclusion, and such properties of objects as their conservation under changes of shape (Sinclair 1987). Others, such as Michael Halliday and his colleagues, have argued that the overwhelming concern should be with the social and interactive processes which enable language acquisition to take place, rather than on the relatively minor role played by genetic factors, since what is important to explain is the fact that language is a social phenomenon, the acquisition of which initiates us into a culture and its social system (Halliday 1975).

There is no dispute about the fact that such social processes do play a role in language acquisition. In the Piagetian case, it is clear that concept development and language development are mutually reinforcing processes. Learning terms and the concepts they represent happen simultaneously and spontaneously, in Vygotsky's sense, as we build a mental picture of our world. Similarly, the fact that we all learn the language spoken around us as children shows the importance of such social and environmental factors in the process of acquisition. In the latter instance, there is also support for the biological basis of the process, since the genetic capacity to learn human languages extends to any of them; the one we happen to learn does not depend upon our specific genetic inheritance the way the color of our eyes or hair does, but on our membership in the human species. The particular language (or languages, since given the opportunity children seem to learn two or three languages at once as easily as they learn one) we learn depends on the historical accident of our linguistic environment from birth to age five or so.

Generative linguists take the strong position, however, that there are language-specific innate properties of our minds which enable us to learn human languages. For Chomsky and his colleagues, these properties are, in fact, the defining characteristics of human languages. That is, such universal characteristics are common to English and Japanese, Swahili and Tagalog, Navajo and Arabic, and while there are enormous differences in the particular characteristics of each human language and corresponding differences in the cultures that speak them, they share certain underlying properties. The existence of these underlying properties of the human mind enables us to learn whichever language is being spoken around us, and these properties we share as a species are what make us more alike than different.

Language Acquisition

From birth to about age five every child acquires a highly complex and creatively flexible native language. Although the system continues to develop in various ways throughout life, its primary mental architecture is built individually and unconsciously, and is fully structured by the time the child goes to school. Language acquisition is an active and interactive process. It depends on the child's being in active contact with speakers of the language she is learning, but each step along the way is essentially initiated by the learner. From the prelinguistic period of cries, facial expressions, gestures, and babbling, each infant is building a cognitive and linguistic system so as to understand the world better and communicate with the other people in it. *The process of first language acquisition depends upon relevant participation in language events employing the language being acquired, but without any deliberate effort either on the part of the learner to learn or on the part of the people she is interacting with to teach the language.*

This statement may be somewhat strong, since the evidence is not all in. There does seem to be some help which parents, peers, and other caretakers do provide and which does seem to facilitate the process. Kenneth Kaye (1982), for example, has shown that the way mothers talk to their very young infants helps set up formats for conversation and turn-taking long before the child can understand the mother's speech. There is also growing evidence that children play an active role even in such contexts by, in effect, teaching their caretakers what tone of voice pleases them by smiling in response to some tones and not responding, or even crying, in response to others. Similarly, Jerome Bruner (1983) has shown that similar scaffolding procedures with somewhat older children function as a means of focusing their attention on the object or activity that their mother is concerned with and therefore help them to learn both object names and such referential expressions as *this, that, here,* and *there.* Bruner has gone so far as to label such assistance as a Language Acquisition Support System (LASS), supporting Chomsky's notion of an innate Language Acquisition Device (LAD).

Some of these efforts to explain language acquisition by means of formats and scaffolding may have conflated the acquisition of the language itself—the mental grammar which permits "I eat shredded wheat every morning" and rules out "Morning every wheat shredded eat I"—with the equally unconscious acquisition of the systems which govern the ways we use it. This fusion springs from a view that because language is so frequently used for communication, learning to communicate is essentially the same as learning language. Givon (1979), Halliday (1978), and others have argued such a case, and, to a degree, it can be found in Vygotsky (1962) as well. The generative position questions the necessity of the connection between language and communication, and argues instead that while language can be and often is used to communicate, its most essential and characteristic function is in thinking, building mental models, and employing them to understand the world. While this capacity does provide the basis for communication, the nature of our minds requires it regardless of whether we ever communicate or not. Although this debate has some theoretical significance, in actual practice children both think and communicate, and each plays an important role in the development of their language system.

Related efforts to minimize the explanatory role of innate factors and inside-out processes in language acquisition have been made by Roger Brown (see his Introduction to Snow and Ferguson, eds. 1977) and others who have studied the "baby talk" that some caretakers use to speak to young children. Dubbing it "motherese," these researchers have argued that caretakers deliberately simplify their speech to children by shortening their sentences, avoiding complex constructions, using proper nouns where pronouns would be more appropriate, and so on. Yet as John Marshall (1987) has pointed out: "We may take it that some children are indeed exposed to 'simplified' or deviant linguistic input. But this fact does not in itself show that 'simplified' input has any effect (good or bad) upon the course of language acquisition. When studies of the consequences of 'motherese' input have been undertaken (Newport, Gleitman, and Gleitman 1977), it has proved remarkably difficult to demonstrate the effectiveness of motherese *qua* teaching aid" (Newport 1977, p. 42). He goes on to point out both that the extent of simplification has been overestimated, and that some of the ways that speech is "simplified," in particular acoustically, have in fact made them *more difficult* to interpret by children even though they may have been highly predictable by adults because of the redundancy of the word within the known (by adults) structure and meaning of the sentence. His conclusion, therefore, is that "although many of the basic facts about 'motherese' are not in dispute, the conclusions drawn from them were often in error" (p. 42, his italics).

Cute acronyms and labels aside, what seems more likely to be going on is that such support does *not* provide the basis for acquiring the characteristic properties of the mental grammar, but may help in providing the relevant exposure necessary for children to acquire those properties of the communicative competence system which will enable them to participate in the particular communication system of the culture they are growing up in. That is, it may help children decide that the language being learned has the properties of French rather than Russian, or learn how to make requests or give directions or behave politely in language. It also provided my son Jack with the necessary input to eventually sort out the differences between the past tense of regular and irregular verbs. At twenty-four, he never makes such mistakes. But to do so, of course, it must be helpful in the sense that it provides each child with a sufficiently rich experiential base to employ their language acquisition device on. It certainly wouldn't have helped Jack if the people he was interacting with had "simplified" their grammar by regularizing all of the English verbs.

Insofar as such formatting or simplifications are not helpful to the child, the effect seems remarkably similar to that of the "simplifications" used in school textbooks and school lessons, discussed earlier and described by Robert Hull (1985). In both cases the simplifications do serve to reduce the amount of input to the child, but in such a way as to rob her of the rich context necessary to fully interpret them, to connect them to her emerging cognitive and linguistic systems, and therefore to make them fully meaningful in any sense. Further, insofar as they are "deviant" forms, structures which do not conform to the system that the child is trying to learn, they may provide the bases for false rather than accurate hypotheses about the target language, and therefore slow down rather than enhance the process of learning it. Given the elusive and subtle properties of the language system revealed by generative linguistic analysis, and the fact that these properties are completely unknown to us as day-to-day language users, it seems unlikely on the face of it that we could provide relevantly simple and nondistorted input to language learners on the basis of our conception of the situation.

Like Smith's (1973) rule for facilitating reading acquisition ("Respond to what the child is trying to do"), the best course of action for caretakers of young children is probably to attend carefully to their emerging understanding and competence. Indeed both Kaye's and Bruner's observations of formatting systems seem to be best explained not as mothers teaching their children but as mothers learning what their children can do and then responding appropriately to their initiatives. Indeed the most helpful mothers Bruner observed seemed to have an uncanny knack of staying just one jump ahead of their children—a feat they could only have accomplished by extremely careful observation of the linguistic and communicative competence their children had already achieved.

This can be called teaching, of course, and indeed it is far closer to my notion of uncommonsense teaching than the traditional commonsense instructional patterns of conscious transmission of knowledge and deliberate practicing of skills.

The lesson in all this for us teachers, therefore, is that in attempting to facilitate the continuing language development of our pupils, we are likely to be most helpful when we watch and listen to them, respond to their questions and concerns, and provide an atmosphere which encourages linguistic (and all other sorts) of experimentation and exploration. Trying to determine in advance what children will need to prompt their language development and building a preset curriculum or set of language-learning activities based on that prior determination, however well intentioned, is actually a recipe for confusion and may end up harming children far more than it helps them.

A program which has been designed to help teachers and parents (and, indeed, students) carefully observe the progress of children as language users has actually been developed in Tasmania, Australia. Called the Pathways program (1987), it provides a wide range of markers for children's growing language competencies in all four modes, and it uses those markers as observational benchmarks which can record what children have achieved in various aspects of language use. What is particularly exciting about the Pathways material is that it recognizes that growth in language abilities is neither steady nor uniform across modes, so that a child may have an extensive reading vocabulary of words she doesn't yet use in writing, or her listening ability may lag behind her speaking ability because she doesn't yet have sufficient powers of concentration to listen for long periods. Perhaps most important, along with the markers derived from observations already made by the teachers who developed the program, it provides blank box markers for teacher-observers to record other evidence of performance and growth not anticipated by the program's initial designers, who were themselves teachers and teacher-consultants. By recognizing the indeterminacy and idiosyncrasies of individual development within the framework of an uncommonsense theory of language, learning and growth, the program provides a sound and practical basis for uncommonsense language pedagogy.

The History and Sociology of Language

Since children are acquiring a particular language in a particular culture and at a particular time, even a psychologically focused conception of language acquisition cannot fully ignore the historical and social context within which the process operates. One of the first truisms that anyone who looks at language historically realizes is that languages are dynamic systems undergoing slow but continual change. It seems probable that the standardization of the written languages through the widespread use of the printed word, together with the somewhat later development of standard dictionaries, has had a braking effect on some aspects of language change for national, and indeed international, languages like English. Nevertheless, English continues to evolve in pronunciation, in vocabulary, and even in syntax.

When languages change on the surface, this also means that the underlying rules must have changed, and there is considerable evidence that the agents of that change are children. This process is particularly dramatic in the case of children who invent a new language, as seems to have happened in conditions where the adults of a language community were communicating with each other by means of what linguists call a pidgin. Pidgins develop as special purpose codes to enable people who don't speak the same language to communicate either for trade, or, as in the case of Hawaii, because people of many different languages have settled there. Pidgins are limited linguistic systems in vocabulary, syntax, and pronunciation, useful for day-to-day business but not complete enough to provide the basis for thinking and other more subtle aspects of communication.

This wasn't a problem for the adult pidgin speakers of Hawaii in the early years of this century. They all had a native language to fall back on for such purposes, whether it was Chinese, Tagalog, Japanese, Hawaiian, or English. But their children needed more, since they needed the language to do all of the cognitive and affective work that languages do, and so they developed a complete language system, now called Hawaiian Creole, which was based on the pidgin but extended it in all domains. Exactly how they did it is still somewhat unclear, and exploring it would take us too far afield, but see Bickerton (1981) for a more compete exploration of this and other creolization processes. The point here is that children take the input they get from the language community they are born into and transform it for their own purposes, thereby changing it in dramatic—as in the case of the pidgin-to-creole transformation—or in subtle ways.

An example of one of the more subtle changes can be seen by returning briefly to the irregular verbs which my son Jack and other children have trouble with. Their regularization of them could be the basis of a language change and indeed already has been if one compares the number of irregular verbs in Shakespeare with those that we retain in common parlance today. Print, combined with the fact that the remaining irregular verbs are both very common and almost entirely residual of the Anglo-Saxon core out of which English developed, has slowed that process somewhat, but it is still going on. *Dive, dived* seems to be slowly replacing *dive, dove,* at least on the evidence of the Olympics telecasts, and there are undoubtedly other examples as well.

One of the reasons that children are so influential in this regard is that they learn their language in an oral community. This means that it is a community where face-to-face contact is the crucial influence and, during the crucial language-learning years from zero to five, one which strongly reflects the speech patterns of family, friends, neighbors, and other local acquaintances. If the community is in some way isolated from other neighboring communities or from the larger regional and national communities, through geographic, social class, ethnic, racial, or other culturally separating experiences, then child-initiated changes can spread to the adults they interact with, but not necessarily to the larger community.

This process is the source of those identifiable variants of language which linguists call dialects. It should be noted that for linguists, dialects are not substandard or degenerate versions of languages, they *are* languages. Everybody learns a dialect (read language) through these processes, and whether or not the dialect we learn is closer or farther from the mainstream standard version is a matter of accident of upbringing. The evolution of a dialect, or set of dialects, as the standard authorized version(s) of a language depends on political, social, economic, cultural, and educational policies, not on the linguistic virtues of one dialect or another. To be sure, once a standard dialect has emerged, children who hope to participate in the culture beyond their immediate oral community will have to acquire it in addition to their more local dialect, but there is nothing linguistically necessary or superior about their choice.

This is not the same as the pidgin-creole distinction; by definition all dialects are linguistically equal even if they are not socially
so. William Labov (1972), for example, showed the linguistic and
cognitive subtlety of the nonstandard dialect of English called the
Black English Vernacular in his paper, "The logic of nonstandard
English," and Shirley Brice Heath (1983) and others have shown
that linguistic differences among oral language communities do not
imply qualitative differences among the dialects themselves. They
may, of course, have powerful educational implications, since the
language of school, and particularly the written language of school,
is the standard version of the culture. School should be the natural
place for all children to acquire that standard language, but they are
less likely to do so if the school acts as though all children already
have it when they arrive at kindergarten, treating those who don't
as linguistic outsiders.

The situation can be diagramed something like what is shown
in Figure 5–1.

While any static diagram cannot fully capture the dynamic
interplay of these various systems, what this one attempts to show
is that some children come to school from mainstream backgrounds, that is, their home and neighborhood languages are
closely allied to the more standard language of school and national
culture, and others do not. Those who come from homes and
neighborhoods which use a significantly different version of the
language will need to participate actively in the school language
culture if they are to add its properties to their linguistic repertoire.
Schools should encourage children to broaden as well as deepen
their linguistic repertoires—that is one of the reasons we have
schools—but such efforts must be done respectfully, in the sense
that they should not denigrate those who don't come to school

Figure 5–1 Interplay of Systems

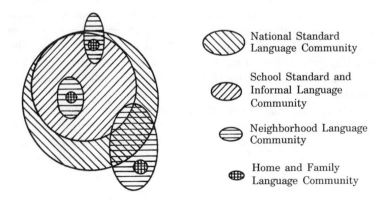

National Standard
Language Community

School Standard and
Informal Language
Community

Neighborhood Language
Community

Home and Family
Language Community

speaking "schoolspeak." Our track record is not good in this area; schools have tended to work better for children who arrive at the door already possessing the standard language than for those who don't.

Ironically, the situation is, in many respects, better for those who speak a clearly distinct language like Spanish or Vietnamese than for dialect speakers. At least no one ever accused them of speaking a bad or deformed version of English. Historically in the United States the acquisition of English by non-English-speaking children was accomplished at the cost of encouraging them to forget or never to use the language of their home. In recent years, various programs of bilingual education have attempted to enable children to learn English while simultaneously maintaining their home language and using it to acquire other skills and knowledge. Although such projects have had admirable goals—including showing respect for the diverse linguistic and cultural communities that make up the United States—they have not been very effective for many children in helping them make the transition to the larger English-speaking community, because they have reduced the need, and crucially, the opportunity to do so.

The lack of opportunity for children speaking both a second language and a second dialect has been the result of the segregation of children into classes, and in some cases schools, with others just like them, thereby greatly reducing the chance for informal, inadvertent, unconscious learning of English to take place in the natural environment of child-to-child interaction. Since peer group interaction is the most powerful language-learning environment for all of us, it can hardly be surprising that children who come from homes and neighborhoods which speak Language A are less likely to learn Language B if they never have to interact with anyone who speaks it except teachers in more or less formal learning situations. The same, of course, applies to dialect speakers, particularly if they are segregated into reading groups (the usual pattern in primary schools) or separate tracks (more common in secondary schools) with people who already talk as they do and thereby are kept from their more standard-speaking peers both educationally and socially. When this situation is aggravated by differences in race and/or social class, the gulfs are still wider and gradually become unbridgeable.

Labov (1972) has shown the power of peer interaction in the development of dialects and has characterized those few children who do manage the transition as "lames," either because they literally are (and hence less valued by the peer group at play) or because of some other familial or cultural pattern which cuts them off from their peers (their parents won't let them play in the street after school, for example). Schools just aren't going to succeed in being the instruments of linguistic enrichment, providing children with the opportunities to add additional dialects or languages to their repertoires, if they continue to treat those children who speak a second language or dialect as not fully worthy of respect and continue to show their lack of respect by segregating children along such lines.

The situation is even more complicated than that. Gordon Wells's (1986) research showed that even when schools try to help children they perceive as linguistically behind the eight ball, their efforts are rarely helpful and frequently counterproductive. The efforts have essentially consisted of commonsense dummy-run drills and exercises removed from the context of meaningful language use. Acquisition of a new language or a new dialect is just as natural a process as first-language acquisition is for young children if it is scaffolded by a meaningful environment of language use. What this means, above all, is that children need to talk with other children, with adults who speak the language being learned, and also with fellow learners.

Language Development in the School Years

Although this chapter has tried to show that the process of first-language acquisition is normal and natural and that it builds a complex mental grammar in all children, we have not explored how the language system can be used and developed in school. To develop their language, it seems clear *that children need to talk meaningfully with each other in school*. Of course, children do talk meaningfully with each other outside the classroom, in the corridors, the playgrounds, and the lunch room, but the commonsense practices of classroom management have severely restricted the opportunity for talk within the classroom. Teacher talk fills most of the time available in commonsense classrooms (most research that has been done on this shows figures ranging from 70 to 90 percent), and students rarely have the opportunity to do more than respond to teacher questions.

Even if teachers didn't talk all the time, the insistence on one speaker at a time in whole-class "discussions" would severely limit the opportunities for an individual pupil to talk. And even if turns were allocated evenly, which they rarely are, thirty pupils in a forty-five minute period would have the floor for only a minute and a half per class. This would mean each child could talk for seven and a half minutes a week, and would have a cumulative opportunity of only four and a half hours of talk a year! Given that the actual time available for pupil talk is more like twelve minutes per period, the usable time drops down dramatically. Further, since the children who most need experience in talking are likely to be the least willing or able to get a chance at talk, the probabilities for either learning a new language or dialect orally or developing their abilities even further in their own language in the common-sense classroom are remote at best.

The solution to this time problem is *to create environments for children to talk with each other in teacherless groups,* but doing so runs head on into the most cherished concern of commonsense teachers: keeping *control* of their class. Control is another powerful meta-phoric concept akin to "covering the curriculum" and "teaching basic skills." Like the other two, it suggests that teachers are, or ought to be, in charge of everything that happens in the class, and it implies that this can't happen unless every child is attending to the same lesson at the same time. Related to the control metaphor are such notions as being "strict" or "firm," being "orderly," "well-organized," and therefore deserving of "respect." What are more or less hidden in the commonsense notion of control are the sources of power and authority in the classroom. Commonsense power derives from the role of the teacher, from the position itself. Chil-dren are assumed in this view to be essentially anarchic spirits who will be up to no good unless they are kept under strict reins. Teachers who are soft or friendly or easy-going will find themselves with classes which have exploded into chaos where, in effect, the inmates are running the asylum.

The dangers of losing control are believed to be most acute for beginning teachers, hence the common advice to neophytes not to smile until Christmas, given particularly by experienced (common-sense?) teachers to those who have been influenced by one of the rare uncommonsense teacher education programs. The common-sense view is that uncommonsense teacher education doesn't pre-pare beginners adequately—paying too little attention to discipline or to learning control techniques—and it thereby contributes to the powerful resocialization of beginning teachers by their more expe-rienced colleagues and by school administrators who in effect say, "Forget what they told you in teacher education, what you really need to learn is how to control a class." There may be truth in some of these complaints, but the major problem is a conflicting set of views about what control means and how it is achieved.

Uncommonsense teachers and teacher educators do not advo-cate chaos. Nor are uncommonsense teachers adverse to order, or-ganization, and respect. But while uncommonsense teachers must possess many of these qualities and are definitely in control of their classes in their own way, the order and respect involved in an uncommonsense classroom are more mutual constructs; the control derives not from the role or positional authority of the teacher in and of itself but from the meaningfulness of the activities in which everyone is engaged. Indeed it is frequently the case that uncommonsense classrooms are more "structured" than commonsense ones, but the structure is more complex, permits a greater variety of classroom configurations, and, most important, does not depend upon everyone doing the same thing at the same time. Although uncommonsense teachers recognize that children, like everyone else, like to have fun and to play, they also believe that schoolwork can be sufficiently engaging and enjoyable to make class time productive even when they are not "controlling" every aspect of student behavior.

Commonsense students do need to learn how to learn in uncommonsense ways in uncommonsense classrooms. The teacher who assumes that they already know how to do so and does not provide sufficient scaffolding for the transition from commonsense studentdom to a more independent, learner-centered classroom will indeed be inviting chaos. Students who believe that the only alternative to "strict and controlling" is "loose and chaotic" may very well decide that the alternative to a teacher-controlled class is a free-for-all. If students have had little or no experience in working in teacherless groups or in doing independent work, they can't be expected to know how to do so. Given the pervasive nature of teacher-controlled classes, the safest assumption for the uncommonsense teacher is that the class needs explanations and models of how to function in the new contexts if they are to become productive learning environments. It is easy enough to curtail such scaffolding processes on discovering that a class can in fact function well on its own, but to assume that they can from the outset can invite difficulties and will make it harder to make the environment eventually productive.

I remember that when I began teaching in junior high school, I assumed that the students would be able to carry on productive discussions either by themselves in small groups or with me in the whole class. When they weren't really very good at doing so, I was at a loss. I didn't have any memory of ever being taught how to do this myself, although I had somehow managed to learn how through having to participate in such discussions. So I tended to fall back on talking most of the time myself, thus preserving the illusion that teaching and learning were taking place, and helping me keep "control" over the class better than small groups could.

With more teaching experience, I gradually learned that I could not take such things for granted and that I had to find ways of helping students learn how to learn through speaking and listening in small groups and in larger ones. For small-group discussion, I found that a fishbowl technique in which a volunteer small group participates in a discussion while the rest of the class sits around them in a circle listening and observing can be very helpful. After ten minutes or so of talk, we all discuss how the group process worked in terms of such "traffic rule" problems as who talked the most, who the least, and so on, but more crucially, we explore how the group worked to deepen and extend its understanding of the topic under discussion.

Another extremely useful way to teach such processes is to tape-record groups and then listen to the tape and discuss it. This requires some auditory privacy for the group being taped, but that can usually be arranged in most schools. Such a procedure works best if the tape has been transcribed, though that involves considerable extra work. The central importance of small-group learning to uncommonsense classrooms, however, makes taking these extra steps worthwhile if we are serious about using this method. Doing so not only helps the students learn how to learn but, equally important, it helps them learn that they are learning. The commonsense perception of students that they only learn from teachers and texts must be modified, or they will not value the group talk appropriately. Similarly, although most commonsense teachers may be able to use talk in these ways for their own purposes, they may not sufficiently value it if they have not had much experience doing school learning in these ways. That's why I've done more and more of my inservice and preservice teacher education using leaderless groups in recent years while also including lots of time for reflection on both how the process works and why it is valuable.

Even the formal or informal lecture can have more value as a teaching and learning method if students are taught how to learn from teacher talk. We cannot assume that they know how to do so, and in my experience even graduate students, who have had lots of practice in college and secondary school, often don't know how to benefit from teacher talk. They take poor notes, they don't ask enough questions, they can't use the lecture as a means of checking their understanding of their reading, and so on. The commonsense solution to this problem usually involves having the teacher dictate notes to the class either through writing them on the board or, in more high-tech schools, on the overhead. Merely copying the teacher's notes, however, not only doesn't much help students learn the material, it actually makes them less likely to develop their own ways of making meaning from teacher talk.

The basic principle involved is *to come clean on the processes involved in teaching and learning*. Too often schools function as though such processes were a secret which only the cleverest could learn, and that to make them explicit would be a kind of cheating. Viewing the situation that way may be to make it seem like more of a conscious conspiracy than a commonsense and therefore unconscious practice, but such has been the effect. A more likely cause is that deliberately trying to teach such things has not been considered part of the common sense of schooling, and as a result little effort has been made in this direction.

One of the reasons this state of affairs is important from an uncommonsense perspective is the hypothesis that *if all students are taught how to learn, there will be fewer differences among them in terms of their capacity to do so.* If many of the apparent differences in learning capacities among students really derive more from a difference in their understanding of how to learn than from some innate distinctions in ability, democratic educators have a responsibility to use this knowledge to close the learning gap as much as they can. And if children do become more effective and efficient learners through attention to how they can learn, in the long run the time devoted to such procedural matters may not be robbed from the time needed to "cover" the curriculum at all.

But in this context the central value of having students talk with each other is that such talk is the best way to provide sufficient opportunities for the kind of speaking and listening experiences which will further develop their mental language systems. For this to happen effectively, this talk can't be talk for its own sake. (This was the problem with language labs, since nobody cared much about whether *la plume de ma tante* was or was not *sur le table de mon oncle:* It was hard to become sufficiently involved to learn the language in that way.) The talk has to be meaningful to the talkers, since like the process of initial language acquisition, *the process of developing one's language system depends on active participation in a meaning-making community.*

Summary

We language educators must continue to try to be informed about the emerging theories of language acquisition and development. This is crucial not because in most cases it will provide material to teach but because it can help us better understand the nature of the system being learned, and the implications for maximizing our pupils' capacity to use it. If we agree with Chomsky that we build a knowledge system naturally and without instruction during the process of language acquisition, what we need do to enhance it is to provide children with the richest possible interactive language environment.

But Chomsky also recognizes that "Two people may share exactly the same knowledge of language but differ markedly in their ability to put this knowledge to use" (1986, p. 4). It is this difference which may be of most significance for us as language educators. In this context it means that it is safer to assume that all of the children we teach have roughly equivalent levels of linguistic competence (this is, after all what is means to call language a species-specific phenomenon) but that they can and do differ in the ways they can use their competence.

An uncommonsense approach to language education would be very wary about using differences in language-using ability as a basis for labeling children in ways which imply that they are different in their underlying language competence. It should be remembered in this connection that most of our diagnostic tests for differences in language-using abilities magnify the effects of relatively small differences among children, while ignoring their overwhelming similarities. When standardized tests are being developed, for example, the questions that everyone gets right are thrown out, so that those remaining will have the maximum ability to distinguish fine differences. This may be useful for some purposes, but as educators we must recognize how much our pupils have in common as linguistically competent young people as well as attend to whatever different abilities they manifest. And when we assume competence rather than incompetence, we can often be happily surprised at children's abilities.

Similarly, the unconscious nature of the processes of language acquisition and language use, in particular our complete obliviousness to the rules we use when we speak, listen, read, and write, should make us question the idea that language development is enhanced by attempting to become conscious of these rules. The commonsense notion that language skills are enhanced by drills finds no support in our growing understanding of the nature of the language system or of how we learned it initially. And this seems just as true for a second language—learned by children or adults during the school years—as it is for a first. There is undoubted security in the illusion that there are rules to be memorized and maxims to be followed, but the evidence is growing that what is needed for maximum language development is the learner's active use of the language in a supportive but not constricted linguistic environment.

Just as it is true for second-language learning, so it seems that reading and writing also can and do develop in the same "natural" or untutored ways as the oral language. Generative linguistics does not deal with the written language very often—although generative linguists have shown that the English spelling system does correspond more reliably, albeit more abstractly, to the mental pronunciation system than most prior theories maintained—but the processes of language learning which characterize oral language acquisition seem quite similar to those which have emerged from research into children learning to write and to read. The properties of the language system itself (creativity, unconsciousness, and so on) are shared across modes of use, and it seems likely that their development is mutually reinforcing throughout the school years. Our tentative conclusion must be that the burden of proof of efficacy must be placed on those who maintain belief in the necessity of conscious learning and deliberate teaching of the processes of reading and writing. We can no longer continue to assume the commonsense view that such processes must be acquired differently from the spoken language. It may prove to be the case that some of them are, but they will be the exceptions rather than the norm.

Language seems to develop to meet the needs of each individual as required for thinking, for communicating, for expressing ideas, and for learning. This process is largely unconscious and responds naturally and automatically to appropriate experiences. What is conscious and intentional are the goals of language use: participating in the family conversation, telling or understanding a story, describing what happened on a recent trip, or explaining how something works. Language education, therefore, must pay special attention to the ends of language use, in the firm confidence that the means will largely take care of themselves.

CHAPTER 6

Language II

How the System Is Used to Make Meaning

The language system so acquired has many uses. Some of them are private, including whatever role language plays in the processes of thought, but most of them are public, or rather communal, in the sense that they enable us to interact with others. Even the private uses of language are influenced by the cultural nature of the particular language system we have acquired, and there is a long tradition in language study of exploring the influence of language on thought stretching, from Humboldt (1836/1988) to Sapir (1921) to Whorf (1956) to Lakoff and Johnson (1980). Anthropologists have long recognized that studying the language of a culture is essential to understanding it, and in some ways the two cannot be meaningfully separated since so many of a culture's assumptions and practices are embedded in and revealed by the particulars of its language system. In the familiar Whorfian examples this can involve vocabulary—the contrast between Eskimo and English terminology for types of snow—syntax—the contrast between Hopi and English ways of talking about explosions (a noun in English, a verb in Hopi)—or semantic properties—how time is expressed relatively in Hopi, absolutely in English.

Although it has proved difficult to substantiate empirically the strong version of the Sapir-Whorf hypothesis that our language categories and forms literally limit or restrict our perceptions, it does seem plausible that our language shapes our typical approach to problems. Our commonsense ways of thinking about language and communication are powerfully influenced by our characteristic language of how they function. So without committing ourselves to a position of absolute limitations, we should nonetheless be alert to the likelihood that our particular culture and the language which characterizes it do provide us with sets of categories and ways of talking which influence our thinking and even, in Berger and Luckmann's (1966) sense, our very conception of reality.

The overwhelmingly common and normal way in which we use language, aside from thinking itself, is to communicate with others. While we can and do communicate by other means, including the way we dress, the way we move and posture ourselves, our facial expressions, and so on, verbal communication through language is such a natural part of our daily lives that only on those occasions when we cannot use it, for example, in a place where we don't speak the language, are we aware of how pervasive and essential it is. The centrality of communication as the major use of language has led some students of language and language acquisition to argue that it is the communicative function of language that provides its essential defining characteristics.

Unlike Chomsky and the generative linguists, for whom internal processes provide the best approach to understanding the nature of language, scholars like Bates (1976), Givon (1979), Bruner (1975), and Halliday (1978) have built theories of language and language acquisition on the basis of the functions of language which center on communication. They have argued, in effect, for the priority of social and cultural constraints on the process of language learning, since children are driven to acquire language out of their need to become part of the language and culture in which they are growing up and to become fully communicative members of the group.

These two approaches are not necessarily incompatible, since it seems clear that both *internal* (hypothesis testing, mental grammar building based on innate constraints) and *external* (learning how to communicate in socially and culturally appropriate ways) processes are operating throughout the course of language acquisition and development. As individuals, we develop our capacity to participate in the culture by learning to communicate both within and against its grain. That is, the culture's ideas, beliefs, and even its language system can provoke dissent as well as assent. One source of language change and the development of dialects, discussed briefly in Chapter V, is individual and small group efforts to rebel against its ideational constraints. To understand language and its uses fully, we will need to look at both the inside-out role of the individual language acquirer and the constraints, models, and influences which come to the learner from the outside in.

Commonsense Communication: The Code Theory

Like the nature of the language system itself, communication and other aspects of language use are generally regarded as straightforward and essentially one-way processes from the commonsense perspective. As Michael Reddy (1979) and others have pointed out, the basic commonsense metaphor for communication is transmission, or as he calls it, "the conduit metaphor." The assumption is essentially what Sperber and Wilson (1986) call the code theory: The speaker or writer encodes her thoughts in language, which is then transmitted by a variety of channels or conduits—voice to air, pen to paper, key to electronic display, and so on—to a receiver, who then decodes the language and receives the thought. As Reddy points out, this conduit metaphor is deeply embedded in our language of language use in such phrases as "putting one's thoughts into words," "getting one's ideas across," "putting one's thoughts down on paper," and so on.

All of these expressions articulate the commonsense theory that communication is a matter of putting one's message or content into words which can then be sent off through a conduit or channel to be received and unpacked by the recipient. As Sperber and Wilson comment, however, "the power of these figures of speech is such that one tends to forget that . . . they cannot be true. In writing [Relevance], we have not literally put our thoughts down on paper. What we have put down on paper are little dark marks, a copy of which you are now looking at. As for our thoughts, they remain where they always were, inside our brains." (1986, p. 1). That is, although the conduit metaphor suggests that it is, literally, ideas which are sent from one person to another, Reddy and Sperber and Wilson are pointing out that what gets sent is a representation of our ideas, not the ideas themselves. Similarly when we receive a message, we must interpret it, not merely directly decode it for the ideas it contains. The conduit metaphor or the code theory in effect omits a crucial step in both the sending and the receiving of linguistic messages. It therefore makes the process seem simpler and more straightforward than it really is.

But it is not only common sense which holds firmly to the code theory; it has been advocated in various forms by most of the Western intellectual tradition from Aristotle through Shannon and Weaver to modern semiotics, which generalizes the code model from verbal communication to all forms of communication. The basic hypothesis of the code theory, that thoughts are directly and literally encoded in sounds (or written symbols), seems so natural that it has been taken for granted by most commentators.

And, of course, it is partly true that language does succeed in communicating ideas, and so it seems commonsensical to assume that it does so by directly encoding them. Expressed diagrammatically, such a model of communication would look something like a game of ping pong. Or if only one side of the process is considered like what is shown in Figure 6–1.

The most striking thing about this diagram is its straightforward unidirectionality and the absence, except for the possible presence of noise, of any source of interference with the communication process, assuming both encoder and decoder are working satisfactorily. Noise is of great concern to telephone engineers and to schoolteachers, thus leading to the commonsense belief that a quiet class is a good class, but it presents no fundamental difficulties in understanding the communication process itself, since it is by definition an extraneous factor.

One of the first things one might notice is that the diagram captures the essence of most classrooms where the teacher is the speaker (thinker) and the pupils are the hearers (receivers). Of course children do get to speak in classrooms on some occasions, but as noted earlier, the basic pattern that has been found consistently in classroom research is that teachers talk most of the time. Even more critical than who is talking is the assumption that if the speaker and hearer are speaking the same language—that is, if they have matching or equivalent linguistic encoders and decoders—then communication of thoughts is essentially automatic. Or, to put it another way, the language directly encodes the speaker's thoughts, and once the language has been decoded, the thought is directly accessible.

Figure 6–1   Code Theory Model of the Communication Process

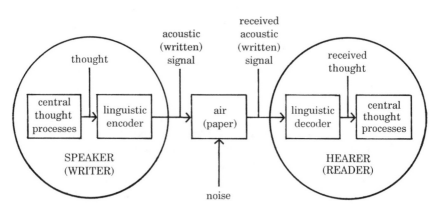

After Sperber and Wilson: 1986, p. 5

What this suggests, in part, is a kind of literalism: *that language means what it says.* And this, too, is part of our commonsense belief system. After all, if I say, "The quick brown fox jumps over the lazy dog," I am clearly talking about a jumping fox, not a jumping dog, and assuming we have equivalent language systems, you can apparently receive my thoughts about this fox and this dog by decoding the sentence. There is something valid about this approach, to be sure, but in what respect does this sentence encode my thoughts? And are your thoughts upon reading it (or hearing it, if we were talking to each other instead of in a writer-reader relationship) the same as mine?

One of my thoughts, which is nowhere encoded in the "The quick . . . etc." itself, was that I needed an example sentence. And since I am a poor typist, the clichéd typing practice sentence came to my mind. If you've practiced typing using that sentence, you may have recognized its familiarity, and, perhaps, remembered times when you used it, read it, or practiced it. In an important sense, therefore, my use of this example needs to be recognized as exemplary, as distinct from literally talking about a particular fox or a particular dog, if my thoughts are to be interpreted more broadly. Perhaps that exemplary thought can be decoded more directly from the whole sentence within which the fox-dog example was embedded, but even that is not certain, since I nowhere say anything about its being an example, and my discussion of it is entirely about what it *says* rather than about what it *means.*

The point here is not that sentences don't give clues to thoughts, but that they don't, as such, exhaustively contain them. The traditional, commonsensical definition of a sentence: "Sentences are groups of words with a subject and a predicate continuing a complete thought," suggests the contrary, of course, but that is only one further example of how our language about language is built on the conduit metaphor. Even if we leave aside the problem of determining completeness of thought (is "Ouch!" a more or less complete thought than *The Decline and Fall of the Roman Empire?*), the problem of the fit between thoughts and sentences remains.

Let's look at another example. Yesterday I engaged in the following dialogue in a computer store.

JOHN: Do you have ribbons for an Imagewriter printer?
CLERK: No, but Computermat might. They're in Brookvale.
JOHN: Where is that?
CLERK: Near the Brookvale Oval, by the entrance to McDonald's.

The problem arose with my second question and his second answer. The thought that I had intended when I asked the second question was not the thought he received. I was asking where Brookvale was, but he answered a different question, something more like: Where in Brookvale is the computer store located? He used well-known local landmarks to identify the store's location, but they weren't helpful to me because I was a stranger in the area. It wasn't a serious breakdown. I did have a map and eventually found both Brookvale and the store (and they did have the ribbon), but it does show us something of the inadequacy of just assuming that thoughts, with all of their associated references and intentions, are directly encoded in language.

In this case part of the problem may have derived from my use of a pronoun (that) whose referent was unclear to the clerk, so let's look at one more example which doesn't involve such a form. This one is taken from Tannen (1986), but I have chosen it because the same problem has often happened to me. A couple is deciding where to go to dinner. The wife asks, "Where would you like to eat?" The husband replies, "I don't care, you decide." According to Tannen, such apparently innocuous sentences can sow the seeds of a conflict which, if not somehow recognized and modified, can lead to divorce. Everything can be smooth in such a case, of course, but if the wife's next statement is something like "If I wanted to decide, I would have suggested some place," or, "You never make a decision," trouble is clearly afoot.

Both sets of problems help us to see that in many if not most instances the words we speak (or write) express (or encode) only the tip of the iceberg of our thoughts. The computer store conversation involved what Philip Johnson-Laird (1983) has characterized as different mental models associated with the words and sentences we used. My mental model was that of a stranger in town, but nothing I said directly revealed that. (My American accent could have been a clue, since this happened in Australia, but that is even more troubling for the code theory unless it includes accent decoding as part of the process.) The clerk's mental model was of the local resident, familiar with both the location of the town and of particular landmarks within it. In particular, both the "Brookvale Oval"—a sports field where the local rugby team played—and "McDonald's" —pervasive even in Australia!—would have had high salience to anyone familiar with the area. His interpretation of my question would have undoubtedly been very helpful for a fellow local, but it did less for a stranger.

In the husband-and-wife example, something more than a mismatch of mental models was probably going on. Tannen characterizes these as a different set of conversational rules. In this particular case such rules govern such things as when a question is an information question, or, more precisely, only an information question, and when the speaker intends that it carry other information as well. Such rules, for example, allow questions to serve as indirect requests, like "Could you pass the salt?," which would be inappropriately answered by "yes" if the "yes" was not associated with any action. Such rules help us convey more than we say, but they only function effectively when the rules are shared by both participants in the conversation. Problems arise when they are not so shared, as in this case where the wife was, in effect, requesting that the husband really make the decision about where to eat and interpreted the husband's attempt to give her the choice as laziness or worse. These rules and the implicit messages they permit are particularly troublesome because, like the rules of language themselves, they function out of the awareness of the participants.

What is even more significant in such cases is that the usual commonsense remedies for such problems—being clearer or saying more explicitly what you mean—are as likely to exacerbate them as to solve them. They may have been of some use in the first example but would be unlikely to be much help in the second. The fact is that *it is literally impossible to say everything we mean, because our linguistic meanings are embedded in a complex web of unstated, and even unstatable, sets of unconscious assumptions and beliefs.* Therefore, any meanings we express are necessarily a selection of all those we intend to convey. The potential problems are further aggravated by the corollary that listeners interpret everything they hear through an equally complex filter of beliefs and assumptions. So even saying more will never be saying enough, and trying to do so helps neither speaker nor listener recognize what role unconscious conversational rules and other unspoken aspects of our mental models are playing in selecting and interpreting the words we receive.

To return to our code theory diagram of the communication process, we can see that the problem lies with its assumption that the process of encoding and decoding thoughts is the same as the process of encoding and decoding language. As we've seen, even apparently straightforward conversations just aren't that simple. This is not to say that the words we choose as speakers or hear as listeners don't signal some aspects of our meanings—their capacity to do so is one of the miraculous powers of our language systems—but rather to insist that there is more going on than just a direct equivalence of expression and thought in the process of communication.

It should also be noted that I have added to Sperber and Wilson's original code theory diagram, in parentheses, using the written language as well as the spoken language to communicate. There are differences, to be sure, between speaking and writing and between listening and reading, but one of the hypotheses of the uncommonsense theory of language education that I am developing here is that the differences are far less significant than the similarities.

The Code Theory Goes to School

This also helps us to see clearly why it is important for language educators to understand that more is going on in communication than the direct encoding of thoughts into language. Commonsense language pedagogy is built on the code theory, as is most obvious in the teaching of reading and writing. In the former, reading has been viewed too often as essentially a process of decoding print. In effect, this commonsense definition of reading involves only adding a second decoding system to the one children have already developed to interpret oral signals. Although more sophisticated theories of comprehension have been developed which recognize the role of inferences in comprehension, even these are frequently viewed as an add-on, something needed for full comprehension of complex texts after the basic process of decoding is completed, rather than as an integral part of the process itself.

What is particularly limiting about the code-conduit view that reading equals decoding is the message it sends to young and inexperienced readers about what they are to attend to and what the reading process involves. If the ideas to be understood or comprehended are all somehow "there" in the text, then the reader must struggle to "get" them out. The only mental activity encouraged in the reading process is that of decoding the words; everything else is assumed to be transparent. Jack Thomson's (1987) research has shown clearly that inexperienced readers see such limits and see few other roles for themselves to play as readers. This is one reason they find texts which are not fully explicit and action-packed boring, and why they are often surprised to discover that it is permissible to struggle with interpretations, to be confused for a while in hopes that one can clear up the confusion later, and to use such things as descriptions of people and places as clues to the possible meaning to be made from the text.

One of the thirteen-year-olds he interviewed described the problem this way:

> I like books that start at point A and go to point B and so on to the end, in proper order. I like to make connections, but lots of books don't have connections. Like some of the ones we have in school. They skip all over the place and you forget things and lose track of what's happened.

Thomson comments: "How easy it would be to help this boy read with some satisfaction the kinds of books he criticizes. In his interview it emerged quite clearly that despite his condemnation of the school texts, he really believed that it was his own inadequacy as a reader which caused his confusion. When he was told that authors sometimes deliberately confuse readers, and that the confusions are eventually resolved by readers who can hold puzzles in their heads while they read, he was quite cheered. It was a completely novel idea to him" (Thomson 1987, pp. 196–197). I would only add that part of the problem may have stemmed from the young man's unconscious adoption from his school experience of the code theory model of reading, which limits the reader's conception of his role to figuring out what the text says and assuming that everything else will be straightforward.

The parallel problem in the teaching of writing has been the value placed on explicitness, implying that it is possible to express everything one means. While young writers do need to learn that writing demands more explicitness than speech, since the writer is unlikely to be available for questioning or further clarifications as a speaker is, it is nevertheless true that no writer can say everything he or she means, nor can one ever be assured that words will be interpreted as they were intended. I am trying to be clear throughout this book, but I also recognize that I may be saying too much for some readers, too little for others; that some may find my tone appealing, others appalling, and so on.

Further, just as we make different meanings from one another as readers, so too, the process of writing is usually more of a discovery process than the transcription-based conduit-code theory would allow. In the code theory the text formation process is entirely internal. Once formed, it can then be transcribed, and, later read, by others. The idea that texts are fully formed and emerge whole like Athena from the brow of Zeus diminishes to the vanishing point the importance of revision and can hardly recognize the possibility that writers can be surprised by what they write. Given the testimony from writers collected by, among others, Donald Murray, that writers don't know what they mean until they see what they say, it seems unlikely that the code theory is the last word on writing any more than it is on reading.

The emphasis on internal formation has also given rise to considerable concern for teaching student writers discourse structures which can be used to format their thoughts. As Jasper Neel (1988) has argued:

> [This] unquestionably subordinates all writing and discourse to thought. Thinking is defined as structure, system, and or-

ganization. Discourse, which is the vehicle for transporting thinking, must be made to fit the thinking that comes to it preformed. Such an idea is rampant in the West and clearly dominates the American composition industry where patterns-based composition texts (those based on such patterns as comparison-contrast and cause and effect) clearly dominate the market. . . . What occurs from the assignment of a cause-effect essay is an essay that says, usually in several hundred words, I am a cause-effect essay that explains the causes and effects of something. The apparent "content" of the essay (e.g., the causes and effects of alcoholism on child abuse) vanishes the moment it appears on paper. . . . The student's goal is not to communicate an idea or opinion; quite the contrary, the student's goal is to demonstrate mastery of the form named cause-effect. (pp. 41–42.)

Many teachers have implicitly or intuitively recognized the inadequacy of the code model as an explanation of verbal communication, but until our pedagogy recognizes it systematically and builds a new approach on a more comprehensive theory, the danger of giving pupils inappropriate signals, assignments to be done only for the sake of a grade or a requirement, and unhelpful advice will remain. In both reading and writing instruction, the dummy-run quality of the drills and other exercises students are asked to do stems quite directly from the combination of the conduit-code theory view that communication is a process of encoding and decoding and from the bottom-up assumption that the skills involved in doing so can be learned out of context. These theories may not be widely recognized, but they are nonetheless pervasive in common-sense practice.

Toward an Uncommonsense Theory of Communication

What, then, might provide the basis for a more adequate theory of verbal communication? Part of the answer springs from the limits we've already seen in the code model: its equating of thoughts and linguistic expressions which encode them, its code-like discreteness and linearity, and its conduit assumption that ideas really travel in their containers. Another aspect will depend on a more comprehensive look at what really happens when people communicate through language. The key notion which must be added to the code theory is that of *meaning making: a recognition that both the producer and the receiver of language are actively constructing ideas throughout the process of communication.* A number of theorists from a variety of disciplines have contributed to the development of a more comprehensive theory including this insight, and what they all have in common is an insistence that the words we produce or receive reveal or provide only some of the bases on which meanings are built.

Let's look at another example or two to see how the process works. Since I am, at this moment, writing this sentence, paragraph, chapter, book, I am, quite naturally, thinking about what I want to say. To do this I have to think about many things: what I know, believe, understand about this topic; what I think my readers know, believe, understand about it; what might be an effective, interesting, and persuasive way to discuss it; what would be the most appropriate set of words to use; and, sometimes, even how to spell those words, whether and when to use commas, and on and on. I also know that whatever words I eventually choose will not fully express all of my thoughts, and that anyone who reads them will not directly receive those thoughts. Writing and reading are not telepathic processes; they do involve a language code, in this the code theory is correct. But they also involve more than that.

What I am really trying to do as a writer, therefore, is to provide a linguistic representation of my ideas and intentions sufficiently rich to allow a reader to reconstruct a representation of my thoughts which will be tantamount to comprehending or understanding what I have to say. Not just any reader will do, of course, since whatever words I choose and whatever constructions I employ, there will be some people who would not be able to read them. Some of them would be people who can't read English (including, clearly, all of the billions of people who don't know English), but even among the universe of people who can read English, my vocabulary or my style could make interpretation difficult or impossible. More problematic still is the likelihood that there will be readers who have no difficulty with the vocabulary or structures I choose, but who find the ideas boring, foreign, threatening, or otherwise repellent, and therefore can't or won't expend the effort necessary to construct a meaning from my words.

This last category of readers is not likely to have stuck with the book long enough to get to this section, but still other problems remain. One of them involves interpreting the various part/whole relationships which are essential to understanding any text (either written or spoken) longer than a sentence. The kind of mental language system we sketched in the last chapter is geared to accounting for the nature of the intra-sentential relations of language, but the nature and structure of larger units is less well understood. Its properties, however, are clearly important to readers and writers as well as to speakers and listeners. Understanding the thrust of the last section, for example, required being able to follow my examples of communication problems and my brief critique of the linearity of the code model of communication added up to a sufficiently damaging view of it to require modification and extension. Whether or not I said enough (or too much) is one aspect of the problem, but perhaps even more fundamental is whether the connections from examples to explanations to critiques were clear enough to be reconstructed.

And if they weren't, who is to blame? Writer? Reader? Both writer and reader? And does the fault actually lie in the text itself or in some other aspects of the process—incoherent ideas on the part of the writer, or inattention, disinterest, hostility, or fatigue on the part of the reader? Or do both contribute in a mutual interaction? And how would we know?

One interesting aspect of these last few paragraphs is that they have been quite surprising to me as a writer. As I was pondering what example to use to illustrate the complexities of communicating, I decided to start with writing because I was doing it, but the extent and nature of the discussion were both unplanned and, I think, unplannable. Further, the whole thing can be scrapped (in which case you'd never get to read it) or moved (to some place I eventually consider more appropriate). One of the major differences between speech and writing stems from these latter possibilities, since if I'd been saying these things aloud, they'd be said, and couldn't be thrown away, moved around, or saved for later. But it's precisely the kinds of thinking and languaging that I've been trying to reveal here which make the code model incomplete and therefore inadequate as a theory of verbal communication. So, if I can't think of a better example later—another one of the luxuries of writing vis-à-vis speech—I'll probably keep some version of this here.

Turning to reading, the active, meaning-making nature of the reading process is frequently less apparent and less in tune with common sense. While even the commonsense view of writing recognizes that writers are constructing meaning, even if it does see them as doing so somewhat separately from the actual transcription process which is, strictly speaking, writing itself, the reader's role has traditionally been viewed as more passive. One thing that makes the activity of either process hard to see is that like most thinking and language processes, they function unconsciously. What we are, and can be, conscious of are our intentions—what I want to say as a writer, what sense you are making of what I am saying as a reader—the actual processes of doing so are largely unconscious, and particularly so when they involve the actual encoding and decoding aspects of either process.

More important in this connection is that we are largely unaware of the ways we use our conceptual storehouse of experience, knowledge, and feelings to make the connections which are essential to the process of interpretation and meaning making. I am not suggesting that we *should* be conscious of such things; in fact, I am sure that trying to be so would be an interference with and not an aid in meaning making. But this lack of awareness of how and when we use them has made them easy to overlook both by theorists and by practitioners. Nevertheless, what you are doing as you read these words is just as complex and active a process as the one I am going through as I write them. We can, often do, and often should reflect back on the meanings we have made and the connections between them and the text. This can provide a means of checking both the congruence of the meaning we have made and the text, and a way of enriching and deepening our meaning. But here, too, *what we are conscious of and concentrate on are the products of our meaning making, not the details of the unconscious processes we went through to make them.*

To start with, you probably have to have consciously decided to read them, although some reading, of the sort Yetta Goodman calls invisible print, like stop signs, product labels, and other environmental words and phrases, is done automatically and without a deliberate choice being made. Once embarked on reading, you bring to bear not only your knowledge of English and your competence as a print decoder but also your tacit theory of reading, your previous reflections on your own reading process, your experiences as a teacher and/or learner of reading, your previous reading of books and articles on this topic, your previous discussions of this topic, and so on. Again, these things may not be conscious most of the time, except when you find me making what your prior experience leads you to regard as outrageous statements or, more dimly, when you find yourself mentally or physically nodding in agreement with what I am saying.

But whether or not you find yourself in agreement with what you think I am saying, the meaning that you are making from the little squiggles you are reading is, in a crucial sense, yours alone, even though to make it you must be part of a social group which shares enough common experiences with me to enable us to transact together to make meaning. That is, the meaning you make from this or any text is a product of your active transaction with it. This process requires that you use your individual and cultural background to build a representation of your interpretation of the text. *Your* interpretation won't be exactly what *I* intended. There will be differences in emphasis, in focus of interest, in connections to your experience as a teacher or learner, and in the assumptions and vocabulary we share (or don't share) as writer and reader. No matter how much I would like to transmit my thoughts to you, I can't do it. You have to make sense of these squiggles on your own.

Although the interpretation each reader builds through this transaction is unique, it should be pointed out that it is neither completely idiosyncratic nor unsharable. The reality is that as we learn a language within a culture and, further, learn the rules of discourse which determine such things as argument patterns or types of stories which can be told, and through them build up a common store of shared experiences, we do build the possibilities of shared meaning making. The fit will not be as perfect as the transmission based on conduit-code theory suggests it ought to be, but there are nevertheless real areas of mutuality. When we share our interpretations with others who have read the same text as we have, we find that their transaction with the text has produced some similar and some different interpretations. So while each reader needs to make individual sense of the text in the primary transaction with the squiggles themselves, he or she can share and extend that meaning by writing and/or talking about it with others. Accounting for both the unique and the consensual aspects of meaning making is what determines how complex our uncommonsense theory must be.

For a theory of verbal communication to be adequate, therefore, it must take into account at least this much complexity; limiting it to a linear process of encoding and decoding, as the code theory has maintained, just won't do. What it ignores, primarily, is the pervasive role of inference in the process, and, further, it fails to provide any account of how the inferential process works. Inference, in this sense, is the process by which we determine which aspects of what people do *not* say must be added to the sense we derive from what they did say to make a more complete picture of their intended meanings. Such inferential processes are essential to every aspect of the meaning-making processes involved in communication.

Cooperating in Communicating

Just as Aristotle, Shannon and Weaver, and many others have developed the code model of communication, the importance of inferential processes in communication has been discussed by many writers. It has played a key role in theories of reading, particularly the reading of literature as explored by such critics as Iser (1978) and Rosenblatt (1978). It has also been a crucial problem for theorists of discourse, both written and oral. Foremost among them in

recent years has been the philosopher H. Paul Grice (1967/forth-
coming), who has developed the view that communication, and
particularly conversation, is governed by a "cooperative principle"
and "maxims of communication."
Grice argues:

> Our talk exchanges . . . are characteristically, to some degree
> at least, cooperative efforts; and each participant recognizes in
> them, to some extent, a common purpose or set of purposes,
> or at least a mutually accepted direction. . . . at each stage,
> *some* possible conversational moves would be excluded as
> conversationally unsuitable. We might then formulate a gen-
> eral principle which participants will be expected to observe,
> namely: Make your conversational contribution such as is re-
> quired, at the stage at which it occurs, by the accepted pur-
> pose or direction of the talk exchange in which you are
> engaged. (Grice, 1975, p. 45)

Grice went on to elaborate his cooperative principle through a
series of maxims of communication which govern how participants
in conversation can enact the cooperative drama of a conversation.
The particulars of Grice's proposals need not concern us here, but
it is important to recognize, as Sperber and Wilson (1986) point out
in their critique of Grice, that "this account of the general standards
governing verbal communication makes it possible to explain how
the utterance of a sentence, which provides only an incomplete and
ambiguous representation of a thought, can nevertheless express a
complete and unambiguous thought . . . to communicate efficiently, all a speaker has to do is to utter a sentence only one
interpretation of which is compatible with the assumption that she
is obeying the cooperative principle and maxims" (p. 34).

What Grice has accomplished, therefore, is to begin to give a
theoretical framework to account for the aspect of appropriateness
in the normally creative use of language identified by Chomsky
and discussed in Chapter V. Even if someone we are talking to
makes what we at first consider to be an inappropriate contribution
to the conversation, our assumption that he is abiding by the cooperative principle helps us try to find a way to make it comprehensible. Consider, for example, the following dialogue:

BERNIE: Would you like to go to the movies?
BARBARA: I have a lot of work to do.

Clearly Bernie needs to do some inferring in order to understand
that Barbara is intending to mean something like: no, I don't have

time to go, but not that she doesn't want to. Depending on how fully they understand each other's mental models and conversational rule systems, this might be the end of the topic, or it might be the beginning of an attempt by Bernie to persuade Barbara to take the night off because the break would do her good. But at the minimum, Bernie would have to assume that the reason Barbara mentioned her workload was cooperatively responsive to his question; and he would then have to use his own inference system to make the appropriate connection and then come up with an appropriate interpretation.

It was not, of course, the only response Barbara could have made. She could have said, with the same, or quite similar, intended meaning:

a. We don't have a babysitter.
b. My mother is very ill.
c. I hate films with subtitles.
d. It's going to rain.
e. That won't solve the problem.

And, of course, she could have said a potentially infinite number of other things. Bernie's capacity to interpret these responses would depend on how fully he and Barbara share the same reference systems: that he knows how difficult or easy it will be to get a babysitter (a); whether or not Barbara is likely to want to be near a telephone waiting for news of her mother (b); that she knows that the film he wants to see has subtitles (c); that the only nearby theater is a drive-in (d); or that they have been having a fight and his suggestion of a movie was an attempt at peacemaking (e). Insofar as he can't make such inferences, or makes different ones, his interpretation may likewise be different, but the point here, from a Gricean perspective, is that conversers have both a vested interest in cooperation in order to communicate, and that they possess models of appropriateness which enable them to make relevant interpretations of potentially or seemingly inappropriate utterances. The meaning being made is essentially dialogic, not monologic as the code theory suggests.

While we can, for example, make some guesses as to what there is about their shared context which enables Bernie to make the inferences he does about Barbara's reply, it is hard to see how to make those contextual principles sufficiently systematic to be a guide to interpretation. What is lacking is a principled way of determining how people make the interpretations they do, and why these are, in effect, the only ones which would be consistent with the conversational rule system.

Relevance Theory

To remedy this weakness and those we have noted with the code system, Dan Sperber and Deirdre Wilson (1986) have developed a combined code and inferential theory which they call relevance theory. It seems to be a more adequate and explanatory theory than any proposed so far, and whatever its final virtues turn out to be, it does contain a number of powerful implications for language education. The essence of their theory is that coded, in particular, linguistic, communication is not autonomous but depends on, and is subservient to, a variety of inferential processes. The principle of relevance enables us to determine which of the possible implications of an utterance should be inferred in order to do the most efficient information processing possible.

For Sperber and Wilson, the relevance theory contains a way of determining how we can make inferences based on the combination of what we already know and what we are receiving. The essentials of their approach are given briefly here.

Some information is old: it is already present in the individual's representation of the world. Unless it is needed for the performance of a particular cognitive task, such information is not worth processing at all. Other information is not only new but entirely unconnected with anything in the individual's representation of the world. It can only be added to the individual's representation as bits and pieces, and this usually means too much processing cost for too little benefit. Still other information is new but connected with old information. When these interconnected new and old items of information are used together as premises in an inference process, further new information can be derived: information which could not have been inferred without this combination of the new and old premises. When the processing of new information gives rise to such a multiplication effect, we call it *relevant*. The greater the multiplication effect, the greater the relevance. . . .

Our claim is that all human beings automatically aim at the most efficient information processing possible. This is so whether they are conscious of it or not; in fact, the very diverse and shifting conscious interests of individuals result from the pursuit of this permanent aim in changing conditions. In other words, an individual's particular cognitive goal at a given moment is always an instance of a more general goal: maximizing the relevance of the information processed. . . . This is a crucial factor in human interaction. . . .

Information processing involves effort; it will only be undertaken in expectation of some reward. There is thus no point
in drawing someone's attention to a phenomenon [through
human intentional communication] unless it seems relevant
enough to be worth his attention. (1986, pp. 47–49.)

Part of the point, Sperber and Wilson argue, is that the principle of relevance is an inevitable part of deliberate, intentional
communication. We don't choose to " 'follow' the principle of relevance . . . [we] could not violate it if we wanted to. The principle of
relevance applies without exception" (p. 162). What we do choose,
as speakers and writers, is what we believe will be relevant on the
basis of our understanding of the social and cognitive context of our
listeners or readers. And reciprocally, as listeners and readers we
use the principle of relevance to make the most significant (multiplicative) meanings we can by using the new information we've
received together with the old we've appropriately foregrounded
in a variety of inferential processes, all of which go far beyond
simply receiving, through decoding, the thoughts of the speaker or
writer.

This contrast with the transmission code-conduit theory is
crucial to education, since commonsense theory, ironically, often
seems to ignore both sides of the relevance equation. Far too often
the oral and written texts of teachers and schools are not chosen
with any attention at all to the social and cognitive context of
listeners and/or readers, but rather in terms of some organizing
principle dictated by the subject or discipline. (And, as noted earlier, decisions about what texts to choose are usually made by
people far from the actual site of the transaction.) The reciprocal
use of the learners' own experiences and prior knowledge is frequently denied to them in school, on the mistaken assumption that
they are not relevant. So rather than being asked to use the knowledge they have already acquired (the "old information") to make
the kind of multiplicative meanings made possible by the relevance
process, such connections are actively discouraged as children are
urged, in effect, to act as tape recorders, merely memorizing and
repeating the information given.

In relevance theory, in contrast, "Communication [is] a matter
of enlarging mutual cognitive environments, not of duplicating
thoughts." In fact, strictly speaking, such duplication is impossible,
since no two people have exactly the same world representations.
They have neither had exactly the same experiences to build on, nor
can they have exactly the same set of intentions in a communicative situation. The success of a communicative event, therefore,
does not depend on exact duplication but on using the principle of

relevance to make our own meaning from the transaction between the received utterance and our own existing cognitive environment. This is, among other things, one of the differences between our minds and those of contemporary computers: We can identify category similarities on the basis of less than identical representations. It is this flexible ability to make category connections which enables us to build relevance connections even though we have not had identical experiences.

Relevance in the Classroom

But regardless of whether or not the text or other content we choose to present has been selected for its relevance, learners will still treat it in relevance terms because, as Sperber and Wilson have pointed out, we have to; it is all we have to go on. Let's turn to two classroom examples to see how this works in practice.

The first comes from a science lesson observed by Mike Torbe and Peter Medway (1981). The twelve-year-old pupils are encountering the scientific use of the term *living* for the first time.

TEACHER: Okay now you're going to classify the various things on that picture into one of the three groups, which are—Karen?
PUPIL 1: Living, once living and er
PUPIL 2: Never lived
TEACHER: Yes, living, once living, and never lived. Right off you go.

[After some group work discussing the categorizations]

PUPIL 3: Sir—sir—
TEACHER: Mmm?
PUPIL 3: Sir, are clouds living?
TEACHER: —er—well what do you think?
PUPIL 3: I think they're not, but Julie says they are.
TEACHER: Oh. Why do you think they're living Julie?
PUPIL 4: Well, they move, and sort of grow and die and that.
TEACHER: Ye-es. What else have you argued about—anything?
PUPIL 5: Is wind living? (p. 30–31.)

This example has many potentially significant ramifications, but let's look at it first as an instance of verbal communication. The first part of the dialogue constitutes a kind of summary, a check by the teacher as to the meanings the pupils have made of the previous talk, and a setting of a task which will enable them to apply their emerging concept and him to assess their level of mastery. Both Pupils 1 and 2 are using their relevance systems to correctly infer the appropriate groupings (even though Pupil 1 doesn't quite remember the third category). The teacher's use of *the three groups* rather than just *three groups* has helped to specify the inference that should be drawn, and the appropriateness of the pupils' replies shows that they have made the right inferential selection.

The second segment of the dialogue shows both that the pupils have mastered the techniques of getting their teacher's attention and their capacity to ask relevant questions. The teacher's reply in the first instance signals that he is prepared to receive a communication, but that must be completely inferred since "Mmm?" hardly encodes it directly. Similarly the teacher's next three remarks—all questions—allow his listeners to infer that, among other things, he takes their questions seriously, that he is asking genuine questions to which he does not know the answer, and that he recognizes that if there has been difficulty with clouds there may be other difficulties as yet unraised. More directly, Pupil 3 must interpret the "you" in "what do you think" as addressed to him or her and probably uses a variety of conversational rules including the probability of eye contact and the fact that former speakers get first right of reply to questions unless there are other cues. Similarly Julie (Pupil 4) knows she is expected to reply to the next question, while the last question is open to any of the pupils for reply.

The last pupil question also illustrates relevance at work as contrasted with, for example, a possible reply about whether it will rain this afternoon, which might have been the subject of an argument but would not be relevant to the shared cognitive environment. This raises another important issue, however, which is that school conversations sometimes seem to violate not relevance, but the normal reality that all participants to a conversation have a mutual share in determining what is or is not relevant. We saw the difficulties posed for the teacher from the pupils' efforts to make relevant connections in the milk discussion in an earlier chapter, which is repeated below:

TEACHER: You get the white . . . what we call casein . . . that's . . . er . . . protein . . . which is good for you . . . it'll help build bones . . . and the white is mainly the casein and it's not actually a solution . . . it's a suspension of very fine particles together with water and various other things which are dissolved in water . . .

PUPIL 1: Sir, at my old school I shook a bottle of milk up and when I looked at it again the side was covered with . . . er . . . like particles and . . . er . . . could they be the white particles in the milk?

PUPIL 2: Yes, and gradually they would sediment out, wouldn't they, to the bottom?
PUPIL 3: When milk goes very sour it smells like cheese, doesn't it?
PUPIL 4: Well it is cheese, isn't it, if you leave it long enough?
TEACHER: Anyway can we get on? We'll leave a few questions for later. (Barnes 1969/1986, p. 29.)

The problem here is not that the students' contributions were irrelevant, from their perspective, but that they were coming from a framework which made their connections to the teacher's mental model of the topic hard for him to trace. He is wrapped up in transmitting the technical terminology of suspensions and solutions, and they are trying to make Vygotskyan relevance connections between what he is saying and what they have experienced. In fact, one way of looking at what has happened is that there has been an explosion of multiplicative relevance connections. Perhaps because he's the capital T teacher, he doesn't seem to see the need to understand the bases for the inferences his students are making and, in Barnes's words, he "hastily continues" to cover the content. What he misses by doing so, of course, is a chance to sort out what is genuinely helpful connection making and which of the inferences being suggested don't work in this context.

What was happening in both the "living" example and the "milk" example was that pupils were finding the new information hard to integrate into their store of old information. The difference is that the "milk" teacher didn't look behind the learners' remarks to explore why they were making the relevance connections they were, but returned instead to what was likely to be even more inefficient attempts at transmission. He thus left the pupils no other choice but to pick up what bits and pieces they could of the new information, if they didn't turn their receivers off altogether. In the "living" example, the teacher recognizes that the pupils are doing the best they can to be relevant, and therefore the confusions they reveal through their questions must be understood and eventually clarified if comprehension is to be successful. He is trying to use the multiplicative possibilities of the relevance system not so that the students can duplicate his thoughts and therefore be able to regurgitate them on demand, but so that, in Vygotsky's terms, they can integrate their prior spontaneous concept of "living" with the scientific one he hopes they will develop.

The principle of relevance underlies all attempts at verbal communication as a framework for drawing inferences. As speakers we have an obligation to be relevant whether we are telling stories or participating in a conversation. And as listeners we have to assume that speakers are being relevant even when we don't immediately see the connection to the previously established context. Another example from Torbe and Medway (1981) exemplifies this point.

> TEACHER: Today we'll be looking at bacteria and viruses and—
> PUPIL: Miss! Did you see *Starsky and Hutch* on Saturday?
>
> As it happens, *Starsky and Hutch* was about a man carrying a plague virus. (p. 35–36.)

As teachers (and as people) we must be willing to give our fellow communicators the benefit of the relevance doubt, and when we don't follow the connections, as we might not in this case if we hadn't seen that particular TV show, we must be willing to explore further to see where they spring from, and thereby reveal more clearly the thoughts that lie behind the utterances.

I've devoted a fair amount of time to relevance theory because I think it helps us to understand some of the inference systems which lie behind our use of the language system. There are, no doubt, many others as well, but the basic principles seem clear. All verbal communication is inferential communication, and relevance is the primary principle which governs our inferencing processes to make our meaning making as efficient as possible. It is not something we are usually conscious of doing, except in cases like the *Starsky and Hutch* example where the principle seems to have been violated. But, conscious or not, it operates all the time and helps us understand more clearly than ever that language does not directly encode thoughts and that interpreting language is not a process of attempting to duplicate the speaker's or writer's thoughts, but of making meaning anew through reconstructing our own sense of them through the filter of our own experience.

This doesn't mean, of course, that the meaning we make will not be similar to that intended by the speaker or writer. The fact that both parties to the transaction are using the relevance principle and more or less equivalent language systems drawn from the experience of living in a common culture is what permits communication to be as effective as it is. But it also shows that when communication misfires, attending solely to the text (graphic or acoustic signal), or even to the text and the systems for encoding and decoding it, which is all that is permitted in the code theory, will not help us understand what has gone wrong. We must, in addition, look at the other systems which are involved in the processes of language use for a more complete account of the process of meaning making as producer or receiver of language.

Metaphors and Schemas: Structuring Our Worlds

In addition to relevance theory, there are a number of other aspects of language which determine how it is used and which have implications for language educators. One of the most interesting and provocative to be developed in recent years has already been touched on briefly, the work of George Lakoff and Mark Johnson, who have together and separately been developing a theory of metaphoric schemas which attempts to explain some aspects of the ways our perceptual and conceptual systems interact with our language system. For Lakoff and Johnson, the key basis for our language and conceptual systems stems from the properties of our bodies. In the words of Johnson's (1987) title we carry *The Body in the Mind* and we use our bodily experiences as the basis for our meaning making, imagination, and reason. This extends from such relatively simple body-based schemas as *up is good, down is bad* to considerably more complex metaphors like *the body as a container*. The former derives from our upright posture and is associated with ideas ranging from growing *up* to a *raise* in pay, and even the traditional location of heaven (*up*) and hell (*down*). The latter, which derives from our sense of ourselves as having an inside and an outside, turns out to structure a lot of our thinking, in ways ranging from the relations of "in-groups" and "out-groups" to the structure of arguments expressed as *journeys from one contained position to another*.

In several instances we've already seen the body as container metaphor in action. The conduit metaphor of communication draws on and extends the container metaphor since thoughts are put into the container of the words that express them and sent out from a speaker to be taken in by a listener. In another sense, the conversation between Elizabeth and her mother about the uses of ashes on the garden showed Elizabeth's mother using her bodily imagination to enable Elizabeth to understand that just as she needs to take a variety of foods from outside into the container of her body to keep her healthy, so plants, too, need to do the same thing. In neither case, of course, is the metaphor deliberately or consciously chosen—like most of the language system, such schemas function completely out of awareness—but our shared experience with our bodies and their relation to the world enables us to use our imaginations to make such connections for ourselves and with each other.

Lakoff (1987) also stresses the uses of such metaphors in our category systems, and through them to the ways we make meaning and develop our knowledge of the world. We develop our initial category systems from the ways we experience the world, but experience does not come to us in neatly prepackaged form; we impose meaning upon it in terms of our earliest bodily experience. For Lakoff, "Meaning is not a thing; it involves what is meaningful to us. Nothing is meaningful in itself. Meaningfulness derives from the experience of functioning as a being of a certain sort in an environment of a certain sort" (p. 292). For Lakoff, the important thing about our category systems is that they are the result of our imaginative minds operating within real bodies by means of metaphors enabling us to see connections and build our understanding of the world.

In the last section of this chapter we saw a group of children and their teacher struggling with the category "living" and doing so by making connections with their own bodily experiences of being alive. Since Julie knows that living things "move," "grow," and "die," it seems eminently reasonable (and, in this sense at least, imaginable) at least to raise the question that clouds may be living, since they certainly move and they do seem to grow and to disappear if not actually die. While clouds may be a decidable case once the criteria are clearer, the discussion itself illustrates that Lakoff and Johnson's approach is speaking to real human problems of the relations between ourselves and our world. For Lakoff and Johnson, there is a real world, but its categories derive not from properties which are exclusive to the things being categorized, but from the relations between the things being categorized and the categorizers; that is, they derive from human beings with human perceptual and cognitive systems speaking a human language.

Of course, much of schooling is to a certain extent a matter of learning categories and the labels for these categories that are assigned by the culture into which the children are being initiated. This is, in a sense, a more adequate view of cultural literacy than Hirsch's (1987) list. Whether the categories are "living, not living, and never lived" or "progressive versus regressive taxes" or "poems, stories, plays, and essays," children learning to participate in a culture must learn the concepts and their associated labels. Further, Lakoff insists, in strong contrast to Hirsch, that these categories and labels are dynamic and interrelated systems which derive from our active attempts to understand the world, not static lists of cultural artifacts and ideas. Since they derive from our imaginative projection of likenesses and contrasts based on our bodily experiences, they are continually subject to modification and refinement as our understanding grows and develops.

They are, in effect, world theories, which develop as we discover their limits and find new explanations more successfully encompassing. The word *atom*, for example, was initially coined to coincide with the view that atoms were the indivisible building blocks of matter. We still use the term metaphorically to mean indivisibility, but as our understanding of the nature of matter has developed, we also understand that atoms are actually composed of a multitude of smaller particles, and even now the precise nature and role of the more fundamental particles is still the subject of active inquiry and considerable scientific debate. As we know more our schemas change, whether we are scientists at the frontiers of human knowledge or more pedestrian human beings trying to understand the world we live in. In fact it is probably the case that trying to understand the world we live in is the real knowledge frontier, and this pursuit is certainly far more relevant than what most scientists do. These ideas are consistent with the notions of Piaget, Vygotsky, and particularly George Kelly (1955), whose characterization of human beings as scientists making predictions on the basis of their interpretation of their experience is consistent with Lakoff and Johnson's view. For Kelly, as for Lakoff and Johnson, our experience of the world does not come interpreted or labeled; we actively interpret and label on the basis of our current understanding. And when our categories or constructs don't help us make accurate predictions, we have the capacity to modify them because we have the imaginative power to build new ones.

For language educators, one essential element of the contribution that Lakoff and Johnson are making to an uncommonsense view of language development is their insistence upon both the experiential (and therefore bodily) basis of knowledge and learning, and their view that such development depends upon our imaginative capacities. Imagination, like creativity, has often been considered a kind of superfluity, a frill, something which is nice but not essential, not sufficiently "hard" to be a subject worthy of attention in school. For Lakoff and Johnson, in contrast, the capacity to form mental images, to image the world and to imagine alternatives and connections, is so basic to our mental processes as to be said to constitute them. For Johnson (1987), "Imagination is central to human meaning and rationality for the simple reason that what we can experience and cognize as meaningful, and how we reason about it, are both dependent upon structures of imagination that make our experience what it is. In this view, meaning is not situated solely in propositions; instead, it permeates our embodied, spatial, temporal, culturally-formed, and value-laden understanding. The structures of imagination are part of what is shared when we understand one another and are able to communicate within a community" (p. 172).

Since language education is preeminently concerned with developing our pupils' powers of thinking and communication, developing their structures of imagination is clearly one of the most natural and effective ways to do so. These imaginative powers derive from our initial bodily experiences of the world but they are then extended as we acquire language and use it to think and communicate. Since the imagination is most naturally developed by the experience of reading and writing narratives, it is also consistent with the best of the traditions of language education, which derive from both the common and uncommonsense approaches. These structures of imagination are part of what we use to make the inferences which relevance theory has shown to pervade the processes of comprehension, of how we relate one thing to another. Similarly the notion that such things are shared within a community enables us to understand how we can use the language which embodies them for meaning making with others as well as for ourselves.

Although I've already argued that narratives function as an important way of structuring our experience as well as communicating it to others, it should be stressed here that narratives, too, are something we impose on our experience. They are constructs, not mere tape recordings of our lives. Even participants in the "same" experience will tell its story differently depending on the interpretation they impose on the events. My own autobiographical accounts of my high school teaching of English, for example, are *my story told from my perspective twenty plus years after the events occurred*. It isn't the story I told about it when the events were occurring, it isn't the story that the other participants in the events would have told then or would tell now, and it is a story I can tell only from the perspective of many years of intervening teaching experience and many years of thinking, reading, writing, and talking about teaching. There would, of course, be some similarities among all those stories, and they all could be mutually shared with profit and understanding, but each story would be a product of the individual's own imaginative interpretation of the meaning of the events.

Uncommonsense language education recognizes that learners are the ones who must do the learning, but that does not mean that teachers, texts, and curricula have no role to play. Our new task is not to present or transmit the world of knowledge to our students, but to find, instead, new ways to help them learn how to do it for themselves. In this role we are not all-knowing experts with all the facts, but guides, coaches, listeners, and questioners who encourage children to stretch their imaginations to understand and solve problems and who build our curriculum to exploit their relevance systems and their intentions.

Functions and Forms of Language Use

We have concentrated a lot on the *hows* of meaning making through language and not so much on the *whats* of either the *functions* which language can serve, or the *forms* which enable us to use language most effectively and efficiently. Since the time of the Greek rhetoricians these aspects have been the subject of intense study and debate, and various category systems have been proposed to account for them. In recent years such concerns have been studied in various ways by anthropologists, by literary theorists, by contemporary students of rhetoric, and by discourse linguists, as well as by language educators.

Sorting out which comes first is in some respects a chicken-and-egg problem, but aside from the intellectual difficulties involved, such decisions have had pedagogical consequences. Those who advocate the importance of forms have tended to try to teach them to writers and speakers. Those who believe in the priority of function have emphasized the prior importance of getting one's purposes clear before deciding on a form to embody it. Either approach has meant that categories tend to become reified and static by the time they are taught in schools. That is, whatever was tentative and fuzzy in the original attempt to distinguish between form or function hardens and takes on an independent existence once it is used as part of teaching. This hardening of the categories is, in a way, another aspect of the common sense of language education, and in educational terms from the formal side it has led to teaching such things as narrative, descriptive, expository, and argumentative or persuasive prose, or the five-paragraph theme, or, from the functional side, transforming descriptive distinctions like James Britton's among transactional, expressive, and poetic writing (1970) into things which should be taught.

While I am sure that we have much more to learn and to explore about these connections and interactions, for the most part the effort seems to be doomed to failure if it is intended to provide a definitive categorization of either forms or functions. Worse, it is pedagogically counterproductive to teach children that there is a finite number of forms which must be employed or functions which can be fulfilled by language. The creative nature of the language system and its possibilities for infinite varieties of utterances, metaphors, and schemas make it hard to pin down the characteristics of particular types or genres of language use. The situation is made even more complicated by the fact that any particular instance of language use is likely to be multifunctional and to mix forms as well. In this book, for example, I have told stories and presented examples of talk, reported on research and theory and explored beliefs and attitudes, been serious and funny, straightforward and ironic, and so on. And this seems to be typical of most language use.

Form, whether it is grammatical—at the sentence level—or rhetorical—at the discourse level—happens almost completely unconsciously during the process of producing language itself. There may be times when we attend to it more closely, as when we deliberately set out to compose a haiku or a sonnet, but even there the consciousness of form is more likely to play a role after some text has been produced than while we are producing it. It is the case, of course, that our experience in producing and receiving language does help us internalize a wide range of possible forms so that they are available when needed. But as Jasper Neel (1988) noted, when we assign a cause-effect essay we get a cause-effect essay, regardless of what its "content" is supposed to be.

Function does seem to play a more active role in consciousness since we are aware of our communicative purposes and intentions, but even there what we attend to is not some category of possible functions, but the particular intention we have to say something to somebody. We don't abstractly and independently choose a function and then embody it (except, of course, in school exercises). And since functions can be achieved by a multiplicity of possible forms, depending on the culture, attending to our purpose and intention does not in itself dictate the form we will use.

At the highest level of categorization into function versus form, that of distinguishing between narratives and arguments, there seems to be widespread belief that the distinction is both psychologically and culturally real. In addition to a long history of such genre distinctions which have been embodied in such commonsense categories as fiction versus nonfiction and creative versus expository writing, it has also been embodied in some of the most thoughtful recent work of language and language education. This distinction is essentially the one Britton (1970) draws between transactional and poetic uses of language, that Rosenblatt (1978) makes between efferent and aesthetic reading, and that Bruner (1986) develops between what he calls "a good story and a well-formed argument" (p. 11).

I find, however, in my own writing and reading that while there are differences between reading, say, Jerome Bruner and Iris Murdoch, there are also some similarities, and even when reading Bruner I find myself unconvinced of the "irreducibility" of the distinction. He is, after all, a great storyteller even in his "logico-scientific" books, (see in particular his *Child's Talk* [1983]), and Murdoch's characters often engage in highly logico-scientific talk.

Because stories value and evaluate experience, and even in some ways help to create experience, they too are a form of argument, and certainly the stories I have told within this text have been intended to further and support its general argument.

This muddying of the distinction exists, in part, because stories always have a point and that point can be expressed in logico-scientific language even though doing so loses much of the storyness of the narrative. I am perfectly willing to grant that there are real differences in standards of truth, or proof, or verification between the two modes. We should observe and understand the different kinds of logic at work in each case. But for me the fact that stories can serve as examples which prove the rule, and that they are so used in normal everyday language use, as well as in more "logico-scientific" discourse, suggests some overlap between the two rather than a rigid distinction. Even science and mathematics can be and are learned through stories, whether of the cause-and-effect sort of physics and chemistry, the word problems of mathematics, or the life-cycle stories of biology. It is important not to think of narrative as an exclusively literary device; its structures pervade all knowing and learning.

My overall conclusion about forms and functions, therefore, is that while they are certainly worthy of exploration and study, they play little direct role in our processes of using language. Language use is multilayered as the centrality of inference in relevance theory has shown. Trying to fit it into compartments denies the possibility that more than one thing is happening at once and focuses our attention on the wrong sorts of characteristics. Just as the traditional distinction between cognitive and affective domains of thought is vitiated by the recognition that every thought embeds a feeling and every feeling is entwined with a thought, so, too, making categorical distinctions can lead to exclusivity and distortion. If we use them at all we must be continually aware of their partial and tentative nature and, above all, of the fact that they are constructed by human beings for human purposes.

This is not to say that children should not be exposed to and given opportunities to employ a wide range of genres to fulfill a wide variety of functions. The inevitable leakage of our category systems, as layers conflict with categories, doesn't mean that there aren't differences of form, style, tone, and means of argument and proof which children should experience as producers and receivers. What it means, instead, is that *we can count on children to internalize unconsciously the useful distinctions of forms and functions as long as they have the opportunity to transact with them for real purposes.* If their attention can keep focused on the meanings they are making as speakers and listeners, readers and writers, the experiences they have will provide adequate exemplars for building their own discourse competence systems in much the same way that they build their language competence systems.

It may be helpful, from time to time, to reflect on those meaning-making efforts, to explore with learners the ways in which their efforts do and don't work effectively. This reflection should not have the goal of bringing them into closer conformity to a preexisting model, but to see how, within the limits of their current purpose, their strategies are enabling them to fulfill it. However, as Vygotsky (1962) has pointed out in respect to other scientific concepts, we can't reflect on that which we haven't experienced, and so the crucial first step always has to be the experience.

Transactions in Action

As the basis for a more fully rounded theory of language use, I have found the notion of *transaction*, in the sense originally developed by Bentley and Dewey (1949) and extended to literature by Louise Rosenblatt (1938, 1978) to be the most fruitful idea available in the uncommonsense tradition. The idea embodies the active inferencing processes of relevance theory, and it is centered on the fact that the meaning-making process depends on both the reader (listener) and the text (utterance). My extension of this idea is to show that, as in relevance theory the same goes for the writer (speaker) since the texts (utterances) we produce do not exhaustively capture our thoughts. They require an active process of shaping and selecting so that the language we produce will, because we use the same relevance principles, permit our auditors to reconstruct a meaning close enough to the one we intend to count as communication.

An additional feature of transactions as distinct from interactions is that they change both parties to the transaction, while an interaction can leave each party as it was originally. Dewey and Bentley's example of an interaction is of balls on a billiard table whose relative position changes, but whose essential nature remains undisturbed. In a language transaction, in contrast, the process of meaning making changes both parties; the producer and the text she is making meaning with and the reader and the text he is making meaning from. The former change is easier to grasp, I think, and I've already explored earlier in this chapter some of the processes of shaping and discovery that writing this text has involved for me. Each morning as I struggle to make meaning on paper, it changes, and both my mental model and the text itself are capable of being changed and modified throughout the process.

Since I am actually composing this text on a computer, its relative fluidity is clearer than ever to me—particularly if I haven't pushed the "save" button when the power goes off, or if, like this morning, I erased ten pages in order to start over on this section and the one before it. And each time I produce something, I am changed through the process. In particular I have had to rethink my ideas, to restructure the ways I have of expressing them, and to reconceptualize how I hope my readers are transacting with my text. The change is rarely dramatic, but each step involves using writing to learn.

With reading, the process of change is somewhat less clear, since the text, as defined by the squiggles on the page, does not change. What changes is our perception of it, the meanings we make from it, what Rosenblatt calls "the poem" we evoke from it by means of the transaction. The best examples of this that I can think of are instances when we reread, after a substantial interval, the "same" text. For me one of the most vivid of such experiences has been *Huckleberry Finn*, which I first read when I was twelve or so, read again as an undergraduate at twenty, and a third time as a teacher at twenty-six. The first time, for the boy John, it was a boy's book, full of high adventure and considerable humor. The second time, partly under the influence of my studenthood, it was a classic text of American literature, full of irony and insight into America's central cultural problems: racism and slavery. The third time, it centered on how my students could be helped to understand it. I was an adult American male, a father, a teacher, a reader concerned with helping my students understand the world they lived in as well as how it came to be that way. Each time the "poem" I made from the book was different, and I'm sure it would be different still were I to go back to it now another twenty years later.

But each time I transacted with it, the squiggles on the page hadn't changed. And while it is easy to see that I had, it is important to realize that, in a significant sense, what I perceived in the text had changed too. It's not that the Duke and Dauphin weren't there the first time, but any sense of their reality had completely escaped me. I'd just found them humorous, nearly cartoon-like caricatures. The second time I found them historically and culturally truer than I had previously, and by the third I was able to recognize some of myself and my own chicanery in their behavior. That rich texts can be read on many levels has been a truism of literary criticism, but the relevance selectional role that the reader plays in choosing which of the levels to respond to, albeit unconsciously, had not been recognized fully until the development of transactional theory.

I had changed in many ways between readings, not only because I had grown older, had more experience of the world, and had changed my status and way of life, although all these are important. But in connection with a transactional theory of language use, what was crucial to those experiences were my linguistic experiences—as reader, writer, speaker, and listener. They had given me a mental repertoire of stories and concepts, of characters and events, of worlds that I had not lived in and lives I would never lead. These intertextual experiences had enriched my interpersonal experiences just as they had been enriched by what we might loosely call my "real" life. For a reader and writer, the distinction is neither very clear nor very important, since in many ways I know the people I've met in literature–Huck and Jim, Ishmael and Ahab, Odysseus and Penelope, Romeo and Juliet—better than I know most of the people I've actually met. And even people who have touched my life have often resonated in my construal of them through echoes of Holden Caulfield, Rabbit Angstrom, and all the rest.

While this sense of knowing people in literature and thereby being able to live more lives and know more people than we ever could in our "real" lives provides one of transactional theory's strongest justifications, it should be emphasized here that this only happens through genuine transactions with literature. By genuine, I mean, essentially, self-selected and self-paced reading as against reading undertaken merely to pass a test or write a book report. As Jack Thomson (1987) has emphasized, the requirement of exam preparation has had a deadening effect on literature read in school, both in sending learners the wrong messages about what is important in the literature they read and in causing them to question their own competence as readers. The whole apparatus of the commonsense literature curriculum—whether required for examinations, for developing cultural literacy, or as an attempt to develop reading skills—must be rethought from a transactional, uncommonsense perspective.

To explore further how the transactional process works, I'd like to share part of a text. The text I've chosen is an ingenious children's book called *The Jolly Postman*, by Janet and Allan Ahlberg (1986). The subtitle of the book is *Or Other People's Letters*, and that is what it mainly consists of: letters, complete with envelopes, written from and to such familiar fairy tale characters as Goldilocks, Jack (of the Beanstalk), and Cinderella. The letters are written in appropriate script and form and are removable from the book so that they can be read. (Jack's is actually a postcard sent to the Giant on the trip he and his mother have taken with the goose that lays the golden eggs. "Better than credit cards," says Jack.) The continuing story is that of the jolly postman as he makes his rounds delivering the mail and staying for cups of tea.

To participate fully in the reading experience of the book, one of the principal qualities the reader must bring to it is this sense of *intertextuality*. That is, the reader must be familiar in advance not only with the characters but also with their stories so that when, as in the first letter, Goldilocks writes to apologize to the Three Bears, we understand what she is apologizing for and can supply the context with our own remembered version of their story. If we are unfamiliar with the adventures of Goldilocks and the Three Bears, we just won't know what is going on, and we certainly won't think it is funny. This is a key aspect of the transactional nature of the reading process, but it plays a role in writing as well, since clearly the shared meanings that the Ahlbergs hope will be built between them and their readers depend on shared textual, as well as cultural and linguistic, contexts of childhood.

Most of the letters are too beautifully penned and illustrated to be reproducible here, but one example may give some of the flavor and allow me to explore further how the transactional process works. It has a typed envelope addressed to:

B. B. Wolf Esq.
c/o Grandma's Cottage
Horner's Corner

There is also a rubber-stamped URGENT in the upper left corner.

Here already the authors are making substantial intertextual demands, but their full implications may not become clear until the letter itself is read.

MEENY, MINY, MO & CO.
ATTORNEYS AT LAW
Alley O Buildings, Toe Lane, Tel: 12345.

```
Dear Mr Wolf,

We are writing to you on behalf of our
client, Miss Riding-Hood, concerning her
grandma.  Miss Hood tells us that you
are presently occupying her grandma's
cottage and wearing her grandma's clothes
without this lady's permission.
```

Please understand that if this harassment
does not cease, we will call in the Official
Woodcutter, and - if necessary - all the
King's horses and all the King's men.

On a separate matter, we must inform you
that The Three Little Pigs Ltd. are
now firmly resolved to sue for damages.
Your offer of shares in a turnip or
apple-picking business is declined, and
all this huffing and puffing will get
you nowhere.

Yours sincerely,

Harold Meeny

H Meeny

Now, for me at least, this is truly marvelous stuff. A thing to
marvel over. Before I discuss it any further, read the letter again and
explore the kinds of connections you make, the kinds of experiences
you bring to the text, and the kinds of meanings you have made.
Like the Ahlbergs, I anticipate that we will all have a lot of shared
meanings here, but try reflecting on yours before I share mine.

Ready?

Read on.

The most brilliant stroke for me here is the synthesis—not
only bringing Meeny, Miny, and Mo to life, as lawyers with an office on Toe Lane, even—but of combining the wolf from the Riding
Hood and Three Little Pigs stories into one Big Bad—abbreviated
as B. B.!—character. (Is Peter's wolf there too? Surely he lurks in
the subtext we bring to the story.) And then, through the civilized
irony of the form and tone of the letter, to deflate the wolf's Big Bad
pretensions into nothing more than "huffing and puffing."

And, above all, it's funny. Or, better, it's funny if we share the
cultural context, the intertextual context, and the linguistic context
sufficiently to appreciate the way the genre of a letter from a firm
of solicitors intrudes incongruously into the world of fairy tales.
The letter works even better because it is entirely serious and formal

on its surface—a faithfully transactional text, in Britton's sense, using all of the formal, and rather stuffy, language appropriate to its genre.

And for those of us who are familiar with the world of the childhood stories of our particular culture, the resonances keep growing beyond those evoked from our memories of Little Red Riding Hood or the Three Little Pigs. Horner's Corner on the address recalls Little Jack, the King's horses and men, poor Humpty Dumpty— recalled by some of us as one of the first advocates of a transactional theory of literature when he counseled Alice in interpreting Jabberwocky and pointed out that we are the masters of the meanings of words, that they do not master us.

What is in the text itself is clearly only the tip of the iceberg of inferential meaning that the reader is invited to make. When one tries this book out, as I have, on readers of different ages and experiential backgrounds, it demonstrates vividly the role of readers in making meaning from texts. Younger, less widely read (or, crucially in this instance, read-to) readers, or almost readers can't make the intertextual connections and thereby lose those resonances, although the format of the book is intriguing even to them, and they like the idea of reading other people's letters. (One of the cultural commonalities they do bring to the story is the experience of the postman bringing the mail and of opening envelopes.) Older children and childlike adults, of whom I proudly count myself one, giggle and sigh throughout. And yet, for them, for all the demands that the text makes on our background and on bringing these characters to new life in the context of our previous familiarity with them, the text, its format, and its subtleties continue to reward our close inspection. We look again and again at the handwriting, the invented spelling in Goldilocks's letter, the stamps and postmarks, the wonderful products advertised by Hobgoblin Supplies Ltd. in the advertisement sent to Hansel and Gretel's Wicked Witch ("Little Boy Pie Mix: for those unexpected visitors when the cupboard is bare").

I emphasize this aspect of the process, for while *The Jolly Postman* makes clear throughout that its full riches will be revealed only to readers who share the background necessary to respond to its relevance connections—the genuine value of cultural literacy—it is the text itself which both provokes and constrains these connections. The transactional theory is *not* saying that texts are like Rorschach blots whose interpretation is completely open-ended. The language we use does provide the basis and the means by which our thoughts and feelings are communicated, but what transactional theory claims is that the text's language is necessary but not sufficient.

The active role of the reader in this process also makes it hard to sustain most of the boundary lines advocated by form and function category systems of the sort briefly discussed in the last section. The reader who plays an active role in meaning construction may in part violate the genre boundaries: taking a logico-scientific text and reading it as a story or vice-versa. Clearly, playing with genres is part of what the Ahlbergs are up to as well, since all of these letters, postcards, brochures, and so on are functioning simultaneously as authentic instances of their form, as in Harold Meeny's letter above, as part of the larger story of the book as a whole, and as part of the larger world of childhood stories, which has both narrative and paradigmatic elements in its claims to truth and meaning. Genres, like texts themselves, are a necessary but not sufficient part of the meaning-making process, and if we don't continue to recognize their layered interconnections as well as their distinctness, we will be behind instead of ahead in understanding how language is used.

To account for how it happens we have had to go beyond the code theory and look at the way we use the coded signals as the basis for our inferencing processes. Relevance theory has provided the key insight into how this happens, and transactional theory provides the basis for seeing how our individual and cultural backgrounds function to determine what we will find relevant in the language we use. If there was ever a text that illustrates the multiplicative effect that language can have when we use it to communicate, *The Jolly Postman* is surely that book. But the point is that all texts, oral and written, work that way, and in each case we bring ourselves to the texts we transact with and are at the same time forever changed by the transactions.

In this case, I was changed because, in some ways similar to my experience of rereading *Huckleberry Finn*, renewing my acquaintance with Goldilocks and her friends in a new context made me see them differently, not only as people who still lived in my mind and heart, but as people who have lives beyond the one encompassed by their original story. Arthur Applebee's (1978) exploration of how children's sense of stories grows, and their sense of whether or not characters like these are "real" or not, seems pertinent here. When he asked children whether a familiar story character was real, in the sense of really living somewhere, very young children often said, "Yes, but it's very far away," or the like. Clearly this insight into children's sense of the reality of such characters is part of what the Ahlbergs are intuitively responding to here. And both adults and children can giggle together over the picture of Cinderella's Prince vacuuming the floor of their new castle wearing a Hawaiian print shirt.

My sense of the role of these stories in helping to form my sense of story, my sense of reality, and therefore my sense of self has been greatly enriched. So too, perhaps, has been my sense of the importance of such shared experiences as part of what is essential for me to call on as a writer as well as a reader. My discussion of my experience of *Huckleberry Finn* depends in large part on my readers sharing at least the experience of reading about Huck once, and certainly on some experience of rereading a book after a long interval. Insofar as those experiences are not shared, I've made the wrong relevance assumptions to guide my meaning making, and your transactions with it will be impoverished as a result. But as writers we have to take that risk, as the Ahlbergs did so successfully for me, both because we can't say everything we mean and because our texts will inevitably be filtered through the experiences of others as they make meaning from them.

The fact that texts are not transparent and don't directly reveal their meaning, or even that their meaning is not fully determinate, should be a source not of worry and concern, but of amazement and excitement. It is what makes our language system so powerful: communicating thoughts, ideas, feelings, and perceptions without directly encoding them. And it is only through understanding these properties of indirectness, of indeterminateness, of inference, and the active meaning-making roles that they require of us as readers and writers that we can hope to be able to help children come to participate fully and pleasurably in these transactional processes.

CHAPTER 7

Integrating the Four Modes of Language Use

Listening/Speaking/ Reading/Writing

This chapter begins with two exemplary stories of language education in action. The two classrooms described below are fictional, composites of my own teaching experience and classrooms I have observed. But even though they're fictional, they're not utopian, since I have either experienced or observed each of the kinds of activities that I'm describing, and in each classroom there are unresolved problems and as yet unmet challenges. Further, they're not intended to be models to be slavishly imitated, but examples of some of the possibilities open to teachers attempting to enact uncommonsense principles and practices in their classrooms. Insofar as they may be useful as models, they would have to be adapted and modified for application in each teaching context.

This last point is, of course, the reason that most of this book has concentrated on a more theoretical discussion of the underlying principles that inform and structure effective language education. One of the most debilitating qualities of commonsense approaches to teaching has always been the attempt to transfer teaching activities, materials, and approaches wholesale from one classroom to another. This is done at the individual teacher level, either informally in terms of what has "worked" to solve a particular problem or through more public routes like exercise exchanges at conferences or in the journal devoted to such exchanges, and more broadly through the use of texts, workbooks, and so on up to employing the full package of a teacher-proof curriculum.

I'm all for teachers talking to each other about their practice; indeed, one of the serious flaws of school structure is to give teachers virtually no professional time for such collaboration. But if such talk is limited to the exchange of gimmicks or recipes for teaching, little improvement and no substantial difference in educational practice is likely to result. Change can only be made possible if teachers explore together not only whether a particular activity works, but what it works *for, for whom,* and *why* it does so. For it is only through exploring and reflecting on the *whys* of practice, which are more or less explicit theories, that we can develop the underlying knowledge we need to understand the essence of a particular activity. And we must understand its essence if we are to be able to adapt it successfully to our own classroom context, and, perhaps most crucially, to evaluate its effectiveness in terms of pupil learning.

In these examples, I'll explore what both the teachers and the classes are doing, and also why they're doing it. I'll consider the why from the point of view of both teacher and pupils, since, in the uncommonsense approach I've been articulating, it's as important for the students to understand why they're doing what they're doing as it is for the teachers. This last concept is even newer for students than it is for teachers, since in most commonsense approaches the only thing the pupils were expected to understand about the whys of school was to have faith that the adults knew best. *One of the challenges of uncommonsense teaching is to help students develop ways to understand the whys of school activities in ways which make sense to them.*

So let's see what two such classrooms might look like.

Peninsula High School: English 11

As visitors arrive at Peninsula High south of San Francisco, they are struck by the huge California live oak tree which dominates the front entrances and by the fact that, unlike most California high schools, most of its buildings are two stories high. The school is well-equipped but not fancy, with a theater for music and dramatic presentations, a large gym, playing fields and tennis courts, a swimming pool, a good-sized library, well-equipped science and computer labs, art rooms, and a number of large and small classrooms. Unlike many high schools, each department has an office with separate office compartments shared by two faculty members.

About 2,000 students in Grades 9–12 attend Peninsula High. They live in the area surrounding the school, which is mostly single-family, suburban housing but includes some multiple-unit apartments and a few houses provided for workers on the few farms that remain in the area. The area is generally prosperous, and most of the students' parents are employed either in the electronics and defense firms that dominate the area or in the retail and service businesses which depend on them. As in much of the rest of the state, and the country, many of the students' parents have been divorced. In some instances the kids live alternately with each of their parents, in others they live with one parent, or a parent and stepparent. The ethnic mix of the student body is also typically Californian, with a somewhat higher proportion of students of Asian and Mexican origin than would be true of the rest of the country. Some of them are quite recent immigrants, for whom English is a second language; for many more English is the second language for their parents and they are to some degree bilingual. Even the native English speakers are likely to have parents who moved there from somewhere else in the United States, although most of the kids are native Californians.

Sports occupy the leisure time of many of the students, either formally on one of the many teams that the school sponsors or informally in neighborhood parks and playgrounds. Other students are involved in one or more of the myriad activities provided by the school, which include several bands and a choir, the drama club, a newspaper, cheerleading, and so on. Many of the students work part-time, typically at one of the many fast-food restaurants which dot the area, or at one of the retail shops in the many shopping malls. For the most part their work is not intended to supplement the family income (although it is in some cases) but to provide themselves with pocket money and to maintain the cars which cram the student parking lot. Like teenagers everywhere, most of their leisure energy is devoted to the complex processes of dating, thinking about dating, talking about dating, dreaming about dating, and so on.

Dan Kelly has been teaching English at Peninsula High for the last four years; for fifteen before that he taught at similar schools in Arizona. He's in his early forties and is just beginning to show a little gray in his hair and his bushy mustache. He still enjoys teaching even though he is now in his twentieth year at it, and he has been invigorated by a sabbatical leave during his Arizona years which he spent pursuing a further degree and by his move to California shortly after his divorce. He likes Peninsula High both for its students, an open and refreshing group of kids, and his colleagues, who are professionally involved and committed. The administration has been supportive of his activities as a teacher and as advisor to the school paper, but also leaves him and the department free to determine their own approaches to teaching English. About a third of the staff, including Dan, have participated in one of the summer workshops of the National Writing Project, and that experience has helped to fuel their continuing efforts to revise and enliven the curriculum.

Dan's eleventh-grade English class is unusual for a number of reasons, but one of them is that, unlike the English classes of most American high schools, it is a mixed-ability group. This is the norm for both English and social studies at Peninsula High, since, shortly after Dan's arrival, both departments decided to abandon tracking in favor of heterogeneous grouping. Like most of his colleagues, Dan was in favor of the idea in principle, as it would mean giving every student a chance at the richest possible curriculum, but a little apprehensive about how it would work out in practice, as he had previously always taught tracked classes. He knew that even the most "homogeneous" classes weren't really all that homogeneous anyway in practice, but he was initially worried that putting the fastest and the slowest learners together would be bad for both levels, as well as putting an additional strain on him. He says his fears proved groundless, however, and he now believes that such an arrangement is best for all concerned and would strongly resist going back to a tracked arrangement.

It is now about six weeks into the school year, and Dan and his class have gotten quite comfortable with each other's styles. This feeling of comfort was accomplished mostly by using the opening weeks of school as a period of mutual orientation, during which Dan and the students had explored together what they were interested in, what they already knew and could do, and what their aspirations were for the future in terms of further education and employment. Each student had written a dialogue journal to which Dan had responded regularly and in which students had explored on paper what they liked to read and write, what they wanted to do in the future, what they expected from this year's English class, and so on. They had all read a novel of their choice selected from the library and shared it with the rest of the class, both by means of a poster which was put on the bulletin boards which line the room and in an oral report to a small group.

Class time was usually spent writing or reading or in small-group discussion of several stories and poems. For the most part Dan had chosen the texts that the class read in common, but he had done this after a process of negotiation and discussion of what themes and issues they wanted to focus on. Some of the whole-class discussions had focused on the processes of small-group discussion. These were based on either a live small-group discussion which had taken place in a fishbowl environment with four students participating and the others observing, or on transcripts of taped group discussions which Dan had made. Although the students had had some experience with small-group work in their earlier years at Peninsula High, Dan felt it was important to develop their understanding of the process more explicitly, because he intended to use it frequently throughout the year, and he wanted to be sure that everyone understood both how to do it and why it was a valuable tool for learning.

He had realized the importance of this several years earlier when he had expected the students to be able to hold independent discussions and they had not been able to. They thought such discussions were just time for idle talk and other fun and games. They weren't, somehow, the "real thing" of commonsense schooling. By reflecting with the class on why they were doing what they were doing, he was able to reassure them and to help them see more of what and how they were learning through their activities, but he had never again taken for granted that the processes he was employing would be taken on faith by the students as worthwhile. Therefore he tried to include discussions of why the processes were valuable, how and what they were intended to help the students learn, and how to involve the students themselves in evaluating their own learning. And he, too, had had to learn that in teacherless groups not all talk would be, strictly speaking, on task, but that student digressions rarely lasted long and served other valuable purposes including getting the group to know and trust each other better.

He knew that discussing the learning processes involved in group work took time away from "covering" content, but he was convinced that such coverage was an illusion if the students didn't understand why they were doing what they were doing. He also believed that what he hoped they would be learning would be unlikely to stick with them permanently unless they were involved enough in choosing what they did as well as why it would be worthwhile. And perhaps most important of all, such discussions were the only way to increase the engagement of the students with the academic processes of the class, since for many years they had been content to remain basically uninvolved in their classes, if not actually hostile to them, saving their psychic energy for out-of-class activities.

Insofar as students had had concerns with the content of their classes, they had mostly been expressed commonsensically in terms of "Will it be on the test?" or, for those with aspirations to attend a selective college, "Will it help my SAT or ACT scores?" Dan believes that such limited concerns with tests and grades has distorted the focus of schools away from genuine learning. Through discussing the whats and whys of learning with his students, he had found that many of them could be reenergized to concern themselves with how what they are doing fits into the larger canvas of their present concerns and future aspirations.

Dan is a confident, professional teacher who functions quite autonomously in terms of his day-to-day life in the classroom. The school, in the form of the administration and his colleagues, places some constraints on what he can teach in terms of subject matter: the literary focus of eleventh-grade English is supposed to concentrate on the cultural heritage of American literature, and the students are expected to write some academic essays as well as other genres. Similarly, both the parents and the community have sufficiently high academic aspirations for their offspring to impose a steady, if usually subtle, pressure on the English department, particularly on those teaching the eleventh grade, to attend to issues of vocabulary development and reading comprehension and thus to assure that the kids do well on the standardized college selection tests. But within these fairly broad parameters, Dan is, in practice, left alone to make his own daily and weekly instructional decisions.

His image of his students is that they are fundamentally nice kids with a fairly wide range of abilities, interests, and backgrounds. What they have in common is that few of them, even the most talented readers and writers, have ever been pushed very hard in school, and most of them have developed the habit of doing the minimum necessary to succeed in achieving whatever grade they (and their parents) have settled on as their "normal" level of achievement. They seem to him fairly passive, having apparently learned through their previous school experiences that if they keep their mouths shut and fill in the appropriate blanks, little more will be demanded of them, and little energy need be expended. When he began the semester he was not surprised, although not very happy, to discover that the most common responses to assignments or suggestions he made were, "How long should it be?," "Does it have to be in ink?," "When is it due?," or "How much does it count for?" There were rarely, if ever, questions about why it should be done or any other aspect of the substance of the task. It almost seemed to Dan as though most of the class had decided that all school tasks were going to be, by definition, meaningless, and the only parameters of interest were therefore those of form and grading requirements.

As they got to know each other during the opening weeks of the term, Dan realized that although there were some differences in reading and writing ability among the students, these were rarely consistently manifested. That is, some of the students who deliberately sought out an easy book to read when given the choice were also those who wrote the most thoughtful dialogues with him in their journals, and one of the most reluctant readers, Kathy, had actually written a powerful short story describing her fears in moving to California and to a new school. Her spelling and punctuation needed work, but her narrative power was both well expressed and extremely moving. Similarly, Frank, whose only real interest seemed to be his motorcycle, had surprised Dan with his thoughtful capacity to discuss the nature and effects of peer group pressures in terms of the various cliques that made up the high school's social structure. Although he had read the novel with some reluctance, even after seeing the film on his VCR, his poster for *The Outsiders* had been one of the best done by the class, and in his oral report he made clear why he thought the book was superior to the movie.

The reality of intra- as well as inter-student differences in abilities, interests, and concerns was consistent with Dan's view that the development of language-using abilities is both a highly complex and a very personal process. From reflecting on his own experiences as a learner, he knew that he worked most effectively and most energetically when he was genuinely interested in what he was doing. He remembered, for example, the time in high school that he had become obsessed with the horrors of war and had done an extensive search for poems about war, even discovering some his teacher had never read. This had led to one of the best papers he had ever written—which he still remembered twenty-five years later. But he also remembered that during that same year in high school he had done some very perfunctory work on books and topics which hadn't grabbed him at all. He certainly recognized that intense involvement would not be possible for all the students all the time. In fact, he was not even sure it would be desirable, given all of the other pressures on their time and interests, but he did hope to find ways to make more involvement possible with everything each student did, and to find as many ways as possible of creating opportunities for intense learning experiences.

Given the real constraint provided by the curriculum's focus on American literature, Dan spent the last week of his introductory unit exploring with the class their interests in American culture, its history, and, from their perspective, its present realities. On the basis of these discussions he discovered that for most students, the primary issue on their personal agendas was their future. This was usually expressed in terms of careers, further education, and family responsibilities, but it also dealt with the nature of happiness, success, and the conflicts they saw around them between personal interests and social concerns. In response to this discussion, he asked all the students to write briefly on what they already knew about the life choices faced by earlier generations of teenagers; they then discussed in small groups what they would like to learn about such questions. Between them they explored the possibilities of examining the history of growing up in America as reflected in the novels, poems, stories, and films of both contemporary and earlier generations.

They also discussed different ways of learning about such things—one suggestion that met with general support was that they could interview their parents, and, where possible, their grandparents, about their experiences as teenagers—and the variety of possible ways they could report on what they found and demonstrate what they had learned. In the course of this negotiation process each student identified his or her own personal learning objectives for the unit and described how the achievement of those objectives would be evaluated. The individual objectives ranged from reading three novels from different periods of American history and writing responses to them to writing a story based on a grandfather's experience of leaving school at age twelve to work in the coal mines of Pennsylvania. Some students chose to work in groups, one of which decided to write a film script for a contemporary teen-age movie which would be more realistic than those currently being churned out in Hollywood.

As a group, the class decided to read a series of short stories dealing with growing up, ranging over several periods of American history, which Dan assured the students he would help select; and a class committee was appointed to work with Dan to select a list of films which might be relevant. Some of these would be shown and discussed in class, others would be recommended for home or library viewing on videotape. For writing assignments, the group decided that it would be fun and useful to write a fictional autobiography describing their lives for the next ten years, and to write learning log responses to the stories they were reading and the films they saw. Some class time was to be devoted to their individual projects and some to the common reading and writing tasks. Grades were to be negotiated between each student and Dan, based on their demonstrated achievement in both individual and class projects.

During the time I was part of the class, the growing-up unit was in full swing. The first day I visited might have been seen by a commonsense observer as one where little teaching was going on. In fact, Dan reported to me after class that in his first year in the school the assistant principal had visited a similar class and decided he couldn't write an observation report on it. "I'll come back another day when you're teaching," he had said. Dan had had to help him see what had been going on, remind him that the reason we have schools is for students to learn, and explain that teachers should "teach" (i.e. present information, lead discussions, give tests, and so on) *only* when those activities are the most effective ways of helping students learn. (This lack of administrative comprehension is a distressingly common experience for teachers attempting to move toward uncommonsense teaching, but its universality doesn't diminish its cautionary power.)

During third period that Wednesday the students were working almost entirely on their individual projects. In addition to the two who were absent, seven students were in the school library either reading or doing research for their projects. The other twenty students were in the classroom, but they were working individually or in groups. The filmmakers were arguing about whether to have a classroom scene in their movie, and once they decided it was important, about who the teacher should be and what kind of class he should have. They decided that they wanted a commonsense teacher (my term, not theirs), but one who was really trying to get the class to work. When I left them, they were trying to decide on the subject she should be teaching. Other students were writing, several were reading, and a couple didn't seem to be doing much of anything. Two were studying together for their math test the next period. Dan was aware of this but didn't attempt to stop them, because the two involved had made substantial progress on their projects earlier in the week.

At the beginning of the period Dan had circulated to try to see if everyone had something to do, and about halfway through the period he went to talk to the two who were staring about rather aimlessly. In one case he suggested that Anne could read Hemingway's "Soldier's Home," which they were going to discuss the next day, and in the other he urged Norman to devote his time to his autobiography if he wasn't ready to work on his project.

During the rest of the period, Dan held individual conferences with six students. He operated with sign-up spaces written on the blackboard beside his desk. He'd filled in the first two names himself in order to get a chance to talk to two of the students whose learning logs on the excerpts from Sherwood Anderson's *Winesburg, Ohio* he had returned at the beginning of the period. In one case he wanted to suggest some additional reading David might be interested in, and in the other, he wanted to find out why Nancy had shied away from the theme of the story and responded only to its events. The other conferences were with students who wanted to consult Dan about what they were writing. Gary wanted to know if he could start his autobiography in the future and work back to the past, Alys wanted some suggestions for material she could read about coal mining and the depression in the thirties to help her understand her grandfather's story better, and Joe and Paul came together to talk about their idea to write their autobiographies jointly in the form of two old friends from high school talking over old times and new at their tenth reunion.

At the end of the period when the students returned from the library, Dan reminded the class that they would discuss the Hemingway story the next day, and that he would collect their learning logs on it on Friday. Following the class Dan had a free period, which he began by making brief notes on the log he kept on the class. His entries, in this case, were on his conferences with the six students, his concern that Anne and Norman weren't making much progress on their projects, and several other observations he'd made during the period. He also made sketchy notes on how he hoped the next day's discussion of "Soldier's Home" would go.

The next day they did discuss the story. The class started as a whole group as Dan asked the students to raise questions about things that had puzzled them in the story or which they would like to discuss. He listed them on the board:

- Was Krebs afraid of the girls in his hometown?
- What had the war done to him?
- How different had he been before the war?
- Why didn't he want to get a job?
- Why didn't he like his hometown? (Was it because they had not given him a parade when he came home?)
- What was it like in the First World War? (How different was it from Vietnam?)

For those who don't know "Soldier's Home," it's a classic Hemingway story originally published in *In Our Time* in 1925. It focuses on the experiences of returning home from the Great War of a young American from Oklahoma who had left college to join the Marines. Harold Krebs finds himself substantially out of step with the mores and beliefs of his fellow townspeople and of his family after his return. He finds people either unable or unwilling to talk about the war, and he himself is not very eager to do so. He doesn't feel the urge to do much except play pool, and even the girls of his hometown seem alien to him as individuals, even though the way they look attracts him strongly. He thinks to himself that the girls of France and Germany were more appealing because one didn't have to talk to them. His father only exists in the story as a shadowy and forbidding presence, and his mother cannot relate to his loss of religious belief, his lack of ambition to get a job and settle down with a nice girl, and his feeling that he can no longer love anyone. Only his younger sisters accept him as a hero, but even they don't seem to be able to understand his lassitude and alienation. His final decision to leave town seems hardly likely to solve his problems, but it will at least get people off his back when he escapes to the relative anonymity of Kansas City.

Dan and the class discussed the questions briefly in order to clarify them, and Dan then told the class to divide into their literature discussion groups. He asked them to discuss the story using these issues as a starting point. The literature discussion groups had been established at the beginning of the unit, and this was now the third story they had discussed together. Dan had selected these groups of four students each to mix up gender, ability, and friendship alliances. He had allowed the students to select their own working groups for the projects and their own writing groups, believing that in those contexts it was important for students to have immediate trust and confidence in their partners. For the literature discussions, however, he believed it was important to have varied points of view to bring to discussing the text, as well as a range of abilities. And he hoped that the experience of staying in the same groups would enable them to build trust through working together.

The group I sat in on consisted of Mary, José, Akiko, and Norman. Mary was one of the class's most articulate students; Dan described her as "a great student to have in class; she never lets you get away with a glib or superficial statement." José, one of the four Mexican-American students in the class, was a bilingual speaker of Spanish and English. Not a very highly motivated reader or writer —his test scores and grades would probably have placed him in a low-track class were tracking still being practiced—José was a talented artist whose cartoons regularly appeared in the school paper, usually poking subtle fun at life at Peninsula High. Akiko had started her education in Japan and almost never contributed to the whole-class discussions, but her reading and writing abilities were solid and growing. Norman's potential abilities were almost consistently hidden by his self-appointed role as the class clown.

Despite their differences, the combination of Dan's overall class style and their previous attempts at working together made the group seem comfortable with each other, and they rapidly went to "their" corner of the room. Norman started the discussion off with a complaint.

NORMAN: I really thought this story was boring. This guy never did anything. All he seemed to want to do was sleep.

MARY: But wasn't that because of what had happened to him in the war?

JOSÉ: But what did happen to him in the war? I couldn't figure that out at all.

NORMAN: That was part of the problem. He didn't want to talk about it, and the story never tells you what he did.

AKIKO: Well it does say that he went to France and Germany. They must have been quite different from Oklahoma.

JOSÉ: Sure, but does it say anything about what he did there?

MARY: (opening book) Well it says on the first page that he "had been at Belleau Wood, Soissons, the Champagne, St. Mihiel, and in the Argonne."

JOSÉ: What are those? Towns?

NORMAN: Maybe they were battles? Does anyone know anything about the First World War?

MARY: Well I remember when we saw *All Quiet on the Western Front* in history last year. That was the First World War.

JOSÉ: Yeah, and it was awful. The soldiers had to sit in these muddy trenches all the time while the guns shot at them and then they had to jump up and charge the enemy.

NORMAN: I remember that, isn't that the one where the hero gets killed in the end just before the war ended?

MARY: Yes, it was a very sad movie, first all his friends got killed and then he did.

NORMAN: But this story doesn't tell us anything about that. Why didn't we read *All Quiet on the Western Front* or some other story about the war? That would have been more exciting.

MARY: But maybe that's part of what this story is about: that coming home after the war would be boring.

JOSÉ: Sort of like my math class which follows this one. It's always boring too. It probably would be anyway, but it seems more so after this class.

AKIKO: I don't find math boring, it's my favorite subject.

JOSÉ: But you're not in my class. All we do is work on word problems. Who cares how long it will take two trains to meet if one leaves Chicago at four o'clock and stuff?

AKIKO: But you need to know that stuff to get into college.

NORMAN: What does all this have to do with the story?

MARY: Well it shows that after you do something exciting, then anything else can seem boring. Look at the second question on the board, it asks: What had the war done to him? Isn't that what we've been talking about?

NORMAN: You mean the story had to be boring because he was bored to be back in this dinky town after going to Europe?

AKIKO: Perhaps, although I wasn't really as bored by it as you seem to have been. At least it was short.

MARY: Well here's what I wrote about this in my learning log:

> Harold Krebs had been changed so much by the war that he couldn't relate to his family, to the girls in the town, or

to any of the other people in town. Somehow he couldn't explain to them what had happened to him and they didn't seem to care. They seemed to expect him to just come back and be as he always had been, as though he only had been away for a weekend, but he just wasn't the same person any more, and he just didn't fit.

JOSÉ: Gee, that's great. It certainly explains how he was feeling, but I still wish he'd told us more about the war.

AKIKO: When was this story written?

NORMAN: Let's see, I don't think it says. . . . Say, Mr. Kelly, when was this story written?

MR. KELLY: In the early twenties. Why do you want to know?

NORMAN: Because that helps explain why he doesn't tell us much about the war. If it had only been over for a few years everyone would remember it.

The literature discussion groups went on for another fifteen minutes or so, and Mary, José, Akiko, and Norman continued to struggle mostly with the question of how the war had changed Harold Krebs. They never seemed very clear about the war itself, but they came to a consensus that whatever had happened to him, he just wasn't able to participate in the world he returned to. They may not have fully grasped why he no longer wanted to get a job and get married, but José did point out that it may have been seeing other people killed that caused him to lose his faith in God, and even Norman conceded that Harold's parents didn't seem to understand him. That led to a discussion about whether or not today's parents understood their children, which was still in progress when Dan called the discussion to a halt and asked everyone to write a learning log entry for the last five minutes of the period summarizing their impressions of what their group had talked about. He also reminded the class that their completed learning logs on "Soldier's Home" would be collected the next day.

In those concluding minutes of the period, Norman wrote:

I still think this is a pretty boring story. I don't think I would have picked it. But I do understand from the discussion that part of it was intentional to show how bored Harold Krebs was when he came home after the war. I think he made a big mistake, though, in not trying to use his hero status to impress the girls in town with what a macho guy he was. I'll bet he could have gotten lots of action if he had and then neither the story nor his life would have been as boring.

I'd like to find out more about the First World War though. Maybe that would help us understand better what had happened to him.

During the group discussions Dan had been available for questions like the one Norman asked—another group had asked him if he'd been in Vietnam—but otherwise he had spent his time eavesdropping on the groups as inconspicuously as possible. When I asked him why he had not participated more actively, he replied that he had found that when he did so he inevitably became the expert to whom the students looked for the "right" answer. Since he wants them to become their own experts, that is to recognize that they have both the capacity and the responsibility for making meaning from the stories without his help, he doesn't want to intrude on the process by being the teacher/expert, and he has found that the students won't allow him to function any other way. That was why, he said, he'd told the group I had joined that I was just there to listen.

He then asked me how I thought the group had gone. I said that it was possible that they had stayed on task a little more consistently than they might have if I had not been there (see, for example, Barnes 1976, for examples of groups that move on and off the topic), but that I had been impressed both by their openness and by their willingness to admit where they were puzzled. I showed him what I had written while the class was writing their responses to the group.

A very impressive discussion. All of the students seemed to play a significant role, and although Akiko had said the least, she did contribute both in substance and in seriousness. Norman's initial concern with the boredom of the story provided a valuable spark to the discussion as did José's willingness to ask questions. Mary seemed to play the closest equivalent of the teacher's normal expert role both when she remembered *All Quiet* and when she read part of her learning log entry, but she did so without arrogance and seemed to be treated by the rest as a valuable but not necessarily superior member of the group.

As far as doping out a meaning for the story went, they were hampered by their lack of a similar experience—at least they never managed to find one except José's analogy with the math class—and by their lack of knowledge about war and particularly WWI, but they did seem both willing and able to struggle with their confusions. They seemed to recognize that the group could be a resource for clarifying their ideas, and the closing discussion about parents and children was moving toward a valuable connection between their own experience as teenagers and the hero of the story when they ran out of time.

I told Dan that I had been impressed by how thoroughly they seemed to have read the story. He agreed that it sounded good, but that in two of the groups he had overheard there were students who didn't seem to have done so, and he suspected that Frank and Cesar, two of the class's less able readers, might have been absent that day because they, too, hadn't read it. He said he'd found, however, that the combination of having small-group discussions—in which one's lack of preparation is harder to hide—and asking kids to write learning logs responding to the story, rather than answer questions he made up in advance about it, seemed to have had a good motivating effect in helping most of the students recognize that they'd enjoy the class more if they were prepared. He said, further, that one of the reasons he didn't collect the learning logs until the day after the discussion was to give those who hadn't read the story by class time a chance to catch up without penalty.

He agreed that time was always a problem, but that he was less worried about having cut off a discussion that was still perking along than he would have been if they'd run out of steam. He also thought it was important to give each student a chance to reflect in writing, however briefly, on what had just happened, to solidify whatever they had learned. He also hoped it would provide a good basis to begin the next day when he intended to have a whole-class discussion on the story and how it related to the overall unit theme of growing up in America. Actually, he said, the most difficult time crunches came in finding opportunities for conferences, for group and individual work on projects, and for everyone to get feedback on their writing rather than in literature discussions.

We could go on indefinitely looking at how Dan Kelly is trying to enact uncommonsense teaching at Peninsula High. The process is not without its difficulties. In fact, the next day's discussion was not a great success, because the students seemed all too willing to fall back into their commonsense pattern of waiting for Dan to tell them what the story meant. Dan recognizes that this is one aspect of his teaching and of the students' learning patterns that he must continue to work on. But overall it does seem to be working, to be engaging the students, and to be helping them develop in all four modes of language use: speaking, listening, reading, and writing.

Uncommonsense Excellence

Some might say that Dan Kelly's classroom can work as it does only because he is lucky enough to work in a relatively prosperous suburban area, where the students are more motivated to learn and come from the kinds of literate homes which give them a leg up on learning how to play the school game. It is certainly true that such factors can and do make a difference, but one striking finding of recent educational research is that in some respects such traditional bastions of academic success have been among the hardest hit by the educational malaise which is a symptom of commonsense schooling in the closing decades of the twentieth century. As Powell et al. (1985) and Sedlak et al. (1986) have pointed out, the reality of virtually every high school in the country is a lack of engagement with learning on the part of all but a tiny fraction of the students. In Powell's *The Shopping Mall High School,* most if not all of the students are being *sold short* (Sedlak's claim) by not being sufficiently challenged in their academic diet.

We've seen some of the commonsense causes for this. By contrast, uncommonsense approaches to language education do challenge students to achieve high levels of competence. Uncommonsense ideas have frequently been criticized for promoting a laissez-faire attitude toward student achievement and for being incapable of embodying high standards, academic rigor, and the pursuit of excellence. While there is no doubt that some advocates of uncommonsense ideas have overemphasized the path or the process without sufficient concern for the goal or the product, nothing in uncommonsense approaches per se requires that standards be lowered, rigor rejected, or excellence eschewed. In fact, as we saw in Dan Kelly's classroom and as we will see shortly in Cheryl Brown's, the level of achievements expected and attained are genuine sources of pride for all concerned.

One major difference in recent years between inner-city schools and those in the suburbs has been the greater feeling of alienation by students in the city than by their suburban peers. This phenomenon has been particularly obvious at the high school level, where enormous drop-out rates testify to the failure of the system to connect with the learners in ways which make them want to stay within the system. Certainly one of Dan Kelly's major advantages over his urban colleagues is that his students are more likely to show up every day and to have come prepared for class. The response to the phenomenon of students' low attendance—and even lower attention—at the typical urban high school and the one that has usually proved the most comforting for school people, has been to, in effect, blame the victims, who are, in this case, the students. Whether the explanation is poverty, drugs, single-parent families, race, culture, or some combination of all of them, schools have often failed to consider their own role in creating rather than solving such problems.

It seems at least worth asking how much the commonsense approaches which dominate American schooling have contributed to current problems by failing to make the school program one with which students can meaningfully connect. I am not suggesting that it will be easy to create a school environment which provides meaningful learning experiences for most of its pupils, or that doing so would solve all of the very real problems that face children who live in a world of urban decay marked by despair and drug abuse, vandalism and violence. But such children are often remarkably hopeful as individuals, and many do succeed despite their environment, so it's too simplistic for schools to shrug their shoulders collectively with a resigned, "Of course, these kids can't be expected to succeed, look at. . . . "

It isn't as naïve as it seems to expect that every student will achieve a higher level of performance by following the uncommonsense path. And it is wrongheaded to assume that the sole path to excellence lies in the commonsense tradition. The built-in elitism institutionalized in the commonsense tracking system means that only students lucky enough to find themselves in the top track even have a shot at excellence. But as discussed earlier, the research evidence suggests that far more students are capable of high levels of performance than the tracking system currently encourages or even permits. Further, the disengagement with school and with learning which characterizes so many secondary students— even many of those with the most advantaged economic and cultural backgrounds, according to most contemporary observations of schooling—suggests that the commonsense tradition has failed to motivate students sufficiently to pursue excellence beyond the concern, "Will it be on the test?"

So as we consider what's happening in Dan's classroom and as we turn to Cheryl's, it's important to recognize not only that the students seem to be enjoying their schoolwork more than they have traditionally in commonsense classrooms, but that this enjoyment has resulted in their achieving higher levels of performance than ever before. Recently I met a group of my former students whom I had taught in high school more than twenty years ago, and one of them said to me that "the thing that stands out for me about you as a teacher was your high level of expectations for us as learners." I was as proud of that now as I had been proud then of the quality of their work. But the point here is not to pat myself on the back as a great teacher, but to emphasize that students are highly sensitive to the expectations we have for them, and that if we don't expect them to seek excellence there is little likelihood that many will do so.

As advocates of uncommonsense approaches, many of us have been so concerned with attempting to reach all students and so convinced that learning processes in schools must be changed, that we have sometimes deemphasized the importance of the quality of students' work. In doing so, we have tended to resist using the language of excellence, of high standards, or of academic rigor. We have avoided such terms partly because we have seen the rigor mortis that commonsense approaches to academic excellence has often produced, and partly because of the too common association between talk of excellence and an elitist, antidemocratic approach to education. The result, therefore, has been to leave talk about quality to our opponents and to be vulnerable to charges of being soft, or easy, or unconcerned with standards. It's high time that we reasserted our view that not only are uncommonsense approaches compatible with high achievement, but they are, in fact, the best way such standards can be achieved for the greatest number of students. Many students have learned powerfully and productively even in restrictive environments, of course, as I tried to do even in Mrs. Wilson's class, but there is no necessary correlation between commonsense practice and excellence, and the pursuit of excellence is no reason not to give uncommon sense a chance.

We've seen some examples of the achievement of excellence in Dan Kelly's California high school classroom. Let's turn now to Cheryl Brown's fourth grade in Brooklyn, New York.

P. S. 71: Fourth Grade

As we approach the school building we are in a different world from that of Peninsula High. P. S. 71 is located on a city block in a neighborhood in Brooklyn that has seen better days, and the school looks like a kind of red brick fortress barely holding its own against the tide of urban decay. Gentrification has not yet come to this corner of the city. Built in the closing years of the nineteenth century, the five stories of the school building make it taller than most of the surrounding multifamily houses, small stores, and businesses. There are what appear to be permanently broken windows in many of them, and the now-elevated subway line from Manhattan can be seen a block away.

The school is surrounded by a high, cast-iron, picket fence, and the playground out back is entirely asphalt, with only grass and weeds poking through cracks in the pavement to relieve the urban scene. There is a park across the street from the school which does provide a visual oasis from the paved landscape, but although the community is making some efforts to reclaim it from the junkies and hookers that have made it their own for more than a decade, the effort has been only partly successful. The school staff have rarely been able to use it for activities, and it is no place for children to venture alone.

Inside the school, the picture is brightened by the copious displays of student work—drawings, paintings, projects, and stories —which relieve the grim corridors with their forbidding wood paneling. These give the school a welcoming atmosphere, as well as emphasize that it is concerned with and proud of the quality of student work which is being produced here. What is evident in the corridors is even more apparent once we enter Cheryl Brown's classroom on the third floor. It is a big bright room in the corner of the building, and every available bit of wall space is devoted to student work. There are sections for math, for stories, for completed work, and for work in progress. There are social studies dioramas in one corner, another is filled with science projects, and a third contains a classroom library featuring a rug on which students can sprawl to read.

Even more impressive than the student displays of work, however, is their display of eagerness whenever they get the chance to demonstrate to visitors what they have been learning. On my first visit to the classroom with a colleague, we were immediately besieged by the class, who couldn't wait to share their pride in their achievements. After the initial burst of enthusiasm had subsided, Cheryl had us sit in separate corners of the room to enable us to meet with small groups of students while others went on with their work after being assured that everyone would get a turn.

The work itself is impressive too. Victor and Jean-Baptiste showed me their mathematics puppet show loosely based on the story of Simple Simon. This Simon is not so simple, however, and his dealings with the pieman not only managed to be amusing, but illustrated the real life uses of arithmetic in buying and selling. The show had been written in such a way that Simon got help from the audience in determining how much things cost, how much change he should receive, and so on. Even though the class had obviously seen it several times before, the group that was waiting to show me their work formed an eager audience, making the required calculations and calling out the answers.

Amanda read me her story of the girl who got separated from her mother in a crowded subway car and had to figure out where her stop was. It sounded like a real life experience to me, so I asked her if it had happened to her. She said some of it had, but she'd added the part about finding her mother on the platform because it made it more exciting—actually she'd found her mother after the train got less crowded and without having to get off the car. I asked her the part of the story she liked best, and she read again:

Julie couldn't see her mother anywhere. All she could see were legs. Black pants, brown pants, long skirts, short skirts. And then she saw the shiny steel pole in the middle of the car.

She squeezed through the legs until she could grab it and hung on as the train lurched through the dark tunnel.

She'd drawn a picture on that page of legs and the pole and it was easy to see from both words and pictures the small child's eye view of a car full of giants.

Roberto showed me his "Bean Diary" which recorded what had happened to ten beans he had planted in paper cups. He had watered them differently with two getting no water at all, two getting watered once a week, two getting watered Monday, Wednesday, and Friday, two on Tuesday and Thursday, and two on each school day. They'd all been sitting on the windowsill. In addition to recording his watering schedule, the first days showed a nine-year-old's understandable frustration over the fact that nothing was happening, or at least nothing was visible. On Cheryl's advice, he had dug up one bean in each group after the first week and described what they looked like. He was very excited to find that:

> March 14: The bean which had never been watered looked just like it had when I planted it. The one that was watered every day hadn't put out any shoots, and it looked like it was rotting. The skin was all wrikly like when you've stayed in the bathtub too long. When I cut it open, it was very soggy and it fell apart. The other three have all put out shoots, and Miss Brown and I talked it over and decided to see what would happen if I planted them again. So I did.

They did grow, as it turned out, and he had six healthy bean plants growing after several weeks, but the best ones turned out to be the ones that were watered twice a week. Once a week seemed to be too seldom, and three times a little too much. Just before Easter vacation he'd dug them all up and found that the beans that looked the best also had the most vigorous root growth. He concluded his project by writing:

> April 10: I learned that plants need water to grow but that too much water is as bad for them as too little. The ones that grew the best had a medium amount of water. They didn't get either thristy or soaked.

When we got a chance to talk to Cheryl during her free period we asked her to explain how she'd gotten the kids to be so involved in what they were doing and so independent in the way they worked. She said that part of it was the result of the fact that except for kids who had moved either in or out of the neighborhood, twenty-two of the twenty-eight children in the class had been with her for two years. She had started with them in third grade and then moved up with them to the fourth. This had enabled her to work slowly with the class to get them used to how she wanted to have the class function, and that by this time, the spring of the second year, everyone was comfortable with the processes involved. She said that keeping classes together for two years was a deliberate policy of the school and that while not everybody operated the way she did, there was enough commonality of approach so that the basic patterns of instruction were common throughout the school. The only drawback to this schedule, she felt, was that she was already anticipating how sad she would be to lose these kids, but she remembered that she used to feel that way even with classes she had had for only one year, and she thought the advantages outweighed the disadvantages.

We asked Cheryl a bit about her background, and she said that she had started out as a conventional teacher relying heavily on the basal series and its workbooks and worksheets, using similar materials in math, and so on. She hadn't been particularly happy with how things were going in her classroom, even though the kids had been doing well on the annual reading tests. She just didn't see much life in the classroom, the kids didn't seem to enjoy the work much, and she was worried about the fact that she didn't seem to have any time to get the kids to do much writing. She was also increasingly aware that in order for her students to become motivated enough to continue to be involved in schoolwork as they got older and faced the growing temptations of the life of the streets, they needed a firm foundation not only of skills but of attitudes toward school and learning. She was worried that the traditional curriculum and approaches were not providing enough of that.

She began to change, she said, when she went to a district in-service workshop on the process approach to writing. Like most teachers who had been teaching for more than ten years or so (she was now in her fourteenth year) she had had very little education on the teaching of writing during either her undergraduate or Master's degree courses of study. Almost all the emphasis had been on reading—which had been the focus of her Master's—and almost all of that had been on a commonsense skills approach. She had taken a course in children's literature, which she had loved, but there never seemed to be time to do much with it in her classroom, and anyway, such books were hard to get hold of, since most of the school's budget went to basal readers, workbooks, and other skills-based reading kits. The writing workshop had opened her eyes to new possibilities, she said, but she was worried about how she could find time for it in a curriculum that was already overstuffed with reading skills and other content in math, science, and social studies.

She determined to try anyway, even though she recognized not only the time difficulties, but also the fact that setting up a writing workshop in her classroom would require her to organize both the physical space and the learning processes differently than she had been. She said that if we'd come to visit her ten years earlier we would have seen the children sitting in desks in rows, not around tables as they were now. The classroom itself would have had neat bulletin boards that she had prepared, changing with the seasons or the month's holiday, but they would have included very little student work. But even more important, at almost every minute of the day the whole class would have been doing the same thing. The students would not always have been reading the same book, of course—she had had reading groups at different levels—but almost everything else had been done with whole-class recitation teaching in which she typically stood at the front of the room and called on children to answer her questions.

The writing process approach hadn't changed all that by itself, she said, but it had been the opening wedge in her process of change. It had been the first area where she helped the students learn to work collaboratively together in groups, to come to trust each other as sources of response and help, and to take themselves seriously both as people who had something to say and as audiences who would help their peers make their texts clearer. She learned through her first attempts that this was a slow process: The kids needed lots of support and models, and they couldn't initially be expected to know how to do it without plenty of structured help. One reason she liked having the same class for two years now, she said, was that it gave her enough time to attend to helping the kids learn how to learn in these ways.

The second breakthrough had come when she began to hear about language, and particularly writing, across the curriculum. She'd taken a summer school course on "writing to learn" and realized that she could use writing in her classroom in many more ways than just having kids write stories, which is how she started out. I'd already seen the results of this in Victor and Jean-Baptiste's mathematics puppet show and in Roberto's bean diary. She'd read Nancy Martin et al.'s (1976) account of a boy's blackbird diary and adapted it to her own science lessons. My fellow visitor had seen Maria's story of the life a nine-year-old might have lived on the farms that covered this part of Brooklyn just before the American Revolution, and Glenda's learning log written in response to her attempts to understand the science book's account of how water transforms itself to ice when it is cooled and to steam when it is heated. In addition to enabling her to expand the amount of class time in which students worked individually and in groups, this use of writing (and the talk and reading closely integrated with it) allowed her to reduce some of the time constraints she faced in trying to cover the curriculum. The children were still writing stories, like Amanda's tale of the subway or Leon's fantasy adventure of robots in outer space, but that was no longer all they were writing.

The third major impetus for change had come through talking with Jane, a school colleague who taught the first and second grades, about the use of children's literature as the basis for the reading program. Jane had explained to her that the program was based on an enormous amount of reading aloud to children—often using big books which everyone could see at the same time, but sometimes using either regular trade books or other small books that everyone had a copy of. This approach had begun to transform the attitudes of the children Cheryl was getting in third grade, making them much more eager to read than they had been, and also, she felt, giving them more in the way of usable skills. They had learned these skills in the context of solving real reading problems; that is, they had really wanted and needed to figure out what the text was saying not because they were being tested on it, but because they wanted to find out how the story came out. And further, since the whole process had been devoted to meaning making, the students were both more confident in their ability to make sense of a new text, and more likely to want to try.

It had taken her several years to do so, but with the support of her principal—a key player in this whole change process, whose encouragement of these ideas had made it possible for Jane, Cheryl, and the rest to try them out—Cheryl had assembled a classroom library of individual books and small sets of books which could be used as the basis of the reading program. They still had sets of basal readers around, but they were now used only for their stories, not for their structure or in the editor's sequence. And the money for buying the books for the library had come from what the school was saving by no longer buying reading or language arts workbooks. The rug that identified the library corner had been found by Cheryl abandoned on the street, and the school's PTA had provided funds to get it cleaned. It wasn't in perfect shape, but it was comfortable and provided a welcoming place to sit and read either for individuals or for the whole class when Cheryl or one of the students was reading aloud.

Cheryl invited us to come and visit for several more days— she promised she'd tell the class we were there just to look and listen, not to be a special audience for their work as we had been the first day—to see how all of these ideas were working on a day-to-day basis. As we returned to Cheryl's classroom the next morning we could hear a buzz of activity even before we got into the room. I remembered vividly my first principal when I was teaching junior high school insisting that all teachers keep their doors open. He believed that a quiet class was a good class, and he used to prowl the corridors listening for noisy ones. I wondered what he would make of Cheryl's class, whether he would be able to recognize the difference between the productive noise of meaningful activity and the distracting noise of chaos.

The class was involved in several different activities: One group was reading books chosen from the classroom library (including, on this day, several that had been written by their classmates), a second group was involved in writing, a third was clustered around a terrarium, and the fourth was divided into pairs working on revising previously written work. Cheryl had explained the day before that this pattern was a common and by now familiar one to the group, and they would often take turns at a set of activities like this during the course of a morning. On this day there was a schedule on the board which announced the sequence of these activities for each group. It didn't have times listed by it, because Cheryl felt that it worked better if she could sense when the natural rhythm of an activity was over and could call for a switch from activity one to two and so on when it felt right. She said she used to do it with a prearranged time sequence, but that now that she and the children were used to it, this kind of flexibility seemed more effective.

Cheryl herself was keeping an eye on all this activity and was available for questions from any group, but she was primarily using the time to hold a series of individual conferences with members of the class. I sat and eavesdropped for a while and found that she used these for various purposes. With Daphne she talked about *A Wrinkle in Time* by Madeleine L'Engle, which Daphne had just finished. Daphne had enjoyed the book, but had found it pretty scary at times wondering whether the children would ever get back home. Cheryl agreed that it was scary, and that she too had been reassured when everything worked out. She asked Daphne whether or not she had ever been lost and had not known how to find her way home. When Daphne said she had, Cheryl suggested that she might like to write a story about that and that she might even try to do it in the style of *A Wrinkle in Time*. Daphne thought that sounded like a good idea, and she said, "I could even begin it with 'It was a dark and stormy night,' like the book." "Good idea," said Cheryl, and after a few more seconds of talk about what Daphne might read next, Daphne went back to her desk.

Cheryl made a few notes about the conference in her ring binder, which contained a section for each child. For Daphne she wrote:

Finished *A Wrinkle in Time.* Clearly enjoyed it and read it with considerable insight. Particularly struck by how scared and lonely the children had felt when it looked like they couldn't get home. Suggested she might like to write such a story based on her own life and use L'Engle's style. Said she would, so I'll ask her about it later. Looks like she'll read *Tom's Midnight Garden* next, which Rhonda had recommended to her. A good choice, similar theme and yet some real differences.

She then called Jared up for a conference and asked him to bring the story he was working on. She asked Jared to read her what he'd written so far. He read:

Once upon a time there was a caterpillar named George. George loved to eat maple leaves. He'd eat almost anything that was green, but he loved maple leaves best. The trouble was when he was crawling on the ground it was hard to tell the maple trees from the other kinds. And, being a caterpillar, he couldn't move all that fast. It was really a disappointment to climb all the way up a tree only to find out it wasn't a maple! Luckily he could make thread come out of his tail and let himself down from trees. At least he didn't have to climb down too!

Jared said he'd gotten the idea for the story by watching the caterpillars in the classroom terrarium who seemed to like some of the leaves they put in but not others. When Cheryl asked him what he wanted to do with his story, he said he wanted to have George figure out how a tree was a maple tree to save him the trouble of having to climb it, but he didn't know how. Cheryl asked him if he could tell the difference, and he said he wasn't sure he could unless he could see the leaves or the little helicopter seeds that maples give off. She suggested that might be the trick. George could crawl until he found a bunch of those seeds. Jared seemed happy with that and went back to his desk to try it.

As she wrote a brief entry about Jared's story in her notebook, I wandered off to see how the rest of the class was getting on. Since my mind was on caterpillars, I thought I'd check first on the group of children who were watching them. They were clustered around the terrarium, and each one had a notebook in which they were recording what they had seen. Anthony was clearly the counter in the group. His notebook consisted mainly of a daily count of how many caterpillars he had seen, classified by the activity they seemed to be engaged in: 4 eating, 2 climbing, 5 walking on the ground, 1 doing nothing, and so on. Teresa was keeping a record of how many leaves were being eaten every day. Patrick was drawing pictures of the caterpillars doing various things: walking, climbing, and eating. He even had a series of pictures of the ways these caterpillars ate a leaf, first showing a whole leaf (a maple!), then others with larger and larger semicircles being eaten out of them until only the main stem remained. I asked them what kind of caterpillars they were, and they said they weren't sure, but they knew that they were supposed to turn into butterflies, not moths, and that they'd have to wait until that happened to know for sure.

It was now time for the groups to shift activities, and I waited for a few minutes for them to get settled before I continued my rounds. I found Maria and Brenda sharing stories by exchanging the papers they were working on. Brenda's was based on a trip the class had taken in the fall to the Bronx Zoo, where they'd visited the world of darkness. She had been so impressed, she said, by the fact that some of the animals only come out at night that she had decided to write a story about people who sleep all day and only come out at night. Here's what Maria had read of the story as it was so far:

THE NIGHT PEOPLE

by Brenda Thomas

When it gets dark most of the people begin to get tired and look forward to getting a good night's sleep. But some people never go out when the sun is up at all. They only come out at night. Because the sun hurts their eyes. Even at night they wear sunglasses to keep the glare down. They also think they look bad with sunglasses on.

I think they look spooky.

They aren't really dangerous, though. When they have children they even have to have schools at night because the little children have the most sensitive eyes of all. They can see even in pitch darkness. And they can hear very well too to warn them of danger. Their ears are much bigger than ours and their eyes are too, but otherwise they look pretty normal.

Maria said that she liked the idea of the story, but she asked, "What is going to happen next?" Brenda replied that she thought she'd try to describe a family of night people and show how they lived.

M: Who will be in the family?
B: Well I thought there would be a mother, a father, and two children.
M: What will they do?

B: I'm not sure yet, I guess I'll just have to keep writing it and see what happens. When I get some more I'll show it to you again.

M: Great.

B: Let's talk about yours. . . .

I left them as they were turning to Maria's tale of her trip to visit her grandfather in Puerto Rico and wandered over to the rug where the former butterfly group members were now sprawled about reading. Anthony was so engrossed in his biography of the young Muhammad Ali that I didn't want to disturb him, but Patrick clearly wanted to talk about *The Wizard of Earthsea*, which he was about a third of the way through. "I think it's cool the way he discovers he has magic powers," he said. "It sure would be nice to have them." We chatted awhile about whether or not there was real magic; Patrick wasn't sure, but he was keeping an open mind. When he went back to *The Wizard*, I asked Tracy to tell me about her book, which I hadn't read. She told me it was about a young girl from the city who goes to live on a farm in the south during her summer vacation. I asked her if she'd ever been to a farm and she said she hadn't, but that her mother had grown up on one and they had talked about it while Tracy was reading the book. She said she'd like to visit one, and since she had relatives in North Carolina who grew tobacco, she hoped she could visit them.

I asked Teresa how she picked books to read, and she said, "Well usually I choose one because someone has told me that I'd like it." This one (a biography of Sacajawea) she'd chosen because they'd been studying native Americans in the fall, and Brenda had read it and told Teresa she would like it too. "But sometimes I look at the cards we write after we've finished a book." She then showed me an index file on a classroom library shelf which contained short reviews of many of the books in the collection, composed by members of the class. She also said that sometimes Miss Brown had suggested books for her, and sometimes she just found them by looking at the covers. She also said that once a week the class got to go to the school library, and that she often found good books there. There was a separate card file for books from the school library, with the same sorts of reviews.

Cheryl then interrupted this conversation to say that it was story time, and the whole class gathered around her on the library corner rug. Although some days story time featured the work of authors in the class, today it was time for another segment of *The Hobbit*. As one might have guessed from the titles of some of the books the children were reading, this was a class that enjoyed fantasy and adventure stories, perhaps because these were also among Cheryl Brown's favorites. Although she later told me that she hadn't read many of these books herself as a child, she had discovered them in her children's literature class and had loved them ever since. I left the group listening raptly to the further adventures of Bilbo Baggins.

Some Obstacles to Integrating Language Education

The kinds of competencies displayed by the children and adolescents in Cheryl Brown's and Dan Kelly's classrooms don't happen by accident or as a result of laissez-faire classroom management. Both teachers run classrooms that are carefully, albeit globally, planned and where careful attention is paid to prepare the children to function independently. What makes the classrooms work, however, is more a function of the pupils' attitude toward what they are doing and why they are doing it than of the teachers' management capabilities. In each case the students come into the room with a seriousness of purpose (not solemnity, or fear, or docility) which makes them ready to begin work because they have learned that they are responsible for their own learning. They have further learned to value their teachers as resources, and as knowledgeable, helpful, and supportive adults who will help them out when needed but who won't do their thinking for them.

Cheryl's class, particularly, benefits from the fact that within a self-contained classroom of twenty-eight children, Cheryl and the class can work together to structure the available time productively. The children do leave the room at least once a day—for gym, art, or music—but for the most part the rest of the schedule is sufficiently flexible to permit the task to determine the schedule rather than the other way around. Although many commonsense elementary schools have become increasingly period-driven in their structure, with a set daily time for each "subject," Cheryl has resisted this kind of scheduling in favor of trying to integrate subjects (as we saw, some of the children were doing science, some reading, and some writing or conferring with others about their writing, all at the same time) while at the same time letting the task being attempted dictate the amount of time required.

Dan and his class, in contrast, are hampered by the usual high school schedule of fifty-minute periods, which only rarely fit the rhythm of the tasks being done. Although this particular class has a reasonably workable enrollment of twenty-nine students, Dan has three other English classes and a journalism class, which means he meets one hundred and thirty-two students every day, five days a week. And each of his students, too, is taking at least four other academic classes, some of them five, as well as gym for all, and art, music and the like as well. In *Horace's Compromise*, Ted Sizer (1984) has argued that the single greatest impediment to creating an effective learning environment in secondary schools stems from the combination of the schedule and the number of minds that teachers must come in contact with every day.

Whether or not it's the most severe problem, it is certainly very serious if one is trying to create the kind of uncommonsense learning environment being developed here. For such an environment to be maximally productive, teachers simply must know their students as individuals. To be able to follow Frank Smith's (1973) precept of responding to what the child is trying to do, each teacher must have opportunities to observe and understand where each child or adolescent is, to read their writing carefully and respond to it quickly, and to be available for individual help where needed. When confronted with wave after wave of adolescents streaming in and out of one's class at fifty-minute intervals, the strain of trying to do all these tasks often becomes intolerable, leading to some of the "compromises" of Sizer's title.

Scheduling is such an integral part of commonsense secondary schooling that it has rarely even been noticed, much less questioned. And even when questioned, it has proved remarkably difficult to change. Even in the small group of secondary schools now working with Sizer to restructure and reconceptualize secondary education, whose faculties and administrations have chosen to attempt change, the schedule has been a particularly hard nut to crack. The group has explored some alternative scheduling patterns where not all classes would meet daily. They have also suggested that teachers and administrators try to understand what the current schedule looks like from a student's-eye view through the device of following one student throughout a school day. The experience is at best confusing, and at worst mind (and behind) numbing.

What is crucial here, of course, is not that such a schedule is necessarily either the best or the worst imaginable, but that in most cases it is one of the unquestioned assumptions that underlie commonsense schooling. And clearly the time we allocate to activities and subjects does reveal, at least indirectly, the value we place on them and the priorities we set. Refusing to think about them or to question established institutional practice means that the scheduling tail will continue to wag the instructional dog. It isn't easy to imagine alternatives, of course, since virtually everyone involved —from the superintendent to the custodian, from the students to their parents—has experienced only the status quo. Further, the amount of time students are in contact with teachers has become institutionalized in the credit system: Carnegie units in high schools, credit hours in colleges.

In my own teaching experience, I happened more or less by accident to participate in two alternative attempts at staffing and scheduling. In the first high school I taught in we developed a modular schedule where classes met in different size groups and for different durations, based on a half-hour module. Large groups met only for one module for lectures or films, other groups met for two to four modules at a time. The schedule wasn't entirely successful and was extremely complex, but it was at least an attempt to fit the schedule to the curriculum, to allow for short lectures and longer labs and discussions, and it put much more responsibility on students, since they ended up with more unscheduled time. It was abandoned after a few years, however, and the school returned to commonsense scheduling. The second high school was in a district where the school board had responded to the recommendations of the National Council of Teachers of English that English teachers should have only four teaching periods a day and a maximum of one hundred students. The attempt here was to ensure sufficient time for teachers to assign and respond to student writing. There was some grumbling from other teachers who felt we were getting off lightly, and I'm not sure we took the best advantage of the reduced load that we could have, but again it was an attempt to put educational priorities ahead of scheduling.

Whether deliberate or not, one of the effects of commonsense scheduling is to put added pressures on teachers to chop up their curriculum into finite bits. If classes are only going to meet for short periods, and if students are confronted with five or six different subjects every day, a fragmented curriculum fits more naturally into such slots than one which attempts a more organic or integrated approach. Since segmentation conforms well to the common sense of bottom-up learning theory, such fragmentation seems less disastrous than it does from an uncommonsense position. It is not unusual, therefore, to see secondary school English classes in which Monday is devoted to language or grammar study, Tuesday and Thursday to literature, Wednesday to writing, and Friday as the day when tests are given and other catch-up activities take place. Similarly, elementary school classes frequently separate reading, writing, and other language arts instruction into separate periods, either daily or spread throughout the week.

From an uncommonsense perspective there are two serious problems with such fragmentation. The first is implied by what we've seen in both Dan's and Cheryl's classrooms: They recognize, implicitly or explicitly, that all four modes of language use are interdependent and most effectively learned in an integrated context. The second problem relates to the first but is somewhat more subtle. In a segmented curriculum the teacher is in more complete control of what students are supposed to be learning. Notice that I did not say what students *are* learning. The commonsense belief that the two concepts are identical is just not accurate. Students learn some very unfortunate lessons from a fragmented curriculum, however, including the fact that learning in school is mostly a matter of jumping a particular set of hurdles on an obstacle course, of learning individual skills which will be individually tested on a short-term basis, and that if it's not going to be on the test it just isn't important.

Some observers, notably Linda McNeil (1986), have gone further and argued that the fragmented curriculum fits the school's primary goal: the control of students. By cutting the curriculum up into bits and snippets and by testing students continually on those bits, teachers keep control of their classes by, in the words of one high school biology teacher, making sure that students get paid (in grades) for their work (Lester and Onore, 1990). Although this approach has the undesirable effect of making it hard to tie large ideas together and to see how one concept relates to another, McNeil's study of high school social studies classes shows that teachers seem willing to make that compromise in order to keep the classes under control.

Even worse, however, in McNeil's view is the fact that the diet of lists and more or less isolated facts that dominates the fragmented curriculum neither enables students to connect what they are studying to their own lives nor provides a forum for debating what are, often, problematic issues. The ironic effect of this, she found, was that where students had experiences or information which seemed to contradict what they were being taught in the official curriculum, the contradictions shook their faith in the whole enterprise. So, for example, if what they were being taught about the depression, or American foreign policy, or the Vietnam War didn't conform to what they thought they knew about such subjects independently—by talking to relatives, seeing programs on television, and so forth—they usually ended up not only not believing the teacher on that particular topic, but also becoming skeptical of what was being presented to them. They were, if they had opted to be school achievers, willing to memorize the teacher's version for the test, but they didn't believe it, and their doubts about the truth of what they were being taught continued to spread.

While student skepticism about the truth of what teachers say and texts write is undoubtedly valuable, McNeil and I believe that it must be expressed and debated publicly, not privately allowed to devalue the whole enterprise. In a classroom where different positions can be articulated, where controversial issues can be debated, and where each participant has the right to an informed opinion, such questioning is not only to be encouraged but forms a vital part of the activities. If the curriculum's lists and facts are only privately rejected, however, no valuable learning is taking place. More open-ended curricula cannot be as neatly packaged and classrooms in such a system are not as orderly, but if education is sacrificed for order, what students will learn is only how to be orderly. Some might argue that this is, indeed, one of the things we hope students will learn in school, but as we saw in Dan's and Cheryl's classrooms, it's possible to have order without sacrificing a commitment to intellectual growth and the search for truth.

Why an Integrated Language Education?

The primary basis for integrating language education, sometimes called a whole language approach (see Goodman [1986] and Newman [1985] for examples and further discussion), rests on the observation that all four modes of language use involve active meaning making and active learning. In normal language use, we switch naturally and effortlessly between reading, writing, speaking, and listening, and in all modes we are consistently trying to make sense of what is happening. In Dan's class, for example, we saw students who had read a story ("Soldier's Home"), written about it in their learning log, and talked about it, both speaking and listening (and, on one occasion, reading aloud from the learning log), with their peers and their teacher. All four modes were mutually reinforcing and interdependent, and all were focused on making meaning from the story. Further, this meaning was, for each individual and collectively for the class, not a process of determining the right interpretation so that the right answer could be given on the test, but one of enriching and deepening their understanding of themselves and their world, including, in this case, such concepts as the effect of war on participants, the nature of American culture in a remote (for them) time, and so on.

This may seem obvious enough, even common sense in the best sense of that term, but as we've seen, it is surprising how little it actually happens in school. It certainly happens more frequently out of school, for children and adults, but the school's fragmentation of the curriculum has made it less natural and less frequent. Partly this situation has resulted from the view that reading and, particularly, listening are essentially passive activities in the sense that decoding is the only activity demanded to receive meaning transmitted from a text (written or oral). This view is similar to the idea that writing and speaking, while decidedly active, are more devoted to expressing or transcribing previously determined meanings than central to the meaning-making process itself.

We've seen the theoretical limits of such views in earlier chapters, but in this instance, it seems clear that Mary's and Norman's and Akiko's and José's struggles to understand the story through all four modes involved active meaning making every step of the way. Whichever mode they were using, their goal was to enrich the sense they were making of the experience, and all the processes of producing or receiving language were an instrumental part of their meaning making.

Perhaps most important from an uncommonsense perspective is that *it is the process of purposefully using language itself which further develops one's linguistic and communicative competence.* As noted when we discussed language acquisition, the process of developing language competence is essentially an indirect and automatic procedure. It depends neither upon deliberately setting out to improve one's "skills" nor upon explicit teaching. It doesn't even require a specific sequence of experiences, since learners seem to be able to acquire what they need from whatever experiences are available. It does demand a sufficient range of different materials to read and write (or speak or listen to), but this doesn't have to be arranged in any particular order.

Integration in Action: Achieving Literacy

Since language acquisition is specific to humans, every human being acquires a highly complex and potentially powerful linguistic system. Although there may be some individual differences in language ability, the similarities in *potential* for each child are significantly more important. It is sadly the case, however, that although this potential is there and is largely reached in terms of the oral language needed for day-to-day activities, the commonsense structures of schooling, which devalue the oral language and place heavy emphasis on the written language, frequently disguise the similarities and stress the differences.

Yesterday I happened to watch a small boy and his mother going fishing as the tide came in on Cape Cod Bay. The boy, who appeared to be three or four, was exploring the water's edge and keeping up a constant stream of talk to his mother—pointing out interesting shells, exploring a boat resting on the sand, showing her a pipe that let rain water flow from the street to the ocean, and so on. His mother was an attentive listener, responding to his questions, sharing his enthusiasms, and occasionally pointing out other things of interest. They were going to fish for crabs with a wire trap baited with stale bread. The process involved throwing the trap into the water, waiting for a few minutes, and then pulling it back in by means of a long rope. In addition to the mother's role as listener and responder, she was also playing the role of student for, apparently, while the boy's father and older brother had taken him fishing with this apparatus, she had never before used it. She cheerfully deferred to his expertise and asked him how to do it, and he just as cheerfully explained what he remembered of the process. Occasionally they ran across something he didn't remember and she couldn't figure out, at which point they joined in collaborative talk as they tried to determine how to open the trap or where might be the best place to throw it.

In addition to being a delightful scene, this kind of adult-child interchange is a nearly perfect example of learning through talk. And such learning is doubly functional because it not only involves learning about what is being talked about—fishing, the tide, boats, or whatever—but it is also the process by which language itself develops. New words are effortlessly learned, new structures are developed and emerging ones practiced in a meaningful context, and the whole interchange gives further reinforcement to the value of language as a means of comprehending the world and of sharing that comprehension with others. Such active learning is most transparent in young children because they have not yet been infected with the dreaded adult diseases of concealing ignorance and enthusiasm, but the same processes are happening whenever we are genuinely engaged in collaborative language use.

This young boy has clearly been lucky, however, in having a mother who values his curiosity and responds so positively to his talk. Not every child is so fortunate, and for some children even the oral world is not as fruitful as it clearly is for him. One of the drawbacks of inadequate day care for children with two working parents, or for children of single mothers who work, may be that such children do not get as many opportunities for adult-child talk as they could use. Similarly, children who spend an inordinate amount of time watching television as toddlers may not be getting the interactive practice they need. But for most children, the oral language does get plenty of opportunities for meaningful use, and it is commonplace for children to come to kindergarten with considerable oral language powers and with a highly sophisticated and complex mental system for using it.

The same opportunities for early exposure to the written language, however, are much less universal. Gordon Wells's longitudinal study of children in Bristol (1986) found vast differences in the amounts children were read to before they went to school. These differences did not seem to have much effect on their oral language capabilities—he found virtually no measurable differences in oral language use among the children at age five—but they had an enormous impact on how the children responded to the literacy demands of the school environment. Those who had been read to frequently learned to read and write with relative ease and speed, while those who hadn't, didn't. Further, and even sadder, the school's way of talking and the subjects being talked about in school were influenced both by the literacy environment and the lack of opportunity for child-initiated talk which is the norm of out-of-school language use for young children, as we saw in the fishing example. So those children who had the least experience with literacy were also least able to use oral language productively in school, and a gap therefore appeared between them and their peers not only in the speed and facility with which they learned to read and write but in their oral language abilities as well.

What seems to be happening here is that commonsense schools operate on a set of largely unexamined assumptions about the literacy experience that children have had before they get to school. These assumptions derive from a variety of sources, including the fact that most teachers themselves came from homes where literacy was valued, were read to as children, and read (or would read) to their own children. Those of us who have had such experiences, and who know what great sources of pleasure they can provide, quite naturally assume that they are nearly universal. Further, when confronted with children who are largely equal in oral ability, we have no direct evidence to alert us to whether or not their literacy backgrounds are equivalent.

Margaret Meek (1983) and others have pointed out that it is impossible to overrate how much children learn about literacy from the experience of being read to. As Meek puts it, "Authors can and do teach children about reading and writing if we let them." Children not only learn such things as distinguishing the front of a book from the back and learning its sequence from beginning to end, they also acquire more subtle properties of texts, such as the fact that they have titles and authors (and publishers), that the texts don't vary from one reading to the next (try skipping part of a familiar book next time you read to a three-year-old!), and, most crucial of all, that the little black marks on the page represent the language the child already knows. Future writers, too, learn other things from books, like the properties of various genres (consider again *The Jolly Postman* as a masterful example of multiple genres within a single text), the nature of stories, and even, eventually, the use of such conventions of texts as capitalization and punctuation.

For the child who has been read to a lot, such learning is not an explicit lesson but rather comes along with the other pleasures of reading and being read to: the familiar place on the lap or by the side of the bed, the humor and sadness of stories, and the chance to live lives other than the one they have. Some of the properties of narratives can be derived from watching television or movies, but neither of these visual media provides the kind of intimate, interactive, and natural opportunities for implicit learning that being read to does, nor do they help one to learn one's way around the printed page. And children who have been read to not only come to school eager to learn to read, which is also usually true of their less experienced peers, they also come far more prepared to take advantage of whatever approach to beginning literacy is employed by the school.

Ironically, one of the reasons that the bottom-up, skills-based approaches to beginning literacy instruction seem to work is that for some children with extensive literacy experience, they do function as a kind of Vygotskyan process of providing scientific labels for already developed spontaneous concepts. Children who have mastered much of the implicit basis of reading through being read to, following along with, and, in many cases actually memorizing familiar books, such instruction works at least to some extent because there is already a sufficiently rich experiential base upon which to build through reflection and analysis. Some children from such backgrounds don't seem to profit from, and may even get discouraged by, drill-based instruction, because it doesn't seem to have anything much to do with why or how they read, so I wouldn't recommend it in an uncommonsense classroom, but in general it is least harmful for those who do have extensive histories of being read to.

Worse, however, is the fact that since commonsense approaches to beginning reading are based on the assumption that such decoding "skills" as sound-letter correspondences and phonics rules are the basics of reading, the children who are likely to get the most steady diet of them in the early grades are those who are least in a position to benefit from them; that is, children who have not been read to. Well-meaning teachers who perceive that some or most of their children don't have extensive literacy backgrounds frequently redouble their efforts to provide them with drills and workbooks consisting of page after page of letter- and word-recognition exercises. In some modern schools these drills have been automated with the use of a computer, which may help somewhat in keeping children's interest, but they are still based on behavioristic part-to-whole approaches and continue to give children inadequate input upon which to build competence as readers and writers.

The cycle of impoverishment intensifies further for those who are identified as remedial readers, since they get pulled out of their regular classroom and given *more drills!* If this helped or solved the problem, there would be no need to be critical of it, but the overwhelming finding of longitudinal studies of remedial readers shows that the achievement gap between them and their peers steadily widens throughout the school years. Children who are a little behind in second grade have become severely so by eighth grade. While drills themselves may not be the only culprit, the time spent on drills is also time not spent on reading real books, for pleasure or for information, so that the experiences necessary to develop both reading competence and a sense of the pleasures and benefits of reading—which can only be learned through encountering real texts, not lists—are inevitably diminished. So children who fall behind are placed in a double bind, and the impact is greatest on those who need positive literacy experiences the most.

What does seem to make a difference, in an uncommonsense contrast, is when schools recognize that *every child, but most especially those who have not had extensive literacy experience, can benefit from being read to aloud in school.* For those who have been read to a lot at home, school is a natural extension of an already familiar and productive learning environment. For those who haven't, it provides a natural and interesting way to learn the properties of print in a nonthreatening and long-term, productive way. Its impact on the long term not only occurs in developing implicitly the actual competencies required to make meaning from texts they are eventually going to be reading privately, but also helps to make literacy pleasurable because it is a social experience. That is clearly one of the meanings of Smith's term "the literacy club," where the literacy experience is shareable with others. In a classroom, having a wealth of shared stories gives all participants a common set of experiences to refer to, and these shared stories also can be the simplest way to begin to get children to read on their own.

Teachers in Australia and New Zealand have taken this process further for beginning readers by using big books for shared class or group reading experiences. The big book format allows every child to follow the pictures and the text as the story is read. And, when supplemented as they now often are, by small copies of the big book for children to read on their own, they provide a natural transition from social to private reading. Such big and little books are becoming widely available now in this country through imports or American versions, and they represent the healthiest publishing trend in beginning reading in years. Similar use can be made of the equally widely available taped versions of children's stories which, when accompanied by the text, can be listened to and read by individual children at classroom listening centers.

Reading big books (or any books) aloud to children is not the sole means by which children will make the transition from oral language to the world of print, but it can be one of the most natural ways of doing so. Books can provide access to a shared experience on making meaning from texts and can be used to introduce children to the decoding process in unobtrusive and meaning-based ways. As the book is reread, and children nearly always want to hear and see it again, particular aspects of the printed text can be attended to depending on the needs of the children in the class. Reading aloud provides, therefore, a natural context for teachers to observe how children are doing as meaning makers and for them to fulfill Smith's rule of responding to what the child is trying to do. (For some detailed suggestions of how this can be carried out, see Hancock and Hill [1988].)

There is no clearer example of the natural integration of all four modes of language use than in the process of reading aloud and its associated activities. Not only does it provide a living example of the connections between the oral and written versions of the language, it provides a natural context for talking about and thereby modeling the process of meaning making from texts. The teacher/reader can further model his or her enthusiasm both for the process in general and the specifics of the particular text being read. Children can share their responses, ask questions, make comments as appropriate, and learn to listen to the written language.

This last provides the crucial link between reading and writing, since successful writers are invariably people who have developed an inner ear for the distinctive rhythms, structures, and vocabulary of the written language. While such an ear for the written language can and does develop through silent reading, listening to mature and polished oral readings provides the most natural basis for the internalization to take place. Children who have been read to begin to develop naturally a story-based vocabulary ranging from such conventional formulae as "Once upon a time" to the use of dialogue, descriptive words and phrases, and so on. If we expect children to write in particular genres, they first must have had the experience of reading them, and for children who are beginning both processes, the experience of being read to provides the most efficacious, as well as enjoyable, means of doing so.

Also in this connection, in addition to the continuing joy derived from the process, older children benefit the most from being read to. They can learn to hear more complex prose (and poetry) than they are able to write yet, and thereby continually enrich their repertoires of stylistic variants in an implicit way. Such readings can also serve as aids to comprehension as well as models of the reader-text transaction. I have already mentioned reading *Billy Budd* aloud to high school juniors, who were able to enjoy and make sense of the text much more richly through hearing it and being able to ask questions as we went along than they would have been likely to when confronted by Melville's prose in a private transaction. I enjoyed the process as well, and because we were all sharing the experience together, the discussions were more lively and purposeful than they were with texts of equal or even lesser complexity which students had read (and in some cases not read!) on their own.

One further caveat should be noted. The benefits of oral reading demand that the reader be a skillful model. Having children stumble through an unfamiliar text in order to read it aloud has been shown to be counterproductive both as a strategy for learning to read and as a way of helping others to do so. It may be useful eventually to have children learn to read aloud well, but that should not be a responsibility entrusted to beginners. In fact, one profitable way to learn to read aloud is to have older children read to younger ones, either stories they've written for them or published texts. Even experienced and capable readers don't sight read texts aloud perfectly, so it helps to have familiarized oneself with a text before reading it aloud. (Other helpful suggestions about reading aloud can be found in Trelease [1982].)

The final reason for the importance of deliberately integrating all four modes of language use is that using one can and should pay important dividends in developing the others as well. Part of the reason for this stems from what I hope I've already shown about their interconnectedness, both theoretically and as exemplified by the integrations occurring in Cheryl's and Dan's classrooms. Another substantial part of it springs from the uncommonsense assumption which has at least been implicit throughout: *that all aspects of language are continuously being developed by purposeful use in all four modes.*

There is, of course, a sense in which people who can read and write are distinguishable from people who can't: That is the essence of the commonsense distinction between being literate and illiterate. But in looking at the actual development of literacy, it proves to be a very hard line to draw for either reading or writing. The research in emergent literacy by Dyson (1983), Sulzby (1986), and many others has shown that precise demarcations are difficult to determine. Further, the more we look at adults in the United States who have limited reading and writing abilities, the less apt the label of illiterate becomes. Even supposedly illiterate or marginally literate adults seem to use print to some degree to survive in our culture and in specific areas of their lives: at work, in church, while using public transportation, or while shopping, they do very well indeed.

Since reading and writing (as well as speaking and listening) are so complex, every time we attempt a language or literacy task we continue to learn and develop with no definable upper limit. I've been reading and writing for a long time, yet the process of writing this book has continued to teach me about all aspects of language, not only because it's about language, but because I am doing it. And of course I'm doing it purposefully: I have things to say that I want people to read. So I'm not only learning how to be a better writer (reader/speaker/listener) by writing it, but I'm learning a lot about how to help others teach such things as well.

CHAPTER 8

Developing Language Abilities in Uncommonsense Classrooms

The nature of the uncommonsense approach to language education is such that it cannot spell out a comprehensive K–12 (or 14 or 16) curriculum with a detailed sequence of objectives with associated activities. The centrality of the meaning and student-centered qualities of uncommonsense learning and teaching precludes such detailed planning outside of the scope of individual teacher-class transactions, and requires that each classroom community negotiate its central objectives, processes of learning, and means of assessment. Even though fully-detailed curricula are not compatible with the uncommonsense approach, there are broad developmental guidelines which uncommonsense teachers and learners should keep in mind as ways of determining what kinds of achievement have already been attained and what might be useful next steps in extending and enriching those achievements.

For any of these developmental guidelines to be useful, however, it should be remembered that *the focus of uncommonsense language education is on student learning rather than on teaching.* Teachers do have crucial roles to play in fostering and facilitating such development, but little of what we can do to have such effects will look like commonsense transmission-based instructional practice. Reflective language education teachers are not so much teaching students about literature or writing or grammar or spelling as they are helping students develop their capacities (including, crucially, their interest) in reading, writing, speaking, and listening. The goals of uncommonsense language education are to develop students' abilities so that they can become increasingly independent learners, thinkers, and language users. Excellence is sought for all, not just for a few, and the best evidence we have is that virtually all students can become more confident and more competent in all modes of language use than they have been under the current commonsense regime. Helping develop such competence requires that we know what it looks like and are able to identify some of the major steps along the way in terms that will be clear not only to teachers and administrators, but to students, parents, and the community at large as well.

Uncommonsense Reading Competence

What, then, does it mean to be a "good reader"? If it doesn't mean getting the answers right on factual tests or being able to identify the initial consonants or choosing the appropriate main idea, what does it consist of? One answer is that being a good reader is not a static concept. That is, a six-year-old who enjoys and meaningfully transacts with *Make Way for Ducklings* is a good reader even though she might not yet be ready for *Charlotte's Web*. To assume that the concept of being a good reader is a static one is to assume that reading is something that we learn once and only once, that, in effect there is a sharp dividing line between nonreading and reading rather than a continuum of increasing sophistication. From an uncommonsense perspective, we are always in the process of becoming good readers since every new text can at least potentially enrich and extend our competence as readers. The key is the notion of a *meaningful and enjoyable transaction with a written text*, but as readers mature and develop, the ways available to them to enact such transactions and to evoke the texts they read should be maturing and developing as well.

While adults can and do meaningfully transact with *Make Way for Ducklings*, particularly when reading it aloud to children, an adult reader's type of transaction with such a text is not the standard we hold six-year-olds to for their transactions. One of the key ingredients in developing the capacity to make more mature and sophisticated transactions has already been identified in our discussion of *The Jolly Postman* as *intertextuality*. And since intertextuality only develops, by definition, through extensive reading, we must keep in mind two interconnected phenomena in assessing reading development: the fact that reading ability develops primarily through the experience of reading itself, and that any individual's reading level cannot be determined absolutely, but only in relation to his or her experience of reading.

The picture is further complicated by the fact that the capacity for meaningful transactions with written texts varies substantially from good reader to good reader, and even within any particular good reader depending on their purposes and interests. I don't read the same kinds of things at the beach that I do at home, nor the same kinds of things for relaxation as I do for information. Personal interest and curiosity, as well as needs and goals, all have an enormous impact on what we can and do read well. So too, unfortunately, does the residue of our commonsense educations, which too often have had the effect of convincing us that particular sorts of texts are either beyond our capacities or are likely to bring few rewards of either enlightenment or enjoyment or both. Most of these individual differences need not be sources of concern, and actually probably should be encouraged, since reading intensely in one genre or on one topic can promote many aspects of reading competence better than forcing young readers to continually transact with texts which repel them in one way or another. Since all of us as readers must make our transactions individually with the texts we read—however profitably and pleasurably we may share the results of those transactions with others when we have done so—our own personal interests and concerns must continue to play a vital role in helping us make the choices of what to read, which will facilitate the development of our abilities to do so. It is also the case that our individuality, too, is a product of our culture, our time in history, and the interactions we've had with others, but out of that cultural mix come the individuals who enact the reader/text transactions.

The most straightforward uncommonsense answer to the question "What is a good reader?," therefore, is that *a good reader is one who reads widely, pleasurably, and consistently, for many diverse purposes and needs*. While other characteristics are important for describing competent readers, from an uncommonsense perspective it would be a hollow victory indeed to claim to have developed such abilities, if by doing so we had so thoroughly turned young readers off from the pursuit of reading that they didn't seek to do it. Therefore, as we look at some of those characteristics in more detail, it's important to remember that they aren't worth developing if they aren't going to be used. Since uncommonsense reading abilities are only developed through the experience of reading itself, however, there is less chance of that happening than through an approach to reading that attempts to do so through out-of-context skill teaching. And, further, the kinds of abilities which characterize uncommonsense reading competence have enjoyment directly built into them.

A clear and comprehensive characterization of uncommonsense reading abilities and the ways they grow has been developed by Jack Thomson (1987) based on his research on teenagers reading. Although Thomson's model is explicitly focused on reading literature, it seems that with slight modifications it can be thought of as a model for reading anything at all. Indeed the distinction between capital L Literature and other written texts has been eroding steadily under the onslaught of contemporary critical analyses which have found that what gets regarded as literature is more a function of the sociopolitical effects of tradition than of the properties of texts themselves. (For discussion see Eagleton [1983] and Reid [1984].) Although Louise Rosenblatt (1978) has made an interesting case for distinguishing between "aesthetic reading" (of those texts which have traditionally been regarded as literary) and "efferent reading" (of those texts which have traditionally been described as informational), she recognizes that the distinction is, really, one of the reader's stance toward the text, not a property of the text itself. While competent readers should develop the ability to do both aesthetic and efferent reading in Rosenblatt's sense, the overall properties of meaning-making transactions with texts which she describes seem to carry through for transactions with both sorts of texts.

Although Thomson's model of the development of the response capacities in young readers shows a lot of insight into the problems they face and have to surmount to strengthen their reading capacities, my principal problem with it is that like most such developmental schemes, it is a stage model. While the capacities he identifies seem like a useful way to identify what is involved in developing reading competence, it seems less clear that they work as a sequence of stages through which children and adolescents pass on the way to maturity. A better way to characterize what developing readers do, it seems to me, is to think of what is happening as a recursive process of deepening and enriching the various capacities required rather than gradually adding them sequentially. Thomson's six general "kinds of satisfaction" that readers derive from reading are:

1. Unreflective interest in action.
2. Empathizing.
3. Analogizing.
4. Reflecting on the significance of events (theme) and behavior (distanced evaluation of the characters).
5. Reviewing the whole work as the author's creation.
6. Consciously considered relationship with the author, recognition of textual ideology, and understanding of self (identity theme) and one's own reading processes (Thomson 1987, pp. 360–361).

Thomson's complete model is a good deal more complex than this since each stage is accompanied by associated process strategies, and within each stage allowance is made for the reader's degree of intensity of interest (ranging from weak/passive to strong/active) and the degree of sophistication of the reader's response (ranging from simple and rudimentary to developed and subtle). Further, he is careful to point out that the requirements for satisfaction at all stages are "enjoyment and elementary understanding."

While these processes do reveal much that would be helpful to both teachers and learners as they observe the sources of satisfaction they are getting as readers, it doesn't seem that one must, for example, empathize with the characters one is reading about before one analogizes about them by, in his terms for the process strategy associated with analogizing, "drawing on the repertoire of personal experiences, making connections between characters and one's own life." It could be the case that one precedes the other, but it seems more likely that it depends on a variety of factors including the experiences of the readers and the nature of the text (and its characters) itself. And the two are hard to separate and probably happen simultaneously. Indeed, a case could be made that it is harder to empathize with characters one cannot connect one's own personal experience to.

Similarly, the process of reflecting, reviewing the work as the author's creation, and considering the reader's processes and relations with the author (and text) vary substantially according to the demands of the text and the experience of the reader—particularly in the latter case—with her experience as a writer (or teller of oral stories). Early experiences with writing stories can have a dramatic impact on the way one reads them, since the process of being in the author's role dramatically reveals the artifactual quality of written texts, including the fact that they could have been written in other ways. Even very young children have been shown to be able to make "authorial" choices of tone, style, and plot structure, and once having done so for their own stories, they clearly bring a different range of sophistication to the process of reading the stories of others than do children who have not had such experiences.

This is, of course, another argument for the integration of language education activities, since it is now well understood that, contrary to the commonsense view, writing is one of the most powerful tools for the development of reading competence, and a strong case can be made for helping children learn to write before teaching them to read. The ideal, of course, is to have both proceed simultaneously, not only at beginning stages but throughout the development process. Ian Reid (1984) has shown clearly that writing a poem or story in response to reading one is one of the most powerful ways to enhance both the sophistication of the reading process and the engagement and enjoyment of doing so for the reader/writer. Similarly, the importance of teachers and other more expert readers reading aloud to learners at all levels, stressed in Chapter VII, also helps to develop both sophistication and enjoyment as well as leading to natural opportunities for the kind of talk about what has been read which can model and help develop the processes Thomson has identified.

Clearly, the sophistication of response can and should be deepening throughout the school years. This depends on a variety of factors including each learner's growing experience of the world— hence, the more connections which can potentially be made to the people and events one is reading about—and the growing repertoire of other texts which have been read which, themselves, enable connections to be made. As we saw earlier with *The Jolly Postman*, a lot of the book's subtlety and humor is lost on readers who don't have an initial familiarity with the stories being referred to. Although most texts do not proclaim their intertextuality quite as overtly as *The Jolly Postman*, one does not have to be a deconstructionist to recognize that through reading (and being read to), readers have internalized a repertoire of textual conventions and genres, as well as characters and plots, and that this kind of cultural literacy plays a role in our transactions with all texts. This is one reason why children who have been read to begin to read on their own with a leg up on their less-read-to peers, but it is also one of the factors in reading development which makes it a never-ending process.

One other aspect of Thomson's research which does deserve special mention in this regard is his discussion of the word *boring* as used by student readers to characterize their response to many of the books they have read, especially those they have been required to read in school. Thomson attributes some of the reasons for their boredom with required texts to the commonsense (my term) ways they are taught, with a heavy emphasis on formal "new" critical analysis involving a "correct" interpretation (which only the teacher and the critics can and/or do possess) and on the formal features of the text itself: images, metaphors, themes, and the like. But even more important, he found, both for books read in school and for those read independently, less sophisticated readers blamed themselves for virtually all the problems they confronted with interpreting those texts which they labeled as "boring." If they had any difficulty at all, they almost universally assumed that it was their deficiency which was causing the problem, and in response they limited themselves to books they were sure they could handle— usually books with nonstop action and little or no description of either people or places—hence his sense that "unreflective interest in action" is the kind of satisfaction sought by the least able readers.

Thomson blames some of this on television and films, whose penchant for action and simplification are well known, and which provide the overwhelming experience of narrative for most of these readers, but he points out that the more sophisticated readers in his study also watched lots of TV and saw lots of movies, and we should be cautious about drawing too rigid a cause-and-effect connection. More surprising to him was the fact that his interview technique for his research not only revealed these things but proved, in fact, to be a powerful pedagogical tool for overcoming them.

Most of the students said at the end of their interview how satisfying they had found it. There were comments like, "I really enjoyed that, I learned something about how I can read better," "I didn't realize so many things happen in my head when I read," and "I realize that sometimes guessing wrong can help you enjoy a book better—as long as you do guess." It was, undoubtedly, a significant learning experience for students because their reflections on texts and on their own reading processes were facilitated and supported in a way that couldn't happen in a classroom of 25 to 30 pupils, at least for such an extended period of time. What the readers found appealing was the respect accorded to their individual responses. They said they found it appealing that their comments were not rejected, denigrated, "corrected," or evaluated in any way, but listened to carefully and accepted as being of interest and importance. Some of those who were reported to have very short spans of attention managed to sustain complete concentration and involvement for an uninterrupted hour, and expressed disappointment when the interview came to an end. . . . The interviews were, in fact, a valuable teaching strategy, for they provided what Geoff Fox calls the "space" which readers need for reflection so that response can grow, or the "middle ground" where book and reader meet:

> It seems useful to note that the "middle ground" exists whether or not an interviewer enters it. . . . It deserves more attention in the teaching of fiction than we allow if our concern is limited to the text. It is the area where the possibilities suggested by the text are "discussed" by the reader. (Fox 1979, p. 34.)

(Thomson 1987, pp. 172–173.)

While Thomson is undoubtedly correct that the normal, even the uncommonsense, classroom does not permit hour-long individual interviews with students, the possibilities for short interviews in the form of reading conferences can be managed in an uncommonsense classroom, as we saw in Cheryl's and Dan's classes. We saw, further, the potential role of small student groups to provide the kind of atmosphere where students can make contributions which will be "listened to carefully and accepted as being of interest and importance" without being "rejected, denigrated, 'corrected,' or evaluated in any way." As Mary, Norman, José, and Akiko discussed "Soldier's Home," they not only provided such an opportunity, but they also found positive value in Norman's insistence that the story was boring. Setting up a classroom climate where students can use such small group talk as a means of learning takes time, patience, and careful modeling, as we saw in Dan Kelly's class, but the payoff is worth it if it can provide the kind of opportunities for the "middle ground" between reader and text to be reflected upon and explored.

So, too, each reader's learning log can provide a written opportunity for such "discussion," initially just by the writer/reader, but later either when shared with the group as Mary did, or as the basis for a private dialogue between student/reader/writer and teacher/reader/writer. Such a written dialogue is neither as spontaneous nor as fast as an oral interview, but it does help to cope with the numbers and time problems, and it can serve the same ends if student responses are treated with the kind of respect and attention that Thomson so rightly calls attention to. And this, once again, is the key to development of as well as continued engagement with and enjoyment of the reading process. If reading is a process of meaning making, then the process each reader has engaged in must be respected even when it may not match her teacher's probably more sophisticated and experienced evocation of the text. The important issue is to find out what meaning the student has made, and to help her reflect on why she has made the meaning she has, not to weigh in with our superior response, which usually has the effect of further alienating precisely those readers who most need encouragement and support if they are to continue to engage in the process.

Another useful antidote to the idea that teachers know the correct interpretation of texts and the students don't, can come through demonstrating with and for students how we read a text for the first time. Gordon Pradl and I have described this distinction between first and subsequent readings of a text as "primary and secondary acts of reading," where the second permits reference to the history and prior critical comment on a poem or story and the first does not. (For further discussion see Pradl [1987].) For the process to work most effectively as a demonstration it helps if the teacher/reader has not only not seen the text before, but doesn't even know who wrote it or when it was written—clues which might not help the class much, but might enable the teacher to sound more scholarly and bafflingly insightful than he would otherwise. The process employed should be that of the teacher reading the text aloud and composing his responses aloud as they pop into his head. After a bit of stumbling about—which has always been my experience when I've tried this, a humbling but nonetheless useful experience for all concerned—it then helps to gradually involve the class in what is, perhaps for the first time, a genuinely collaborative effort at meaning making.

This not only helps demystify the teacher/reader's pretensions of expertise, but more significantly it provides a genuine model of the kinds of things the students Thomson interviewed were surprised by: how much goes on in my head when I read, how important it is to guess even if the guesses are off-base, and the like. So much of commonsense teaching involves the presentation of polished meanings and previously worked-out interpretations that it is rare for students to ever feel anything but failure and deficiency when they compare their halting efforts to those of the experts. Just as it's important for teachers to write with students—sharing our crossouts, our hesitations, our false starts, our revision strategies—so, too, it's important to share such primary acts of reading, and to use them to help student readers reflect on their own processes—not to show them that they are inadequate, but quite the contrary, to show them that there is no other way to do it.

To develop reading competence, therefore, enjoyment must be kept at center stage, but readers at every level must be helped to see that they can learn to broaden the range of texts they can derive pleasure from and to deepen their capacity for response to them. This isn't a speedy process, and while it's happening over the school years students should be encouraged to continue to read, independently and confidently, those texts they are most comfortable with. Every school reading/literature program should include some sort of wide-reading plan which encourages students to read many books of their own choosing with only minimal "reporting" requirements. (One of the most deadly aspects of commonsense reading/literature teaching has been the Book Report, which has, too often, destroyed most if not all the pleasure derived from reading by demanding a sterile and useless—to both the writer and the reader—formal report.) If reporting is to be useful, it should be done as Cheryl Brown encouraged her students to do, through short cards addressed to fellow class members which they can then use as a basis for making their own reading choices.

It may be discouraging to many teachers to see students reading, in effect, the same book over and over—whether it's one hundred or more Nancy Drew stories or all of Encyclopedia Brown—but while students can and should be encouraged to broaden their choices, many adults continue to derive pleasure from book series, and their popularity should tell us something about both the legitimacy and worth of the familiar even as we try to encourage experimentation with the novel. My daughter, who was a prolific reader almost from the start, did and does read such series books and books by familiar authors, but this is not her only reading. With students for whom it is the exclusive reading diet, the opportunity for conferences and/or learning log dialogues can be used both to suggest alternative titles and to probe their sources of satisfaction with the types of books they're reading. Such insights will not only provide teachers with valuable information about how to suggest alternatives, but can also help the students see that they need not be always limited to the familiar.

Books read by student groups or, more rarely, by the whole class, can be used to broaden and deepen student reading competencies if the process of doing so is based on reflecting on the meanings already made. We are trying to help students to acquire the strategies that good readers use and to shed those which limit their meaning-making powers. But, as with most of uncommonsense teaching, we must be careful that we don't commonsensify the process of doing so by making the strategies into ends instead of means. The commonsense structures of schools are so powerful that we must be careful not to turn reader-response transactional strategies into the kinds of dummy runs which have made even the potentially useful reading strategies of the new critics so stultifying and restricting. If class or group texts become occasions for prediction exercises, for deliberate analogy drawing, for identifying the intertextual elements in a work, and so on, the slim candle of enjoyment through personal transactional meaning making can be snuffed out just as surely as through exercises in symbol hunting and tone identification.

This will be easier if whole-class teaching of the same text becomes the unusual rather than the norm that it has usually been in commonsense schools. While developing readers do need to learn how to collaborate in their meaning-making processes and to check their emerging meanings with those made by others, this is done as effectively by groups reading the same text as by the class doing it together as a whole. As we saw in Dan Kelly's class, groups can do this very well, and the process works better without the teacher/

expert than it does with her, except when she, too, is engaged in a primary act of reading. Part of the reason whole-class teaching of literature has remained the norm derives from the control factors discussed earlier, which make whole-class teaching of anything the norm. But with literature, there is also the not so hidden common-sense assumption that if the teacher doesn't finally deliver the essential interpretation, somehow the kids won't "get it." And if they don't get it,—the teacher's meaning—what was the point of reading the book anyway?

If the real point is to be able to give back the right answer on the test, then whatever lip service has been paid to students developing their own meaning-making capacities has been a sham. In an uncommonsense classroom, we have to recognize that students won't always (ever?) get *our* meaning from a text, and that that is not only inevitable but actually desirable. It's inevitable because of the nature of reader-text transactions and the various factors that influence them, which means that texts read by six- or ten- or fifteen- or even twenty-year-olds won't have the same resonance for them that they do for adult teacher/readers. It's desirable since, while we hope that the discussion processes we promote will help student readers deepen and enrich the meanings they're making, they are not intended merely to support a pretense that students are the meaning makers, while we, the teacher experts, wait to either seduce students into our interpretation or demand it through our testing/grading power.

In fact, it seems hard to justify literature tests at all in an uncommonsense classroom if their purpose is either to check on student recall of the text's facts or to require that students rehearse a previously developed interpretation. While writing about books we read can be a valuable adjunct to and support of the meaning-making process, doing so to "prove" that we've read a book or to demonstrate that we've got the "right " interpretation distorts it. In fact, as Rosenblatt (1978) has pointed out, treating literature as content to give tests on is one of the factors which transforms the potentially aesthetic experience of reading a literary text into the efferent experience of treating the literature as though it were a mine of information. While we do, undoubtedly, gain information from even aesthetic reading, we do so incidentally, and to focus on the information as the reason for reading aesthetically inevitably distorts the process.

Rather than relying on tests to check on the progress of student readers, we and they would be far better served by a cumulative reading record of some kind which identifies the texts students have read—in and out of class—along with a running commentary to be shared with the students on their overall strengths and weaknesses as readers. If the class is operating on the kind of explicitly negotiated basis that Dan Kelly's class exemplified, the criteria for evaluation will be sufficiently clear, explicit, and public, and thus students can participate in the assessment of their own progress in concert with their teacher. Such record keeping can take many forms, but in all cases its focus is on the development of each learner as a reader, not on the short-term particulars of how much they remembered from *A Tale of Two Cities* or *Treasure Island*.

Uncommonsense assessment, therefore, does not depend upon the illusion that daily or weekly marks are either the fairest or the most accurate means of student evaluation. While daily/weekly grading fits neatly with the bits-and-snippets pattern of common-sense instruction, where each individual skill or bit of knowledge stands alone and therefore can be tested and graded independently, uncommonsense instruction is seeking the long-term, the cumulative, and the permanent. If the primary identifying mark of competent readers is that they read, any teaching or testing strategy that makes that less likely to happen is not worth supporting. There is time for the intensive analysis of texts and for reflection on our reading processes throughout schooling, but they should not be done before there is a solid basis in pleasurable experience with reading.

The ideal situation is for students to initiate the times for deeper exploration by being able to express their own puzzles and problems with a text they are sufficiently intrigued with to want to understand it better. If we listen to their questions, observe their reading processes, and recognize the importance of their engagement, those opportunities will come. They won't always be predictable or plannable far in advance, but the uncommonsense teacher has her antennae out waiting for the teachable moment, when the zone of proximal development is the middle ground between the text and the reader. If we remember then that it is still each student who must make the reading transaction, we can help deepen and extend it rather than close it off by substituting our meaning for theirs. Their questions provide the key. And the uncommonsense classroom must be a receptive environment for them to be asked— out loud and on paper—in the full confidence that they will be given the respect and attention they deserve.

Uncommonsense Writing Competence

As we've already noted, writing develops most effectively in tandem with reading but, at least for products of commonsense schools, writing remains both a less common and a more frightening activity. While it seems natural enough to characterize a good reader as one who reads, the parallel description of a good writer as one who writes seems much less appropriate. This stems from the pervasive experience of being taught writing as a kind of civil defense preparedness drill that most of us had in school: something we might have to use in some future emergency, but of no real consequence to our current lives. Fewer teachers (and parents) think of themselves as writers than they do as readers, and so children and adolescents are less likely to see writing as a continuing part of the lives of their adult mentors. Whatever invitation they get to join the "literacy club," it is much more likely to be an invitation to become readers than writers.

This attitude has had a variety of effects which we've already discussed. Learners are more likely to be taught about writing— rules of grammar and usage, spelling and punctuation, and rhetorical form and structure—than they are to do it. When students do write, they are more likely to be evaluated on the form of what they've written—consistency with the rules of grammar, and so on—than on what they've said; and when writing is required in school, it is almost universally a dummy-run experience—written on demand, for a teacher to evaluate, about a topic the writer didn't choose and doesn't care much about—rather than a struggle to make personal meaning on paper in order to communicate with a genuine audience. These effects have been mutually reinforcing to the point that few graduates of American schools (or colleges) feel comfortable, confident, or competent as writers. And fewer still think of writing as something they do for pleasure or relaxation, while many feel that way about reading.

Indeed even the word *writer* itself seems to denote someone special. Within the commonsense tradition, writers, particularly those who write fiction and poetry, are those who write for a living, and even people who do a lot of writing—of letters, articles, research reports, memos, and the like—don't normally describe themselves as writers as freely as they would be likely to describe themselves as readers. Indeed at New York University, a heated controversy developed several years ago when the writing program faculty, in a self-study, characterized what they were attempting to do as the development of writers. Many of the rest of the faculty were horrified by that characterization, which smacked of a bellelettristic and creative writing focus. They were clear that they didn't want the program to develop writers in this sense, but to seek more utilitarian goals such as enabling students to be able to write papers in their subsequent courses with appropriate scholarly and linguistic form. And this attitude, ironically, sprang from a faculty who not only write as part of their normal course of academic lives, but whose whole system of rewards for tenure and promotion are based on successful writing.

While it's perfectly permissible for such faculty members not to regard themselves as writers if they don't want to—and similarly for business executives and managers, scientists and lawyers, and doctors and politicians—the notion that writing is a special competence, available only to the creatively talented (or the dilettantish), and not a real requirement of the daily work lives of hardheaded professionals and business people, has continued to support the commonsense approach to writing instruction which has had such crippling consequences. In particular it supports a dichotomy between thinking and meaning making on the one hand—as done in research, problem solving, and getting the real work of the world accomplished—from the task of writing itself. Writing can then be regarded as a technology of transcription (utilizing the sorts of rules taught in commonsense schools) which one ought to learn how to do, but which is not regarded as intimately connected with the processes of learning and meaning making themselves.

From the uncommonsense perspective, everyone who writes is a writer just as everyone who reads is a reader. The uncommonsense position does not make a fundamental distinction between the writing of utilitarian texts like lists, memos, recipes, or reports, and the writing of imaginative texts like poems and stories. From the uncommonsense perspective all genuine writing is creative, because all genuine writing—writing that is other than copying, doing a fill-in-the-blank exercise, or writing an essay for the sake of a grade—involves the creation of personal meaning in order to communicate with a reader or readers. The struggle to create meaning—and even for the most experienced and competent writers, there is always struggle—involves all of our linguistic, cognitive, and affective resources in order to explore and express our ideas in a way which will be relevant to and therefore communicative with our readers. This intimate connection among the thinking, learning, and writing processes makes writing far more than a technology of transcription, and at the same time makes it both more rewarding and more challenging.

The commonsense approach to writing instruction has been based on an implicit developmental model which moves from:

> **correctness** (in the sense of conformity to the conventions and rules of standard written English—SWE) to
> **clarity** (in the sense of making one's meaning as transparent as possible, as though prose could be adjusted to be universally more "readable"—a position advocated by E. D. Hirsch (1977) before he moved on to cultural literacy (1987), and after

he had advocated the possibility of verifiably correct interpretations of literary texts (1967)—if Hirsch hadn't existed to
articulate the commonsense position, he probably would
have had to have been invented) to

fluency (in the sense of talented performance—a level of
achievement that the commonsense position believes only
those born with special talents are likely to achieve).

The uncommonsense position, in effect, turns this developmental model on its head by arguing that development should
proceed from:

fluency (in the more expansive sense of a feeling of comfort, confidence, and control of the writing process, not built
on an absolute assurance that one will always succeed, or that
the effort will not involve struggle, but rather on a sense
that the process itself is worth it for the learning it brings and
the potential rewards of meaning making and communication) to

clarity (in the sense that through the struggle, and the
nearly inevitable internal and external revisions that it involves (Murray 1978), writers can become clearer about what
they mean and can make their meanings more accessible—
even if never completely transparent—to readers who share
their universe of discourse and relevance systems) to

correctness (in much the same meaning as in commonsense, but with the recognition that the conventions of SWE
are means to the end of meaningful dialogue, not ends to be
sought in themselves, and they are therefore properly subor-
dinate to and supportive of the processes of meaning making).

This uncommonsense pattern of development is a recursive
one, unlike the commonsense view which does seem to be stage-
like in practice if not in theory. In a sense, each time we try to
write—and, in particular, each time we try something substantially
new as a writer: writing to a new audience, in a new genre, or about
a new subject—requires a cyclic recapitulation of the process of
development. Even experienced writers can become dysfluent
under such conditions, and that makes their struggle to be clear
even harder, and frequently even causes them to seem to have
slipped back in their mastery of such things as spelling and punctuation, to say nothing of the more complex aspects of rhetorical
structures. This is part of what makes writing hard work, but for
writers who expect such difficulties and yet have enough underlying confidence (fluency) that they will achieve a sufficient level of

success to make it worth trying, the process can be rewarding as well as challenging. The difference between frustration and challenge is, as often as not, a matter of attitude as much as competence.

Viewing such processes as recursive rather than linear has important consequences for the teaching of writing and the related assessment of students' development as writers. Most important, it means that writing, like reading, can't be thought of as a "skill" one acquires once and then is able to use. Correlatively, it means that everyone who writes is in the process of becoming a writer (or a better writer). There is no reason to believe that everyone cannot achieve a sufficiently satisfactory level of competence during the school years to have developed that underlying level of confidence which enables them to approach writing with a feeling of potential success rather than nearly inevitable failure. There might continue to be only a few people for whom writing becomes such an important source of pleasure and stimulation that they choose to become writers in the commonsense use of that term, but even this is not clear in view of the commonsense experience of learning to write that most people have endured. In fact, even with that experience, the testimony of editors of those "little magazines" which publish poetry and prose suggests that there are many more writers out there than readers, at least if the relative figures of number of works submitted are compared to the numbers of subscribers to such publications.

To answer the question of who's a good writer, therefore, the uncommonsense position would be: *A good writer is one who has sufficient confidence to approach a wide variety of writing tasks with assurance that the experience will be valuable and that the product will be relatively, if never perfectly, successful both as self-expression and as communication to readers.* This definition may be too overqualified and cumbersome, and certainly I would like to be able to simply say: *A good writer is one who writes.* But for this to be true, there would need to be a far more similar recognition of the potential for pleasure and success in writing as there now is much more commonly for reading. In such a circumstance, more people would be comfortable being characterized as writers, and writing would cease to be the forbidding and frustrating experience it now so often is.

This transition will not be easy to accomplish. But under the influence of teachers who have themselves had recent positive experiences with writing, some progress has already been made in this area, and there may be more to come. The influence of the National Writing Project, which has run summer programs for teachers at more than one hundred and fifty sites for over a decade, has been particularly salutary in this respect, as have the many similar programs sponsored under other auspices by school districts as well as universities. The experience of writing in a meaningful and supportive atmosphere to an audience of peers who serve as responsive and collaborative readers—the hallmark of the writing project summer institutes—has served as a useful antidote to the commonsense experience most of the teacher/students had in school themselves.

Unfortunately, from my perspective, the positive experience that teachers have had in the writing aspect of such summer programs has usually not been sufficient to transform their teaching when they return to their schools. This is true partly because the Writing Projects themselves have been deliberately atheoretical in their approach to teaching writing. (For discussion, see Blau [1988], who is, as a writing project director, generally sympathetic to this fact.) This avoidance of theory has been justified in the name of eclecticism—where so little is known, we must avoid an adherence to any single theory or approach—and based on a conviction that theorists really didn't have much to contribute to the pedagogy of writing. Rather than relying on university "experts" as the sources of wisdom for writing instruction, therefore, in addition to the writing experience itself, the basic model of instruction in the summer programs has been one of "teachers teaching teachers"—that is, sharing with each other successful approaches to the teaching of writing which they have used.

While it is clearly important for teachers to share with each other both our problems and our solutions and to generally recognize the value of our own experiential expertise—what North (1987) calls our "professional lore"—the irony of the Writing Project approach as a basis of instructional reform is that the approaches and lessons being shared are inevitably based on the teacher's practice *before they have had the positive writing experience of the institute.* So, for the most part, although not exclusively since many teachers have been the source of uncommonsense theories and practices, the lore they share fits comfortably within the commonsense framework. And, not too surprisingly, the teachers' practices following the institute are eventually, if not immediately, domesticated within that framework as well. This domestication, which has been documented by Judith Langer and Arthur Applebee (1987), involves slipping back to using teacher-chosen writing assignments done for a grade. An even more severe distortion is the grading of such things as journals, learning logs, and other writing experiences whose only raison d'etre is that they are exploratory and therefore, by definition, not able to be evaluated in the same ways as commonsense writing exercises are thought to be.

So while the uncommonsense writing experience the teacher/students have had in the institutes has helped positively change some aspects of the teachers' attitudes toward writing, it has not been sufficient to reform the overall pattern of instruction in uncommonsense directions. For that to happen we need to better understand the theoretical framework which underlies the uncommonsense position on writing, and to sufficiently deconstruct the commonsense framework of schooling to be able to fight against its domesticating power. To achieve this will require a reflective practitioner stance which draws on teacher's reflections on our experience in classrooms, on the best we can discover through theory and research about how writers write and how writing ability develops, and on historically sensitive explorations of how classrooms can work as developmental language workshops.

The connections between research and practice are not direct or simple. One of the best recent examples of the failure of research—even quite innovative and insightful research—to directly provide solutions to educational problems has been recent attempts to apply research into the composing process to classroom practices. Emig (1971), Perl (1975), Hayes and Flower (1980), and many others have shown us that writers employ a complex, recursive discovery process when they compose texts. They engage in a wide range of percolating, drafting, revising, and editing behaviors and shift rapidly among them as they struggle to shape their text. Such research discoveries seriously challenged both the then-current rhetorical theories of the composing process and the commonsense pedagogical strategies based on them. These involved a more linear transcription view of composing, heavily dominated by such practices as making an outline before writing, choosing a thesis statement for one's essay and topic sentences for each paragraph early in the process, and following strict genre and mechanics guidelines for the form of the final essay.

While the research done by Emig and her successors does show us important new insights into the mental processes involved in composing, it has definite limits in terms of direct application to classroom practices. Like most such research in the technical/rational tradition, these studies of the composing process of writers—both students and adults—were done out of the context of the teaching and learning processes of the classroom. We've seen that classrooms are complex social environments which exist within even larger and more complex social structures called schools. Defining or setting the pedagogical problems to be solved is done by a large number of people on the basis of a wide variety of constructs of what schools are for, how learning takes place, who's in charge in the classroom, what's going to be on the test, and so on. The pedagogical problem which might be characterized as "how to teach writing" carries with it a lot of that conceptual baggage. These ideas include the belief that writing is a valuable thing for all students to learn and that it can be directly taught, as well as particular understandings of what writing means and what it means to be able to do it.

In commonsense composition teaching, teachers assign topics for students to write on, give them time limits to complete the work, and specify the form and length of the final product. Further, the teacher is the primary audience for the student's text, since she is the one who evaluates it, and that evaluation is usually based more or less explicitly on the formal features of the paper—spelling, punctuation, presence or absence of topic sentences, and so on—with little if any regard for its effectiveness as a genuine effort at communication.

When these dimensions of composition teaching are not modified, as has usually been the case with most if not all of them, then introducing a "Writing Process" pedagogy, which claims to be an application of this research by Emig et al., has usually meant both linearizing and trivializing it. It has been linearized by setting aside specific and separate times for prewriting (usually accompanied by a set of teacher-framed activities), for drafting, for revising, and for editing. Recognizing the importance of revision is probably the most positive change in such implementations, but doing so mechanically can lead to such parodies as the second graders who almost seemed to compete with each other to see how many different openings they could create for a particular story. Further, it fails to recognize that some pieces need not be revised at all (they are too good, too private, or too awful to bother with), and that in some ways fluency will be more greatly enhanced by a lot of drafting with no revision at all. But most important, revision is never going to be genuinely undertaken by a writer who does not care sufficiently about her piece to want to work toward communicating through it as effectively as possible. Achieving this level of commitment is rarely possible in a teacher-dominated composing framework where the student perceives the teacher as the final arbiter of the nature and quality of the text.

Making effective use of the insights of composing process research in a pedagogical context, doing so artistically in Schön's sense, requires more than merely changing the labels of the stages of the composing process. Changing the labels seems to be virtually the only effect in the new edition of *Warriner's Grammar and Composition* series (1986), the all-time American best-seller of its kind. Nothing much else in the books has changed. It's still the same old prescriptive grammar and presentation of maxims for effective writing involving topic sentences and the like, but now there are new labels and equally prescriptive activities for prewriting, drafting, and so on. Without a more comprehensive understanding of the nature of the language system and how it develops, and the artistic implementation of that understanding to substantially change the students' and teachers' roles in the classroom, only limited effects can be expected from changing to a "Writing Process" approach.

Beginning writers should learn that the first thing they write down need not be immutable, since revision is not only possible but desirable. Similarly, distinguishing between revision—for substance—and editing—for form—and learning to recognize that there is plenty of time for both, can help writers avoid premature concern for error, which is the principal paralysis facing those writers who arrive at adolescence or adulthood with the conviction that they can't write (Perl 1975). But while learning to exploit the various aspects of the composing process can help give writers more of the sense of confidence and control they need in order to approach writing tasks competently, doing so through the implicit message that one must perform these tasks in a fixed and linear order, that they are completely independent and separable from each other, and that everything one writes should follow such a sequence, is probably more constricting and restricting than liberating and confidence building.

Indeed, as researchers have looked more carefully at the composing process (see, for example, Berkenkotter [1983]), they have found that while the subroutines of the process are often present, they are frequently intertwined as writers shift rapidly between them. For experienced and proficient writers, the shifts are so rapid, the number of factors impinging on the production process so many and complex, and the impact of any one on all the others so powerful, that the notion of a linear, or even a simply recursive process seems less and less tenable. The implication of this for teaching writing is not that composing process research has no value for the teaching of writing; it has and it does. But what it suggests is that the distinctions among subprocesses and the overall notion of the composing process itself must be taught not as a commonsense lock-step model to imitate in advance of writing, but as part of a reflection on experience, a process akin to the other aspects of Vygotskyan uncommonsense development of scientific concepts built on a spontaneous concept base.

This derives both from the uncommonsense learning theory advanced here and from understanding that in order to learn to write, the focus for the writer must be on *what* she is trying to say and on *whom* she is trying to communicate with. All of the other factors that involve the *hows* of getting it said appropriately and effectively must be properly seen to be the means to doing so, not ends in themselves. As we've seen throughout, language ability, including writing ability, develops in response to meaningful experiences of using language. The great virtue of writing process instruction is that it has slowed down the writing process for many learners, given them a greater sense of control over its pace and intensity, and provided opportunities for writers to get meaningful feedback before they think they have completed the paper. (The single worst aspect of commonsense writing instruction was that teacher "corrections" and comments were made on final drafts and returned so long after the paper was complete that the comments had little or no impact except to further convince those writers whose papers were bleeding with errors that they couldn't write.) But if the papers being written are no more meaningful to the writer than those written under the old regime, slowing down the process of composing them will, finally, have no more utility in helping develop writing abilities.

Creating appropriate occasions and opportunities for meaningful student writing is not easy in commonsense schools. The pressures of grades, time, numbers, schedules, and so on all have a negative impact. So does the growing disengagement with the curriculum as a source of personal meaning making by students. When everyone expects writing in school to be a dummy run, it's hard for it to be otherwise. But if, as uncommonsense theory suggests, only meaningful writing will develop writing competence, then we must find a way to create such occasions even if it means a substantial change in normal practice for students as well as for teachers.

Doing so, however, will require that we really take students seriously and that they take themselves seriously as well. The former means, essentially, *that everything students write will have to be self-initiated.* While there can be negotiation about various aspects of such things as when writing should be done, possible issues to be explored and propositions to be debated, genres to be attempted, and whatever other constraints the overall curriculum requires, in the final analysis, students must make the final choices in all of these areas if they are to have sufficient commitment to the products they produce. One doesn't learn about revision, for example, from being required to revise a paper which doesn't say anything anyway; one only learns about revision from struggling to find a more effective way of saying what one really wants to say. While seeking a good grade may motivate some of us to try harder, under such circumstances we are mostly trying harder to do what the grader wants done, not learning to trust our own developing sense of how best to say what we want to say.

The necessary commitment is most likely to be developed in a context where the writer is communicating with genuine readers as well. While teachers can serve as real readers, and one of the goals of the uncommonsense classroom is to create a context where that is more likely to happen, the teacher's additional roles as expert and grader make that a difficult situation to achieve. Even teachers who would like to be treated as, in Britton's phrase, "trusted adults" know that it is hard to be such if they also have to grade the resulting products. Other students in the class are less likely to be perceived as experts, and hence more likely recipients of genuine communications, particularly communications of an informational sort, and every effort should be made to create the kind of classroom community where the meaning-making process is collaborative and mutually supportive in both reading and writing. Students can and do enjoy communicating with each other both orally and on paper in such a climate, and the feedback they can provide each other about emerging texts can be a valuable source of learning both of how to improve the text being written and, at a more meta level, of the kinds of things that are effective (or not) with readers.

One's fellow students are not an effective audience for all student writing, however, particularly for adolescents whose sense of privacy can be acute and whose sense of a need to create and maintain a particular image with one's peers can be threatened by writing which exposes one's real self too nakedly. Writing, like reading, can be one of the ways that we can explore our emerging selves, consider alternative values and life patterns, express our deepest and most sensitive feelings, and in other ways delve into our private spaces. But in order to do so, we must be confident that we will have readers who will respect our privacy and our tenderest feelings. While writers who publish their work have to take their chances on anonymous readers, the very anonymity of their response provides more protective cover than can be found in a high school classroom for a student who may not want his classmates to know his deepest thoughts and feelings. This is a situation where teachers can play a useful and professional audience role by encouraging students to write in such ways if they want to, and then respecting their privacy and integrity when they do so.

It may be that some students will eventually want to share such texts, but like the other aspects of the writing process, going public with one's work through some sort of classroom or wider publication should be a decision made by the writer not by the teacher. There's no doubt that publication of various kinds provides an important motivation for writers who really want to share their ideas and texts with others. Putting student work on bulletin boards, producing class magazines, publishing stories in book form, and even reading texts aloud in class can have a motivating effect on increasing commitment and on developing the pride in craft which is the only factor which makes writers care about editing. But students must control what gets published in these ways, and there should also be plenty of opportunity for nonpublished, even nonrevised, writing of all sorts, from journals to poems, from stories to essays.

There is no doubt, however, that engaging in genuine writing is a risky business. As Jasper Neel (1988) has pointed out, "as writers write, they produce something different from what they expected" (p. 130). This can be frightening, particularly for students who have acquired the commonsense "theological belief in the disembodied existence of knowledge" (p. 131), and genuine writing threatens that belief because "in writing the perception upon which they have built their understanding of the world gets called into question" (p.131). Students (and teachers?) who are fearful of threatening their belief systems retreat into what Neel calls "antiwriting," which amounts to a declaration accompanying each paper that:

> I am not writing. I hold no position. I have nothing at all to do with discovery, communication, or persuasion. I care nothing about truth. What I *am* is an essay. I announce my beginning, my parts, and the links between them. I announce myself as sentences correctly punctuated and words correctly spelled. (p. 85.)

The attractiveness of such antiwriting, Neel argues, is that it leaves one's existing belief structure unthreatened by the unexpected, or by recognizing either the slipperiness of knowledge or the intertwining of knowledge with expression. And when confronted with such dummy-run antiwriting, all teachers can respond to are its formal features, since neither writer nor reader can take it seriously as a meaning-making endeavor.

Teaching writing as a process can either lead to antiwriting in its commonsense domesticated version, where the attention still remains focused on producing "essays," or it can lead into thickets of discovery. There student writers won't find some independently existing absolute meaning or knowledge, but their own partial and changeable meanings and personal knowledge. In this uncommonsense position, writing is not a technology for transcribing meanings that exist prior to and independent of the process of trying to express them, it is part of the daily struggle to make sense of the world by representing it. In doing so, we are inevitably influenced by, while at the same time we are participating in, the great intertextual conversation. This means not only that our representations share those of the texts which have preceded ours, but that our readers bring those texts to bear in interpreting ours. Just as readers of literary texts must transact with them to make meaning from them, when we begin to write we learn that our meanings do not slip transparently and effortlessly into the minds of our decoding readers (as the code theory would have it), but are subject to all of the vagaries of transactionalism as well.

This process is one of the major routes through which writing can be a means of intellectual and ethical development. Whether our terms of reference derive from Piaget (1967), from William Perry (1970), from Carol Gilligan (1982), or from anyone else, the full development of what Neel calls the capacity "to make choices in a world of probability . . . [that is essential to] the process whereby the individual develops an ethical self" (p. 207) derives from an understanding of the contextualized quality of knowledge and belief. And that in turn is best learned from the experience of genuine writing, of struggling to make sense for oneself and others, of participating in a community of meaning makers who can share each others' probabilities rather than resorting to some nonexistent, independent source of truth.

Like reading controversial texts, engaging students in such genuine writing communities will be perceived as threatening by those who hold one kind of truth or another to be absolute and independent of human agency. Such a community calls for what Neel labels "strong discourse" which, among other things, includes the notion that it never exists alone, but only in vigorous competition with other strong discourses which seek to persuade us of their value. In such a community, the discourse of the teacher is merely one voice in the conversation, with no more privileged status than any other voice. Such a classroom is pluralistic and democratic as well as non-teacher-centered, since it insists that authority be earned by argument and not granted by fiat. Most of us have to work hard to overcome the commonsense habits and beliefs which make such a classroom community threatening, but if we can begin to do so, the uncommonsense prerequisites for the genuine development of the two faces of the language-and-thought coin will be created in ways that would otherwise seem impossible.

As with student reading development, student writing development cannot be effectively assessed on a paper-by-paper basis. This is partly because, as noted, the factors influencing whether or not a particular paper is successful vary according to such things as the writer's experience with writing other, similar texts, her motivation and commitment to the topic, the amount of time and effort available, and so on. This makes the process of writing development—like the process of reading development—not a straight line reaching ever upward, but a very lumpy curve indeed. Even revision itself, as Onore (1983) has shown, does not guarantee improvement, since sometimes in "solving" one problem we create others which are even more troubling to our readers. This is a distressing reality for those of us who teach students for only one year—and worse for those who have students for only one semester, as is the norm in college and university writing courses.

Like tests on literature, giving separate grades on each essay or other student text distorts the nature of the writing process and short-circuits whatever learning can be expected on the basis of the experience of writing the text. The goal for the writer inevitably becomes getting the best grade which, in turn, takes the responsibility for choosing how to most effectively compose a piece away from the writer and cedes it to the teacher/grader. Experimentation is therefore restricted, and everyone sticks as carefully as possible to those prestructured genres of antiwriting which have proved themselves the safest path to good grades. If writing develops best through self-initiated writing, then the assessment of it must be self-initiated as well. This doesn't mean that the teacher has no role to play, but the teacher's role is to help the class to articulate and understand the criteria to be used to assess writing effectiveness. This can be best done by modeling for students how to be involved in responding to and assessing their own and each others' writing and by having them involved in the judgment process. (For further discussion and some examples in this area see Mayher, Lester, and Pradl [1983], especially Chapter 7.)

Since writing development is also long-term and cumulative, even if not linear, the assessment system too must work in these directions. Writing folders which accumulate the work students have written over a term can play a useful role here, but only if students have learned how to choose whatever pieces they think best represent their growth as writers. It does no good for a teacher to ask students to pick out their best work unless they have developed some criteria for "bestness." Doing so when they have not been addressed causes panic in the class, as I learned the last time I taught college freshman composition. But the process of discussing such criteria using examples drawn from the texts students have already written is the best example of teaching writing. In such a reflective context, all of the issues teachers have traditionally wanted students to attend to in writing can be addressed, but it can be done in a way which is both purposeful and accessible.

And, like reading, the final judge of the effectiveness of a piece of writing has to be the writer. Her readers may not make similar judgments, of course, but that is the risk all of us run when we say or write anything. But finally it's our sense of the adequacy of the text which must determine whether or not it will ever see a reader other than ourselves. Until we say "Here it is," we can always change it, destroy it, or leave it for another day. It is learning to develop our own sense of judgment that will finally determine our own sense of confidence, without which we will never become competent. And if the development of students' writing competence is our long-range goal as uncommonsense teachers, helping them to learn to assess their own work, to be their own most important reader, is a crucial step in the process.

Uncommonsense Speaking and Listening Competence

Implicit in the preceding discussion of the development of reading and writing abilities has been the inseparability of talk from either process. While it's common enough for both reading and writing to be silent activities while they are actually being accomplished, the talk that precedes and follows—and even, quite frequently, interrupts—them is crucial for their development. And, further, it's the talk that surrounds them that enables others— peers and parents as well as teachers—to play a role in promoting (or, unfortunately, in retarding) this growth by interactions within Vygotsky's (1978) zone of proximal development. In the case of reading, the principal developmental role of talk is that of creating what Stanley Fish (1980) has called an "interpretive community" through which readers share the meanings they have made and/or are making of a text and work toward an interpretive consensus. In writing, the most direct role for talk comes both in the process of exploring initial ideas prior to writing and, most crucially of all, in providing writers with useful reflections of their text's impact and an opportunity for discussion of its strengths and weaknesses.

Through these various collaborative uses of talk to support the reading and writing processes, learners can develop their capacities to produce and share meanings, to raise questions about the texts they're reading—both for the sake of meaning making and for giving feedback to the writer—and by doing so to deepen and enrich their own meaning-making process by participating in the processes that their teachers and peers are using to make their meanings. One of the crucial insights of the language and learning research that has been done in the last two decades, particularly by Douglas Barnes and his colleagues, and James Britton and Nancy Martin and their colleagues, has been the recognition that *the production of oral language is a crucial means through which we learn*. We have seen examples of that already in the examples of student-to-student talk we've looked at from a number of classrooms, but the point must be reemphasized here in order to stress the importance of providing time for exploratory talk in classrooms.

No other single factor so clearly distinguishes uncommon- and commonsense classrooms than the relative range of opportunities for student talk in each. The contrast between the teacher-dominated commonsense classroom and the more learner- (and, I would add, learning-) centered uncommonsense class can be seen starkly in the percentage of time allocated to student talk, the primary audience for student talk, and the purposes for which it is employed. In the commonsense class, not only do teachers do most of the talking, but most student talk is addressed to the teacher, and it largely consists of answering teacher questions or in some other way providing a reporting of what the students have already learned. In the uncommonsense class, by contrast, students normally talk with each other during most of the typical class period—usually without a teacher present except, perhaps, as an eavesdropper—and the talk is intended to be one of the major processes through which learning occurs, not merely a way of reporting prior learning.

There is some teacher-student talk in uncommonsense classes, to be sure, even some whole-class discussions, but even these are—or ought to be—structured to serve as learning opportunities so the teacher's voice is regarded as one among many and not as the last word. And some of the student-teacher talk in uncommonsense classrooms takes on other functions as well, including serving as the principal vehicle for negotiating the curriculum and its associated assessment system, for mutual reflection on what and how the class has been learning, and, crucially, in individual student-teacher conferences. In addition to the quantitative and addressee differences between common- and uncommonsense approaches, the major distinction is that of exploratory talk versus reporting talk.

Exploratory talk is vital for all aspects of learning. It's the major path through which we find our way into content learning: checking our emerging sense of what we've read or heard or seen by sharing our perceptions with others and learning further from their similar explorations. One of the problems with Vygotsky's (1978) formulation of the zone of proximal development is that it seems to suggest that learning still descends, in a sense, from adult and more experienced peer to the learner. Barnes (1976), Hull (1985 and 1988), and others have shown that this process can be a mutually beneficial one in which no one has to play the "teacher" role, and equally inexperienced learners can pool their resources through collaboration, with the result that all gain through the process. While it is likely that in any student group, one or more students will have more relevant background in the topic being

discussed or more skill at using the collaborative process for exploring it, nevertheless it is often the case that even the least experienced learner can play a vital role in the group as a whole. This can
be particularly true if they are willing and able to ask questions
about those things which are troubling them, a process which can
spur their peers to reexamine their own understandings and to
articulate them to others.

This "teaching" role, in a more general sense, is the role that
productive language use generally plays as an aid to learning: By
having to articulate what we understand, we make new connections, reveal gaps or confusions in our knowledge, and literally
create new meanings. By having to defend a position, we are forced
to deepen and extend our understanding of its implications. By
asking questions, we take the most crucial step of all toward solving problems, since to frame a problem is to accomplish most of the
hardest work involved in solving it. By probing another's argument
for weaknesses, we come to understand both the argument and our
own position more clearly. And, by doing all of these things, we are
learning how to learn as well as learning more about the substance
we are discussing. While we can learn much about content and
thinking processes by listening to others, we do so much more
effectively in a system that permits open give and take among
equals than we do in a context where our major learning task is to
try and memorize and be able to recall a teacher's monologues.

And, incidentally but nonetheless powerfully, the process of
engaging in such dialogues is the fundamental process through
which we further develop and enrich our language system. It's the
way we learn new vocabulary, because we have the opportunity to
hear it and produce it in a context where its appropriateness can be
tested not in a punitive atmosphere, but in a mutually collaborative
attempt to clarify the meanings being made. It's the best opportunity we have for enriching the complexity of our syntactic repertoire by being in contexts where complex ideas naturally demand
the use of complex structures by speakers and listeners, but to do
so in a context where questions can be raised when the complexity
level causes confusion.

In particular, of course, the vocabulary and structures we are
learning through such occasions for use will, eventually at least, be
those of the academy: the languages of the natural and social sciences, the arts and the humanities. Acquiring such vocabulary and
structures is also a traditional goal of commonsense teaching, but
the difference here is not only one of means, doing so in a context
where the terms and structures are organically tied to the ideas
being explored and the meanings being made, but significantly
also one that permits the terms themselves to be deconstructed—
questioned for their validity as explanatory labels, related to the

experiences of the learners, and seen in the context of their inter-textual echoes. Although no one can become a member of a culture or subculture without comprehending its language, the process of acquiring its terms can be done either through rote imitation of the transmissions of others or through a critical process of collabora-tive examination and discussion. The latter path is the uncommon-sense route, and it has the benefit not only of making the learning more likely to be permanent, but also of actively reconstructing it for each student generation.

Such occasions for active exploratory language use are also the most effective ways for students to acquire either a second language or a second dialect. For those students—and there is an increasing number in American as well as in British, Canadian, and Australian schools—who don't come to school speaking English or the more public dialects of English, engaging in exploratory talk provides both the occasions for and the means of acquiring a fuller command of public English. For this to happen most effectively, however, such students cannot be segregated by language or dialect into groups where they have no native models to transact with: another strong argument against tracking, segregation, and language separation. Peer-peer interaction is the most powerful vehicle for language development in school-age children and ado-lescents, but it cannot have its maximum effect unless learners have easy access to speakers whose dialects more closely approximate the regional and cultural norms.

In addition to providing an effective context for language learning and development, such student-student exploratory talk groups also enable this development to happen in a context which is, insofar as possible, free of denigration of the learner's prior language. While students can indeed be cruel to one another—and one of the crucial teacher-modeling roles in such classrooms is to try to create a supportive rather than a personally critical context for such talk—their cruelty is of a different sort than the "official" criticism implicitly or explicitly delivered by teachers. In the atmo-sphere of racism and other intergroup discrimination systems that still operate in our society, it would be naïve in the extreme to pre-tend that student-student talk in uncommonsense classrooms will singlehandedly solve such problems. Even if schools were really unsegregated and heterogeneously grouped, problems of ethnicity, sexism, and classism would still remain. But commonsense class-rooms haven't and won't solve such problems, and may even go on aggravating them. So the potential for exploratory talk to contribute to their solution is real if incomplete.

From the uncommonsense perspective, the development of speaking and listening competence, like that of reading and writ-ing, is a lifelong process. The language-using experiences we have during our school years can and do play a crucial role in influencing the course of that lifelong process as well as in determining our access to further educational opportunities and to employment and other aspects of a productive life. To ensure that this development is encouraged during school, learners need access to opportunities for productive exploratory talk so that they can develop the capacity to recognize its value as a means of learning and growth. While the experience of talking to learn will, itself, provide much of that sense of worth, like many other kinds of implicit and indirect learning, it will be most fully appreciated if it is also reflected upon.

Such reflection functions in two ways: first, as we've seen, as part of the process of modeling which is essential to help learners make the most productive use of opportunities for such talk, and second, as a way of helping them (and their teachers) assess their development. The general neglect of talk in commonsense classrooms has resulted in what, for once, is a happy absence of a testing industry shadow falling over the enterprise. (Britain is planning to assess oral ability in their new school leaving testing program, and it will be interesting to watch the effect of doing so on school practices.) There are no tests for speaking and listening skills and consequently there is little teaching of them or drilling on them either. While this makes it easier to emphasize that they must be assessed in holistic and context-sensitive ways, the lack of attention they have normally received means that most teachers—even uncommonsense teachers—have little or no idea how to do so.

The basic mechanism is one of reflection through observation and discussion. Tape recordings (which work best accompanied by transcripts, however cumbersome and tedious the transcription process can be) are the best means of doing so since they ensure that the conversations examined will have been genuine examples of student discussion. Looking at the process of student-student talk is not initially easy—although Douglas Barnes (1976) has provided some excellent guidance for how to do so—but since participating in conversations is something we do all the time and have done since before we even began to talk ourselves, we do have a large tacit store of background and experience to draw on. Once both students and teachers start to look at talk exchanges, they rapidly learn to follow their dynamics, to identify the various roles played by the participants, to see examples of helpful and nonhelpful contributions, and so on.

There are more complex and theoretically sophisticated analysis systems available to help where necessary (see, for example, Barnes and Todd [1977], and the ethnographic work done by Judith Green and her colleagues [Green and Wallat 1981], and by David Bloome et al. [1987]). But for the most part, useful analysis can be done by looking for the meanings being made and the ways each participant does or doesn't contribute to the process. If goals of oral language development are to enrich and extend the language system of all learners, to deepen their capacity to learn through language, and to enable them to use their oral language system to interact with and support the development of their competencies with the written language, then these should be the aspects of oral language use which teachers and students try to recognize, identify, and eventually assess.

Like the assessment of the development of written language competencies, the assessment of oral language development should be holistic and long-term. By emphasizing the positive achievements of all learners—an easier prospect in oral language than in any other area in schooling, since all children come to school with, as we've seen, an already highly-developed and sophisticated oral language system—assessing oral language development can be a positive experience for all learners. And for children and adolescents to recognize the potential power of their own oral language system can give them the necessary confidence to use it in new situations and to continue to develop it throughout life: in the workplace and at home, for courtship and recreation, for learning and for growth. The oral language is useful for everyone every day. Developing its full potential, therefore, must be a high priority for an uncommonsense educational system.

CHAPTER 9

Uncommonsense
Teaching in Context

Toward Uncommonsense Schools

Creating the kind of climate for learning that enables uncommonsense teaching and learning to take place will require major modifications of the internal structure of schools and substantial changes
in the ways that schools are regarded by the communities that
support them. In both cases, however, the changes may be more
possible in the current climate of public and professional opinion
than they have ever been, and at least in some places efforts to
move in uncommonsense directions are already underway. Given
the stability and inertia of current commonsense structures of
schooling, no one should be too sanguine about the ease of making
sweeping changes, but the potential rewards for all concerned are
so great that the effort has to be made.

Internally the most important overall change is to place student learning back at the center of the school agenda and to encourage teachers to reclaim their rightful control over the processes of
teaching and learning that take place in every school. Teachers and
administrators who come to recognize the potential of uncommonsense approaches for teaching and learning have the power to
change what they are doing. Despite all of the restrictions currently
in place in many school districts, curricula can be changed, tests
can be deemphasized, teacher-proof materials no longer need be
bought, and so on. Teachers who fall back on "*They* won't let me do
it" as an excuse to avoid change must be challenged to specify each
"they" and then to see if it's really true either that "they" won't
permit experimentation, or that "they" exist at all. Although any of

this is hard for an individual teacher to do, groups of teachers within a building have enormous potential power to change their teaching strategies and approaches if they have a coherent plan for doing so and if they can unite together to win administrative and parental support.

Administrators will rarely, in my experience, provide the leadership necessary or run the risk of upsetting the status quo to get the process started, but they are, by the same token, usually happy to support a group of teachers who take collective initiative toward change. Of course, there are some administrators who are out front on these issues, and we must be grateful for that. But whatever the local situation, collective action by teachers can provide a powerful impetus for change. Getting one's fellow teachers mobilized to do so will not be easy, of course, since many are more than satisfied with the status quo and more than comfortable with the teaching routines they have developed. But it has been my experience that most schools have a cadre of teachers who are already raising uncommonsense questions and who are prepared to move in uncommonsense directions if they can be supported when they do. And, most important, most teachers are genuinely committed to improving student learning, and if they can be helped to see effective ways to do so, they will at least be willing to try some of them out.

Some will resist the whole effort and most will resist some of it, but we're not talking here about a process that can or should be quick or simple. For teachers to gain (or reattain) their rightful professional autonomy and responsibility will take a long period of exploring the basis for their commonsense beliefs and of trying on and trying out more uncommonsense ones. Both Dan Kelly and Cheryl Brown started as commonsense teachers, and they are still evolving toward being more uncommonsense ones. So, for that matter, did I begin that way, and I too am still exploring alternatives and struggling to find better and more effective alternatives, as are my colleagues around the country. But the fact that the process will be a long and difficult one can't be allowed to prevent us from beginning it.

Making time available for teachers to talk with each other will not be easy and it will require imagination, flexibility, and, to some extent at least, money. The money can usually be found if there is a substantial reason for spending it and if teachers and administrators work together to do so. There have been large expenditures for teacher development in many districts during the last decade or so, but the funds have generally been spent on programs or approaches which have had the effect of what Michael Apple (1986) calls the "de-skilling" of teachers. This has been done through the imposition of teacher-proof curricula and programs, of demanding a lock-step approach to instruction, or through creating a new testing program to evaluate pupil learning and, concurrently, hold teachers accountable for it. The main characteristic all such programs have had in common is that they have been imposed from above with little or no teacher input. They have also usually employed expensive outside consultants to transmit the word.

While teachers often need and deserve outside help and support in the process of changing, such support must be jointly sought by teachers and administrators if it is to have any long-term impact. Further, the program should be designed in such a way as to encourage teacher leadership throughout the process and to gradually shift full responsibility onto the teachers themselves. Just as uncommonsense teaching hopes to promote student autonomy and independence, so uncommonsense inservice education for teachers should be promoting their ownership and control of the process of change. If the goal of teacher education is to promote reflective practice by reflective practitioners, then the scaffolding of the education process must give way as soon as possible to teacher/learner control. (For further discussion and a detailed case study of how such a long-term inservice education project can work, see Lester and Onore, 1990.)

The process of creating a climate for change within a school will be greatly facilitated if parents and other members of the community—including the press—can become supporters of the change process. The extent to which this is possible varies substantially from community to community, depending, among other things, on their level of commitment to commonsense ideas of schooling. In most cases, however, the safest course is to assume that the community is interested in providing a better education for their children, but that they tend to define better in commonsense ways: emphasis on values such as discipline, high standards, student respect for adult authority, and the like are frequently as important to the community as they are to teachers. Anything that seems to threaten such values will be regarded as potentially dangerous, and proponents of uncommonsense ideas must be clear that they are neither promoting anarchy nor lowering standards.

Whatever the local situation, the best approach includes a process of parent and community education which involves them in the process of change as well. In the program Lester and Onore describe, for example, each of the three years of inservice workshops involved a school board member and a building principal as well as teachers from all grade levels, and each year's efforts culminated with a report to the whole school board at a public meeting. Many parents are aware of the fact that children who are eager to

go to school in the early years become less and less so as the years
roll on, and this phenomenon can be used to account for much of
the motivation for schools trying to change their approach. Further,
if parents can get involved in the processes of language education
by becoming partners with their children in such learning activities
as reading aloud, discussing books that the child has read, and
reading their written work, the process of uncommonsense learning will be strengthened for all.

Even those parents who are the most vigorous supporters of
the educational status quo are often, ironically, those who didn't
much like or benefit from their own commonsense schooling, but
who became convinced that they were at fault for not being diligent
enough. Sometimes such parents are impossible to convince until
they see some genuine signs of success in their children, but they
must, nevertheless, be approached and listened to whenever possible. They and all parents must also be convinced that uncommonsense ideas do not follow the easy and slipshod path. Seeing
teachers who don't correct every spelling error or who permit students to choose many of the books they read may seem to some
parents as sloppy and irresponsible. Pretending such conflicts are
not going to happen won't avoid them in the long run, however,
and they are less likely to become confrontational if the change
process and its rationale are developed with parental and community involvement rather than only within the school itself.

My last book, written with Nancy Lester and Gordon Pradl,
closed with a chapter called "surviving together in the real world,"
which featured a series of vignettes about the difficulties faced by
anyone trying to change the ways writing is taught and learned in
schools. The risks to be run by anyone trying to implement the
more sweeping changes toward uncommon sense advocated here
will be at least as great and maybe greater. The only advantage, I
think, comes from the fact that the change called for here is more
comprehensive. That may seem paradoxical, but I am convinced
that exploring and revealing the inadequacies of the common sense
of schooling which are so deeply rooted in all of us has a better
chance of success because it is more explicitly devoted to examining
why we do what we do in schools than the earlier book was. I am
convinced that until such beliefs are examined and alternatives explored, no meaningful change can happen in schooling.

Teacher Autonomy?

When James Britton (1980) declared the 1980s as "the decade
of the classroom teacher," he was optimistically espousing the be-

lief that teachers working together could build a new pedagogy which would effectively enact the best that we know about language and learning. We could do so on the basis of our practical knowledge and experience and our growing participation in the process of knowledge generation and classroom research. I share that optimism—if I didn't I wouldn't be writing this book—but as the 1980s have unfolded we have seen a variety of forces at work whose net effect has been to limit, not enhance, teacher autonomy; to downgrade, not celebrate, teacher competence; and to make schools less enjoyable and exciting places in which to work.

These pressures have led some observers of schools, like Stanley Aronowitz and Henry Giroux, to characterize the situation as *Education Under Siege* (1985), and others, like Frank Smith, to see what he calls "the bureaucratic invasion of American classrooms" as an *Insult to Intelligence* (1987). In some respects, these conflicts are not new; there has been consistent debate about the nature and purpose of public education and attempts to control teachers since it began, but accompanying earlier waves of criticism of schools and attempts to modify them to achieve some broader social, economic, or political purpose has usually been a positive level of faith in the general competence of teachers, which is strikingly absent from most media and political comment in the current perception of a crisis in education. Indeed, as Henry Perkinson (1968) has shown, the most common response to earlier social crises in America was to place still another burden on schools to solve the problem, whether it was equal economic opportunity, racial discrimination, or the Americanization of new immigrants.

As Perkinson's title, *The Imperfect Panacea*, suggests, schools were not capable of solving the problems thrust upon them by public, press, or politicians so that some of the current loss of faith in schools may be the result of their failing to achieve goals they could never have been reasonably expected to meet. Nevertheless, throughout its history, the United States has led the world in its faith that effective education was not only the keystone of democracy and freedom, but the means by which the social and economic benefits of our society could be assured on the one hand and made available to most if not all of the population on the other. Even the current crisis, brought most powerfully to public awareness by the publication of a federal report significantly titled *A Nation at Risk* (1983), continued to emphasize the central role of schooling in determining the future course of American society. The problem is not that schools are not important, but that they are so important that their failures threaten to destroy the nation.

In discussing these issues in the current context, however, I also want to make clear that they are not new problems which have suddenly emerged in the 1980s. In particular, in terms of their impact on teachers and teaching, they are, in many respects, old wine in new bottles. Larry Cuban's (1984) fascinating history of the nature and structure of American classrooms from 1890 to 1980, on which I have drawn heavily, makes it clear that the traditions which help to structure teaching and define the nature of schooling have deep roots in American culture. Despite the widespread view expressed by many of the current critics of schools that first John Dewey and progressive education and, more recently, the criticism and reform movements of the 1960s, had destroyed American schools' commitment to such fundamental educational aims as broadly achieving high levels of literacy and numeracy, Cuban makes it clear that such reform efforts actually had a very minor impact on patterns of teaching and learning. For Cuban, teaching, circa 1980, is more like teaching in 1890 than it is different. This may indeed be a problem, as I believe it is, but it is not the problem identified by critics who see American education as having gone to the dogs under the influence of the progressives.

This belief among the media and educational policy makers— politicians, administrators, researchers, and federal and state education bureaucrats—devalued the professional competence of teachers and strengthened the view that major educational decisions should be made not by those who were working with children, but by people who were supposed to know better about such things as how children learn, how school systems should be managed to guarantee successful outcomes, and, most importantly, how to package instruction and test for results. This opinion emerged clearly in response to the earlier crisis in America's confidence in its schools which resulted from the Soviet Union's launching of the first Sputnik in 1957 (which was discussed in terms of some of its effects on English teaching in Chapter II).

In an attempt to solve the problems that were perceived at that time, two major solutions were developed: federal and foundation support for the continuing education of teachers, and the development of what were called teacher-proof curricula. I've already discussed the first approach, so I won't dwell on it extensively here except to point out that it gradually withered and died, in part because of the drain on the nation's finances caused by the Vietnam War, but even more significantly because the second solution really took off and has been growing steadily ever since. And, clearly, the second solution contradicts the premises of the first since, if curricula were to be teacher-proof—that is, to be employable by teachers with equal effect regardless of the teacher's level of competence—then there was no need for worrying further about how competent teachers really were.

Although the development of such curricula, which really meant prepackaged instructional programs which would include all of the materials and activities needed for a particular grade or subject, neatly structured and sequenced, is in some respects a substantial change from an earlier more laissez-faire approach to such matters, they could not have had the influence they have had or been employed as widely as they have been if they had not fit quite neatly into the existing structures and ethos of schooling. As Cuban (1984) has shown, the consistent pattern of instruction in American schools has been a teacher-centered one, by which he means:

- Teacher talk exceeds student talk during instruction.
- Instruction occurs frequently with the whole class; small group or individual instruction occurs less frequently.
- Use of class time is determined by the teacher.
- The classroom is usually arranged in rows of desks or chairs facing a blackboard with a teacher's desk nearby. (p 3.)

To which I would add the assumptions of common sense that we have already explored, including significantly the code theory of communication and the behavioristically-based learning theory that learning proceeds from the bottom up and can be most sensibly sequenced in small, atomistic bits. This last is, of course, the key to understanding both the nature and the cause of the development of such instructional packages. They were developed largely by people who believed in the behaviorist account of learning.

We have already looked at the flaws of such a conception of learning and I will not rehearse them here, but it's important to understand in this context that such packages have had an almost completely restrictive effect on teacher autonomy. That is exactly the effect the packagers intended them to have, since the clear, if not wholly explicit, message being sent to teachers was: *You* cannot be trusted to make instructional decisions, therefore *we* (who are wiser and more responsible) will make them for you. No matter that you may know your children better than we do, no matter that you may have different ideas about how children learn, no matter that such instruction will remove nearly all of the human contact in the classroom either between teacher and student or student and student, we know better and we will decide. As an added bonus for teachers (who were known to be lazy anyway; why else would they be willing to work such short hours and insist on all those vacations), employing such programs would make the job even easier because no thinking and little effort would be required. *And*, and here was the stick that went with the carrot of making teaching easier, we will hold you accountable for student progress by testing your charges so often that we will be aware of any deviation from following the approved program.

The *we* here were largely people well-removed from the realities of classroom life: bureaucrats and administrators, educational publishers and test makers, think-tank researchers and instructional theorists. It is also probably significant that they were and are largely men, while classroom teachers, particularly at the elementary level where such packaging has been most pervasive and most pernicious, were and are primarily women. It is indeed ironic that during a period when women have been making substantial gains in entry into other fields and professions, their autonomy and authority in the profession that has always been most open to them was being significantly eroded. Is there a cause-and-effect relationship here?

It's tempting to hold the packagers and publishers responsible for the problems these approaches have created, and indeed they do deserve a fair share of the blame for not actually developing the real expertise they have claimed to have. But those closer to the classroom, administrators at the school and district levels (also largely men), and even teachers themselves must shoulder a fair amount of the responsibility for embracing such programs so eagerly. So, too, teacher educators (more men!) must bear a substantial part of the blame for not helping teachers develop the confidence and the competence necessary to resist the onslaught. But apportioning blame is not really the issue here; there is plenty to go around. Instead, we must look at the effect of such programs.

testing, Testing, TESTING!

One of the major effects such packages have had is to dramatically increase the amount of, the impact of, and the reliance on testing at all levels of schooling. While schools and teachers have always wanted to know how their pupils were doing and have used tests and a variety of other assessment measures to do so for a long time, never before has testing played such a dramatic and pervasive role in all aspects of the curriculum. In one sense, virtually all of the instructional processes involved in teacher-proof curriculum packages are themselves tests: worksheets, workbooks, exercises, drills, and so on are all designed to measure student achievement and, especially, to determine what the student doesn't know. These, in turn, are supplemented by more explicit tests: diagnostic tests at the beginning of an instructional sequence, mastery tests throughout it, and a final, cumulative test at the end. These test processes are, themselves, designed really as practice for the *real* tests, the standardized tests of reading, language skills, mathematics, and so on which are used to assess student achievement on, usually, a yearly basis. And these tests are, in turn, supposed to provide the basis for the ultimate tests: the SAT or ACT tests which determine college and university entrance.

In addition to the mind-numbing frequency of such testing, several other things should be noted. The most crucial, in this context, is that the yearly standardized tests are explicitly designed as instruments of school and teacher control. They are mandated by schools, districts, and, more and more frequently, by states, as a way of checking up on educational progress. The test scores are frequently published in newspapers and used to make comparisons, much in the way that batting averages are used to compare baseball players. Principals whose school's scores are judged to be too low are under enormous pressures to raise them, as are districts and even whole states. In addition to leading to fraud and cheating of various kinds, such pressures have been directly translated to teachers with the explicit or implicit message: *Teach to the tests so the scores will go up.* Even when the message is delivered subtly, everyone involved understands that, in a climate of intense scrutiny and pressure to produce results, anything that can be assumed to increase test scores will be judged good and worthy of investment of time and money; anything that can't be so guaranteed will be phased out or eliminated.

Now this might not be a terrible thing if the tests were any good. It would still not be desirable to create a school structure which so successfully restricted the capacity of teachers and students to determine their own educational processes and priorities, but it is made far more disastrous by the fact that the tests themselves are almost completely invalid. *They just don't test what they purport to test.* That is, in the area of language education, the reading tests *don't* validly test reading ability, the writing tests *don't* validly test writing ability, and so on. (I'm not sufficiently expert in such fields as mathematics or science to be sure that such tests are as bad as those in the language area, but from what I've read, they seem to be.)

There are a variety of reasons why this is so. Some of them stem from the fact that the test makers are the ideological cousins of the curriculum developers in that their learning theory is behaviorist, and their conceptions of reading and writing are based on both abilities being the result of an aggregate of atomic skills. Tests that focus on such skills are only as valid as the theoretical framework which embodies them. We have already seen some of the weaknesses of that theoretical framework from a learning perspective,

and the more one understands the holistic, transactional, and purposeful quality of both reading and writing, the more it seems clear
that standardized tests are the ultimate dummy runs. What this
means, of course, is that a student's capacity to correctly identify,
say, the right initial consonant of the word which labels a picture
of a ball may or may not have anything to do with her capacity to
read. And, similarly, the young writer's capacity to write a business
letter ordering an imaginary item from an imaginary company, or
to write an essay arguing an invented opinion for an invented
audience, may not have much to do with whether or not such a
student can write in any real sense.

Some writing-testing mavens have argued that you don't
really need to have students write at all in order to test their "writing ability." They base this judgment on the fact that there is a very
high correlation between scores on writing sample tests and scores
on multiple choice, machine-scorable tests of grammar and usage.
The correlation is, indeed, very high, usually well over 80 percent,
but most writing teachers prefer actual writing samples, since they
seem to have more validity. One of the advantages of using writing
samples is that it is more likely to encourage schools to require
students to write rather than just teaching grammar and usage.
This can be a positive change, as it was, for example, when New
York State introduced a writing sample for fifth-grade students,
thereby dramatically increasing the concern for and amount of
elementary school writing. But from an uncommonsense perspective, perhaps the correlation can be better explained by the fact that
both kinds of tests are so artificial that neither really tests much
except test-taking ability, which, given the pervasiveness of tests,
may be a valuable thing for students to possess, but which is not to
be confused with genuine achievement.

A further limitation of such testing is that it can only ask
questions which have a right answer. This certainly seems consistent with common sense, and it certainly has a long history in the
pattern of questioning typical of teacher-centered classrooms, but
it's seriously flawed in language education. It limits language testing from two directions: First, it can mean that questions get asked
because the right answer can be determined; and second, and most
important, questions that don't have right answers, and short ones
at that, can't be asked at all. The significant flaw here is that if we
want to know how well someone has read something, what we are
concerned with is how well they understood it. This doesn't depend on how they have decoded it, which can be assessed by a
right answer format, but it depends on the meaning they have
made from it, which can't be tested that way. Since meaning is

dependent on individual inferencing, based on using the principle of relevance in a transactional process of active meaning making, questions about what someone has understood do not have universal right answers and must be asked in an open-ended, not fill-in-the-blank or multiple choice, format.

Indeed, the principal flaw of standardized tests in reading and writing is that they almost completely ignore the fact that both processes are individually meaning centered. We don't write to write or read to read, and yet that is exactly what students are asked to do on reading and writing tests. That's why they are the ultimate in dummy-run activities, and, as such, they just don't tell us anything about the capacity of the same student who may do poorly—or well—on such tests to perform in meaningful reading and writing contexts. Indeed, in an effort to make such tests "fair" to all students regardless of previous background or experience, their out-of-context quality has to be strengthened so that no one will have a special advantage in taking them. The reading passages will be equally foreign to all students' experiences, the writing prompts equally boring, and the vocabulary words equally obscure for all.

What is particularly ironic in view of their claims to fairness is the fact that most of these tests are built to assure that a substantial number of students will fail them. In some cases, this is because the tests are norm referenced, usually by grade level, which means that they are built on the assumption that half of the fifth graders who take them will be reading below grade level, and therefore, in that sense, to seem to have failed to make normal progress. What makes this kind of test even more insidious is that such "grade levels" themselves are not determined by any meaningful assessment of what fifth graders ought to be able to do, but by giving the test to a supposedly "typical" population of children and seeing where the fifth graders' average performance happens to fall out.

Despite such flaws, which are well known, the concept of "reading on grade level" has entered the realm of educational common sense not only within schools and publishers' offices, but outside of them in the language of parents and the press. When the public looks to see whether or not schools are doing well, the number of students reading on grade level is frequently taken as a useful benchmark of progress. Since school people are well aware of this, they have often taken to exploiting the vagaries of the norming process by selecting their tests from those known to have less rigorous norms. Since the scores are reported with equivalent language—the ubiquitous grade level—the public's apprehensions can be assuaged by being able to report higher scores without following the more tedious route of actually trying to improve the reading ability of the children. It is hard to avoid sounding cynical about such manipulations, but they certainly show, if nothing else, the insidious effects of an overreliance on testing.

Even beyond the problems involved in developing such "norms" for the wide variety of students in American schools, it also must be remembered that in constructing such tests, standard practice is to eliminate all questions which everyone gets right (or wrong) and keep only those which "discriminate" because some of the kids get them wrong. This has the effect of ignoring whole ranges of achievement which everyone has mastered and over-magnifying whatever differences remain. In principle, therefore, it would be possible for all fifth graders to have mastered, say, 75 percent of what an independent judgment might characterize as what should have been achieved by ten-year-olds. None of what everyone has learned will be reflected in the test scores because all of the items used are those which competitively distinguish students from one another in the remaining 25 percent of the learning objectives. So if, for example, after reading the paragraph that precedes this one, all, or virtually all, students correctly (or incorrectly) answered a question like either (24) or (25), the question would be thrown out.

24. In the passage above, *assuage* means:
    a. aggravate b. calm c. soothe d. urge e. assume
25. The best title for the paragraph above is:
    a. Grade level accurately determines reading achievement.
    b. Grade level scoring leads to educational fraud.
    c. Grade levels are now part of educational common sense.
    d. Grade levels can be manipulated by choice of tests.
    e. Grade levels distort reading achievement reporting.

Although I made up these questions and they are, therefore, not strictly representative of such tests, they are illustrative of their format, and the deliberate level of difficulty of the "distracters"—testese for the wrong answers—is quite typical. The second type of question—the reading test maker's format about asking about the "main idea" of a passage—presents particularly tricky issues since determining the main idea of a passage is always dependent on the particular meaning made in the particular transaction with the text by a particular reader. In question 25, although I expect there would be little difficulty in ruling out (a) as a possible answer, a good case could be made for each of the other four. If pressed I think I would choose (e), but I would respect arguments for any of the other three. In keeping with the transactional perspective taken here and consonant with relevance theory, part of what determines what any reader will think is the main idea of a passage is the extent to which they find particular parts of it "new information." Since new information will be more striking, hence more noteworthy, than the information we already had before we read the passage, it may very well strike a reader as the "main" idea she is getting from the passage, whatever the author's intent or whatever other readers may construct for their meaning.

Lest anyone think that the vocabulary type question is more "objective," what choice did you make? I may have cheated a bit by including both "calm" and "soothe" as answers—would "heal" have been a more or less "fair" alternative? What I had in mind was more like soothe than calm, but again, a good case could be made for either. And neither is completely "objective." And worse, the more usual practice is for no context to be provided at all.

This may seem to be making more of the problem than it warrants, but since test makers have been forced to make their tests public by New York State's truth in testing law, it has not been uncommon for contradictions and ambiguities to be revealed. In some cases, test takers' complaints have revealed that there was more than one "right" answer to a question, and in a couple of instances they have shown that the test makers' chosen answer was actually either wrong or at least not the best choice according to independent expert opinion. Even such revelations have not squelched the general faith in such tests for their accuracy and objectivity, but it must be remembered that even the most carefully-prepared tests are subject to all of the subjective variety of the human meaning-making process. If language is never completely transparent as to its meaning, no test made with language and/or testing the understanding of language will ever be completely free of subjectivity.

This problem is dealt with somewhat better by so-called criterion referenced tests, which establish their achievement criteria in advance of students taking them. In such tests it would be, in principle, possible for everyone to pass, or, conversely, for everyone to fail. Such criteria are not absolute, however, but are developed by testers and bureaucrats in response to educational and political realities, and therefore for such tests, too, the criteria are either set to assure that some will fail and most will pass, or adjusted later to give the same result. Criterion referenced tests undoubtedly have the potential to be more useful and fairer in their assessment of children's learning, but they will not really be so until the criteria are based on a more valid understanding of learning and language development than they are now. As long as the construction of such tests remains in the hands of the behaviorists, they will usually be no better than their norm-referenced counterparts because the criteria they embody will be based on the same faulty conception of learning to read and write that the others are.

By building failure into the test results, several other negative consequences occur beyond the stigmatization of those individuals or schools that have "failed." One consequence is that they are used to identify children who need "remedial" help who are then, typically, removed from their regular classes and, again typically, almost never catch up despite the additional help. This happens partly because the help has tended to be more of the same, and partly because by being removed, children are confirmed in their negative self judgment and frequently give up. Perhaps even more insidious, the provision of extra personnel to schools for such remedial help is usually determined by low test scores, which gives the school at least some motivation *not* to succeed, because to do so would mean a loss of staff and a consequent increase in class sizes. And, of course, structuring the tests to guarantee failure confirms the general expectation that some students are genetically or environmentally marked for failure, and therefore provides a continuing rationale for the tracking and grouping which is so much a part of the common sense of schooling.

A particularly insidious effect of such tests has been their use as instruments of teacher control. This has made even teachers who know better, and many if not most do, teach to the tests out of self defense. Although it would be hard to prove, in my experience of working with practicing teachers, no other single factor has been as responsible as mass testing for the steady diminishing of teacher autonomy which has marked this decade. Tests drive the curriculum and teaching practice and hamper efforts at change because the all-too-common statements of teachers are: "We must prepare children for the————(state, district, Regents, SAT, or whatever) test," and anything that does not directly seem connected to doing so can't, or won't, be done. And, ironically, under the guise of accountability, such testing has increased teacher responsibility for the outcomes of student learning while simultaneously decreasing their autonomy to make the professional decisions which might be able to influence it.

Unfortunately, I must also stress the fact that the short-term prospects for reversing the testing trend are bleak indeed since more and more educational jurisdictions are developing and using them in a growing range of areas. Worst of all, most of the newer tests being developed are explicitly designed to test what are called "minimum competencies." Even if they were based on the real basics of competence, which they are not, they have had the counter-productive effect of making what were intended to be the flooring underpinning schooling into the ceiling for most student achievement. Even teachers, either on the job or as a prerequisite to certification, are increasingly being tested by minimum competency tests of the same format, which are equally invalid as assessments of teacher competence.

Even tests of this sort could be made more valuable if they asked students to explain and justify their answers, but then they wouldn't be machine scorable and their actual lack of objectivity would be revealed for all. We certainly can't count on the emperors of testing to reveal the scantiness of their intellectual clothing, and, indeed most of them, like the legendary emperor, aren't aware of it. But those of us who have come to understand it cannot sit by and assume that the problem is insignificant or that it will somehow go away. If the trend is to be reversed, everyone involved must come to the recognition that *testing is the problem, not the solution.*

Uncommonsense Assessment

Nothing in the preceding discussion should be taken to mean that assessment of learning is not an important aspect of teaching and learning. The uncommonsense approach to assessment has several significant differences, however, which can be briefly sketched. Among the most important is that uncommonsense assessment is based on positive achievement rather than on deficiency identification. Uncommonsense assessment is, further, individual, holistic, and cumulative, and although it is criterion rather than norm referenced, the criteria used must be based on explicitly negotiated standards.

The importance of the last point—that the criteria must be understood by all concerned: students and parents as well as teachers and administrators—can't be overstressed. I remember teaching tenth graders some years ago, a class that had been following my first approximation of an uncommonsense approach. The group had been reading novels, poems, stories, and plays. They had been writing and talking about them in large and small groups. And they had been writing other sorts of things as well: sometimes their own stories or poems, sometimes essays and reports on subjects they chose. What we hadn't done was bring out the grammar books and do the kinds of grammar exercises which had been a staple of their junior high school experience. The combination of the absence of grammar and the lack of any discussion about why we were doing what we were doing eventually made them nervous, and early in March they caucused and appointed a class spokesman—who happened to be the class clown; I'm sure they and he figured he couldn't get in more trouble than he already had—to say: "Now Mr. Mayher, we don't want you to think we aren't having a good time in here, because we are. But when are we going to get to English?"

The question caught me up short, but it made me realize then and since that I could not take for granted that my goals for teaching and learning, or my criteria for assessing student progress, were clear to my students. As we talked further, it became even more evident that while the students had enjoyed much of what they had read, written, and talked about, they hadn't seen it much as a learning experience—or, particularly, as a *school learning* experience. This was partly true simply because they had enjoyed it, and for the most part school learning had been anything but: boring, tedious, hard, drudgery were some of the words they used. So I had to assure them that enjoying something didn't mean they were not learning; quite the contrary, I said, since most of us learn most effectively when we are enjoying what we are doing, at least in the sense of surmounting a challenge, and wherever possible, in the sense of actually attaining mastery of something we value.

Most important, however, I realized that I had neither been sharing my goals for learning with them nor helping them see how well they were achieving them. To do so I asked them to collect the papers they had written in the fall, and the next day in small groups they looked at their own and each other's work to see how it had changed. They were quite surprised and pleased to see that they were generally prouder of the papers they had written in February than of those they had written in September. They even were able to identify many aspects of why this was so. Not only were the papers generally longer and more fully developed, but they were more interesting and more carefully argued, with better evidence and a more readable structure. They also noticed that their progress had not been strictly linear, that is, each paper was not necessarily better than the one before. Too many other variables including, particularly, the difficulty of the task and the amount of interest they had had in each, had had an effect. We also talked about the books we had read and even about how the class had learned how to talk with each other, and they were able to see improvement in both their reading and talking competencies which paralleled their writing improvement.

The result of this process of reflection was salutary for us all. They had come to see more clearly what they were accomplishing, and I had come to learn how essential it is to make these criteria explicit. So often students feel that teacher grading is arbitrary and capricious, that they have lost or never acquired their own sense of responsibility for their own learning and its assessment. Further, such reflection enables the teacher to enact the role of coach which Sizer (1984) and many other contemporary commentators have seen as the ideal teacher role. *For the teacher to become a coach, the key ingredient is that the standards of achievement to be mastered must be public, explicit, and shared by both teacher and student.* By leaving the standards to be achieved and the criteria by which successful or unsuccessful performances were to be evaluated shrouded in mystery, I had not enabled the students to gauge their own development.

Once this is accomplished it places the student exactly where he or she ought to be: responsible for his or her own learning and for the assessment of that learning. This principle in turn implies two others: that the curriculum should be subject to negotiation between teacher and learners and that self-assessment is the key to learning. In a sense, of course, all schooling involves these principles to a certain extent. Powell et al. (1985) and Sedlak et al. (1986) have made it clear, for example, that contemporary high school classes are based on tacit "treaties" between teacher and those being taught as to the amount of work which will be required in a given course. Once the treaty has been established, the students agree to do the required work and to be orderly in class, but the teacher cannot exceed the demand level which has been tacitly agreed to without risking rebellion. Both the Powell and Sedlak research teams, however, report dismay over the low level of achievement which is routinely required under such treaties. Courses where high demands are made and met are extremely rare even in "good" schools with "good" students.

Negotiating the Curriculum

The kind of negotiation being advocated here, however, is quite different, and when I was teaching those tenth graders I had no real idea of how to do it. This uncommonsense approach to negotiation is exemplified most clearly in a collection of papers edited by Garth Boomer (1982) describing how it can be done called *Negotiating the Curriculum: A Teacher-Student Partnership.* Boomer and his colleagues attempt to demystify the processes of curriculum selection and the evaluation of learning by making them public, explicit, and based on genuine student choice. Although Boomer and his colleagues recognize and build into the negotiation process whatever external constraints are placed on the learning situation (from the established curriculum, from external tests, and so on), *the specific learning experiences of the curriculum, its pace and structure, and the means of evaluating what had been learned are all potentially subject to negotiation.* We saw such a process in action in Dan Kelly's process of working with his class to determine the short story unit they worked on as a whole class, as well as in the process of determining the individual and small group projects they were engaged in. The negotiation process begins with the identification of a general topic or area (these are often determined by the overall curriculum). Once that has been decided, the process then involves four questions:

1. What do I (we) know, believe, assume about X?
2. What do I (we) want to learn, find out about X?
3. How am I (are we) going to learn it?
4. How will the learning be demonstrated and evaluated?

Each of these questions goes to the heart of the teaching/learning process, and by making them explicit and subject to negotiation not only is it more likely that students will find something within the broad topic that they are genuinely interested in pursuing, but also the process itself can be educationally significant. By exploring what individuals and the group already know about a topic, the redundancy and repetition that so often characterize schooling can be minimized. Further, since at least some of the group's beliefs and assumptions are likely to be incomplete or inaccurate, it provides a basis for deeper explorations which can extend, refine, or challenge them.

By making the choice of what is to be learned and how it is to be accomplished subject to negotiation, students can learn how to select manageable areas of inquiry and develop a wide variety of strategies for carrying them out. Commonsense teaching usually involves the teacher making all of these decisions, which not only diminishes the possibility of student commitment to the topic, but, more important, robs the students of an opportunity to learn how to make such choices. If our goal is to have students become independent, life-long learners, the negotiation process facilitates this development by demanding that students learn to choose responsibly in an atmosphere which encourages risk taking. In the early stages of such processes students frequently set themselves tasks which are more challenging than they recognize and some unanticipated problems almost always turn up. But in a classroom built on negotiation, such difficulties can be resolved through renegotiation, and the lesson can be a valuable one rather than an experience of failure.

The experience of teachers and students who have participated in such negotiations is more often than not a positive one, even though the students find they are working harder than ever before. One of the great commonsense myths, in fact, is that if students are given a voice in such decisions, they will inevitably choose the easiest possible path. While this can happen if the teacher is not clear about the constraints required for the quality and quantity of work to be done, it seems more characteristic of commonsense classes where implicit treaties are arrived at than in negotiated ones where the process is explicit and public. In a school setting where the rules of the game are to get the highest possible grade with the least possible effort, students frequently do appear to be eager to take the low road. In a negotiated setting, in contrast, where the students have asked questions they are genuinely interested in, they seem more likely to err on the high effort side than on the lazy side.

In the schools studied by the Sedlak and Powell teams, the key problem for all seemed to be the lack of engagement with the curriculum on the part of the students. This was just as true in the blue ribbon suburban schools as in those in the inner cities, and in each case it seems clear that one of the keys to the lack of engagement was the students' sense that they had no voice in determining what they learned or how they learned it. Those still willing to play the school game were content to amass the tokens of success needed to permit entry to the next level of schooling so that eventually they could be done with the whole thing and be able to get on with the real business of adult life. Those who had lost faith in the possibility that schooling would be the ticket to personal prosperity were either anticipating dropping out or were so completely alienated as to remain in school only because their friends were there and it was easier than working.

While negotiation itself will not fully solve all the problems of lack of engagement, by putting students in the center of the process of determining what and how they are learning, it provides a context for making connections between the learner's personal concerns and the school's notions of what ought to be learned. Given the fact that, in language education in particular, the connection between student purposes for reading and writing (as well as speaking and listening) and the development of higher levels of achievement is clear and explicit, negotiation must play a central role. Unless students have a voice in determining what they read and write, they will have little motivation to improve their competence in doing so. Few students, for example, will bother to genuinely engage in revising their writing if they are not genuinely committed to finding the best way to say what they want to say. And yet we know that writers must learn to revise if they are to develop high levels of achievement. So if revision is one of the keys to writing development, then student writers must be committed to their written efforts, and that can only result from their involvement in the process of choosing what they are to write about.

Further, negotiation is the natural way to make the criteria for assessment explicit and mutually shared. When students are involved in the process of determining what would be sensible ways of demonstrating and evaluating what they have learned, the standards of judgment to be used must be understood and agreed to by all parties. Further, such assessment need not be limited to the conventional processes of quizzes, tests, and teacher-marked papers. All kinds of other demonstrations (posters, panel discussions, films, audio and video tapes, oral reports, dramatic enactments, and so on) can be used in addition to more conventional papers and written reports. And, in addition, both the learners individually and the class as a whole can be directly involved in the processes of assessment. This last concept is crucial since part of the negotiation process demands that the students recognize the standards of quality being employed in such judgments, and that they too share in the responsibility of assessment rather than leaving it solely in the hands of the teacher.

In some respects this is the hardest aspect of negotiation to learn because it is the most direct violation of the principles of commonsense schooling. It not only violates the implicit rule that teachers require work and students try to do as little of it as possible while pretending to be killing themselves, but it puts the burden of responsibility directly on the students' shoulders. No more "I got an A" versus "He gave me a D." Further, it challenges the notion that schooling is a zero-sum game where a reward to student X diminishes the chances of rewarding student Y. No more grading on a curve! This has been a particularly hard thing for successful students to unlearn (as well as for those teachers whose sense of power and control depend upon being the sole arbiter of quality in the room), but the negotiation process offers the possibility of getting all of these assumptions out in the open so that they can be discussed and modified where appropriate.

Also, it is this aspect of negotiation which makes it more rather than less likely that levels of excellence in achievement will be higher in an uncommonsense environment than in a commonsense one. By making the standards both public and reasonable, in the sense that all parties agree that they can be feasibly reached, both effort and levels of performance rise. The feasibility caveat is an important one since it does no good to set high standards if all they mean is that everyone will fail. No matter how much I'd like to run a four-minute mile, it's just not going to happen and setting it as my standard would only guarantee failure. But one area where almost every critic of the schools agrees is that standards are probably not high enough. This problem cannot be solved by merely raising standards arbitrarily, but it can be solved gradually by mutual negotiation. Students have no desire for low levels of achievement in areas they care about, so the key is to ensure that they care about the levels of genuine achievement that they attain in school.

Schools and the Economy

While there have been many kinds of pressures, both external and internal, that have led to teachers and teaching being under increasing control by tests and testers, one of the most significant is the perceived connection between education and the economic health of the nation. The logic of this connection goes something like this: Schools educate the people who run and work in the economy. The American economy of the late nineteenth century and the first two-thirds of the twentieth century was the most powerful the world had ever known. Therefore the schools must have been doing something right. Since then, the American economy has been slipping and now seems increasingly threatened by such allies (and former enemies) as Japan and Germany. This threat is particularly apparent in what used to be our major pride and joy, the development and use of technology. Therefore the schools must be doing something wrong. This was, in essence, the logic of *A Nation at Risk.*

Expressed at this level of generality, this logic makes a certain amount of sense, but it has serious flaws as well. It probably overplays the impact of schooling in both directions. Neither the success of the economy not its failures are attributable solely to schooling; too many other factors have and continue to play significant roles, including the overall state of the world economy during the period, the effect of two world wars and of the massive expenditures on defense since World War II by the United States but not its competitors, the effects of prosperity and success on motivation to achieve, the effects of various media—in McLuhan's (1964) sense including the automobile, electricity, and the telephone as well as radio, television, movies and, most recently, the computer—on people's lives and work styles, and so on.

Such a logic also frequently confuses correlation with causation so that, for example, when census data revealed that people with a college education made more money over their careers than their less well-educated peers during most of this period, the assumption has been often made that a college degree caused their economic success. Other explanations, which didn't provide such an instrumental role for schooling as such, have been unseen or ignored. These probably include the fact that until very recently the percentage of people who earned college degrees was so small and college education so costly that other factors may have accounted for the observed correlation. One might make the mildly heretical observation that those who got college degrees were already the economically-advantaged segment of the population, and they might have had the same big career earning powers even if they hadn't gone to college.

The simplistic connection between level of schooling and individual economic success does seem to have become less common in recent years. There aren't ads in the New York City subways any more saying: *Stay in school and you'll get a good job.* The ones that say *if u cn rd ths, u cn gt a gd jb* are still there, but that says something about an employable skill, not levels of schooling. And, of course, this is the rub: To what extent should schools be concerned directly with producing people who will be good workers, technicians, managers, and so on?

No answer to this question will provoke universal assent, but in my view it is the wrong question. That is, the kinds of goals for language education that I have expressed here would, if enacted, educate people through learning experiences which would help make them flexible, capable of coping with change, and able to understand themselves and their culture both broadly and deeply. They would, further, possess a wide range of competencies as language users in all four modes and other related abilities, including having learned how to learn and having had enough positive experiences of learning and language use to want to continue to learn. Many of these abilities will be vital prerequisites for a wide variety of jobs, but for the most part they are not directly or narrowly vocational. They will not fit people well for jobs which involve mind-numbing routine and little chance for either individual initiative or critical thought.

And this last point may be the real problem. Some of the more conspiracy-minded among us have found the criticism of progressive approaches to education to be expressing not a worry that standards have been abandoned by such pedagogies, but a fear that they might actually succeed in providing students with critical faculties and intellectual skills which would make them unwilling to tolerate the normal conditions of employment in a mass production/service economy world. As David Cohen pointed out in his chapter of *The Shopping Mall High School* (Powell, Farrar, and Cohen 1985): "Perhaps high schools teach students what they most need to know: how to endure boredom without protest" (p. 303). And as Bluestone and Harrison (1982) have pointed out, the number of jobs which pay good wages and require the kind of intelligence and language-using ability uncommonsense teaching hopes to develop has been decreasing in recent years. Indeed, Giroux and McLaren (1986) have noted a striking absence of the rhetoric of democracy and of the need to produce democratic citizens in the recent criticisms of schools, and from the uncommonsense perspective, *enabling students to become critical citizens in a democracy is one of the most salient of educational goals.*

Whether or not it has been the intent, the effect of instructional packaging and frequent testing has been to reduce both teachers and students to people who monitor and perform the filling in of essentially meaningless blanks. Such instructional routines have taken the spirit and meaning from schooling and further emphasized its lack of connection to the meaning-making processes of real life. Such experiences may be a useful preparation for some kinds of mindless employment, but they are hardly likely to provide the basis for the kind of reinfusion of creative energy and imagination which the same critics who bemoan the loss of educational standards see as the essence of the revival of the economy. Further, they provide no basis for the development of pride in craft or the investment of commitment necessary to see that a task is not just finished but completed with pleasure and a sense of accomplishment. Such competencies can only be developed by being involved in projects which have meaningful outcomes for the learner, and this is impossible in the kind of instructional routines which typify teacher-proof curricula.

It may be that many people outside of schools see sorting people in terms of their fitness for future employment as the major function of schooling, with a small elite getting what I would characterize as a real (uncommonsense) education, and the rest learning to show up regularly and on time prepared to endure boredom. This position may be rooted in a genuine conviction that only a few are genetically endowed with the capacity to profit from more independent learning, or it may stem from a desire of the parents of society's haves to maintain their economic advantages and pass them on to their children and, perhaps, the most deserving of the lower orders, or it may be a combination of the two. As has been argued throughout this book, however, the genetic argument has no firm basis in fact, since human learners at age five are far more alike than they are different, and democratic schools in a democratic society need not be a party to elitist values and practices.

Challenging the assumptions that underlie these practices will not be easy, however, particularly as the kinds of instructional packaging and skills-and-drills teaching they embody have been justified and defended precisely because they are the same for all students and are therefore perceived to be fairer and more democratic. They are assumed to provide equal opportunity for all, but this assumption is seriously flawed because it is based on a transmission/code model of instruction which ignores the role of readers and listeners (not to mention speakers and writers, because opportunities for either are seriously limited in such instructional schemes) in the meaning-making process. The net effect of them, therefore, is to reinforce whatever social class differences there are in the background experiences necessary to fully participate in literacy activities. Those who come to school with extensive experiences in being read to, for example, may not be helped much by such programs, but they are not hurt by them as much as those who don't have such experiences and who, it is claimed by those who argue that such programs are fair and democratic, are supposed to benefit the most from them.

If schools are to fulfill their democratic mandate for equal opportunity, and to do so in ways which will be helpful to, if not directly vocationally related to, the health of the economy, programs which set everyone the same tasks without regard for what the learner brings to the situation or the meanings she may, or may not, be making from performing them, will not do the trick. In fact, if we are to prepare students to have meaningful choices in their vocations, *we must concentrate more on equality of outcomes than on equality of opportunity*, at least for those aspects of schooling which can be characterized as general education, of which language and literacy education certainly are an important component. And, ironically perhaps, the worst way to assure equality of outcomes is to have everyone do exactly the same things in school.

Worst of all, for teachers and students alike, the experience of spending period after period, day after day, and year after year on tasks that were developed by "experts" outside the classroom context robs learners of one of the major learning experiences that they ought to be getting in school: contact with teachers' minds and hearts. One of the great traditional sources of implicit learning by students has always been that of working with teachers who were living examples of people who used the competencies schools hope to develop in meaningful ways in their own lives. If teachers are people who read and write with power and acumen, who care about the world they live in and its problems, who use language as a means of continual learning, who are in short, learners themselves, then students can see the goals and values of the critically literate community enacted and embodied. If, on the other hand, teachers are only perceived as workbook dispensers and correctors, as test givers and evaluators, and as people whose own control over what happens in their classrooms is radically limited, then what students learn is, in effect, that the kind of education teachers give lip service to is essentially hollow, since it has not been able to free them to be their own person in their own classrooms. So that when students reject such education, they may be making a positive choice, however disastrous its societal consequences.

Teacher autonomy is important because it is the only basis upon which student autonomy can be built. Students learn as much or more from the structure and processes of classroom life as they do from its content. And if teachers don't strive to retake control of those structures and processes and to become responsible for their own teaching, students will continue to learn that the skills schools are trying to develop have little value. The pressures for right answers, for short-term, testable objectives, and for uniform teacher practices won't be easy to combat, but unless and until we try to do so, the kind of general education and language education that learners receive will continue to be mind limiting, not mind expanding. And such a course not only threatens the future health of the economy, but the very basis of democratic society.

The Role of Teacher Education

In my discussion of the common sense of teaching and its historical tradition, I don't want to let my colleagues in teacher education off the hook for our significant failures in affecting this situation. While the socialization processes and more or less formal apprenticeship systems that operate in schools have certainly played a major role in perpetuating the conservative quality of the culture of teaching, it is nevertheless the case that virtually every teacher in America has had some kind of explicit teacher education in an institution of "higher learning." And we have simply not done an effective job.

Or maybe it would be more apt to say that we have had exactly the effect we deserved. Insofar as the structures and learning processes of our classrooms have been teacher-centered, we have taught our future teachers to be teacher-centered. Insofar as we have taught future teachers instructional techniques and provided them with activities to teach with and classroom management skills to order and organize their classrooms, we have taught our students to manage instruction, to concern themselves with materials and activities, and to survive in the real world of schools. Insofar as we have eschewed theory, taught behaviorist learning principles, and have not been models of people who critique their own practice, we have taught prospective teachers that theory doesn't count, that behaviorism accounts for learning, and that they need not reflect on their own practice. Even when we may have *advocated* different approaches to instruction or a different theoretical framework underlying it, insofar as these alternatives have not been *embodied* in our own practice, our students have easily learned to discount them; to do as we do, not as we say.

Since it is well known that teachers teach as they were taught, some teacher educators have tried to shift their own burden of responsibility to the school experience prospective teachers have had as students and even to our higher education colleagues. While certainly such models do provide a powerful influence in shaping eventual teacher beliefs as to "the way it spozed to be," those of us who are directly charged with preparing future teachers and who are, for the most part, the ones involved in most inservice education for practicing teachers, have a special responsibility to provide alternative models of beliefs and practices if we ever hope to see change in teaching practice. If future and practicing teachers have never had an active, implicit, and purposeful experience of *school* learning, they will not have any models at all for making connections between the kinds of spontaneous concept learning they have done in their out-of-school lives, and the ways that kind of learning can be embedded in a school context and combined with the active learning of scientific concepts, which is the special province of schooling.

I have been struggling during my years in teacher education to make my practice more congruent with my principles, to reveal and discuss my own frustration with the constraints of time and grades and other factors which make it hard for me to do so, and, in general to practice what I preach. It hasn't been easy and I am by no means satisfied with my efforts. The old habits die hard and the expectations of the students die even harder. I like to lecture, to transmit, to listen to the power of my own explanations as much as anyone. And my students have become so accustomed to looking to me for assessment of the worth of their learning that they are nearly unable to make such judgments of themselves for themselves. And, in many cases, they don't feel they are getting their money's, or their time's, worth if they are not being transmitted to.

In a recent summer program for experienced teachers, where my colleagues and I were trying to enact an uncommonsense learning structure, these problems manifested themselves with the additional dimension that some students felt hesitant to disagree with what they perceived to be the pedagogical position we were advocating, because they were fearful that such disputatious behavior would lead to penalties on the final evaluation. We solved the evaluation problem by negotiating with the students an evaluation system which protected their final grades, but which guaranteed each student a final conference to explore as honestly as we could our assessment of what they had achieved and where they still needed to improve. This solved some of the problems, particularly those of making a climate which permitted argument, but it didn't solve them all since in this domain many people, and many teachers especially, have not had enough experience with argument to be able to distinguish the *idea* being argued about from the *person* being argued with. And, further, given the nature of their prior school experience, some students continued to place more importance on what one of the teachers said than on a more interesting or significant point made by one of their peers. So, even in one of the best teaching/learning environments I have ever been lucky enough to be part of, it wasn't utopia, but unless we continue to try to change our practices as teacher educators, we certainly cannot expect anyone else to.

"Teaching and Learning: A Profound Confusion"

The title of this section is taken from a fine paper by Judith Wells Lindfors (1984) which explores her somewhat surprised realization that when asked to describe instances of student learning, many experienced and even expert teachers describe instances of teaching or of instructional activities. Her examples are drawn from a doctoral student, a primary teacher, a sociolinguist, and, most depressing of all, from her own second grade son, Erik, who showed her the power of the ways this confusion can be transmitted from teachers to children. In each instance, the examples dealt with reading, although she points out that they could have been drawn from many other areas, and in each case there was no recognition of "the difference between *teaching*—what teachers do, the instructional activities and sequences they design with the intention of increasing children's ability to relate language meanings to printed symbols—and *learning*, what children do to make print make sense" (pp. 601–602, her italics).

In the case of her son, he had described himself as: "I'm not good in school. I'm not good in reading." She was astonished because he "was not simply a child who 'knew how to read' but he was a reader, one who *did* the thing—avidly and with many purposes, his own purposes—whether for fun or information about dinosaurs or TV programs or how to assemble a toy." Probing further she asked, "What makes you think you're no good in reading? You read me stories lots of times."

Erik replied, "Yeah, but at school I don't finish the workbook pages and I'm no good at vowels."

She then goes on to point out that this is the same confusion in which a child "who had so effortlessly and confidently and naturally learned to read saw himself as an inadequate *learner* because he did not successfully move through the instructional sequence provided by the teacher. . . . He believed, wrongly, that his learning *was* the business of carrying out the teacher's sequence. He believed he was doing *his* thing badly (learning) because he was not doing *her* thing well (moving through her instructional sequence)" (pp. 603–604, her italics).

Reading her paper made me newly aware of the fact that I'd been noticing the same thing myself in a variety of contexts, but hadn't fully recognized it. In an earlier book (Mayher, Lester, and Pradl 1983) we describe a sequence of activities for exploring how writing to learn activities could be developed in various curricular areas. The first step was: "Define a learning objective in your discipline which is appropriate for your students." We went on to discuss the fact that one had to "be sure they are objectives rather than activities, a confusion we've frequently encountered when we've done this" (p. 90). I realized after reading Lindfors that these were the *same confusions*. The teachers who'd given us activities when asked for goals were focusing on what *they* were doing, not on how their students were learning. They did so not because we had given unclear directions but as a result of a much deeper and more profound misinterpretation of the relations between learning and teaching. We'd usually taken the blame on ourselves, willing, as teachers often are, to take responsibility for the problem which may, in some ways, be another instance of the same confusion: "If only I'd taught it better . . . "

In thinking about why this confusion exists, I've reached the tentative conclusion that it is consistent with the commonsense justification for teacher-centered instruction. In particular it derives from the axiomatic belief that:

• Whatever is learned must have been taught;

and its corollary:

• Students learn (only) what teachers teach.

Adherence to these two beliefs makes it natural to assume that there is no meaningful distinction between teaching and learning, and therefore it is perfectly appropriate to describe instructional activities when asked to describe learning.

As Chapters IV and V have shown, neither of these beliefs is true. Although it certainly can be true that teaching can facilitate learning, lots of learning, particularly language learning, happens without any teaching at all. Although students can learn from teachers, what they may be learning, as in the case of Erik, is not, say, reading—which he already knew how to do in any case—but that they aren't very good at something because they are unable to succeed in achieving within the context of the instructional sequence. Or, as noted in discussing teacher autonomy, students may be learning that teachers aren't very interesting or competent people because they don't seem to know that reading is for meaning, but think it is based on a boring process of filling in worksheets.

The Common Sense of Teaching

These beliefs are crucially important to recognize and understand because they help to explain some of the most pervasive qualities of what I have characterized as the common sense of teaching: that teachers transmit knowledge and skills to pupils, that in order to do so they must have sufficient authority and control to determine the nature and sequence of instruction, and that student learning achievements, particularly those demonstrated by test scores, directly reflect teaching practices. These elements of educational common sense go a long way toward accounting for why instructional packaging and testing has fit so neatly into the commonsense patterns of schooling. Even though such practices may undermine teacher autonomy, they do provide plenty of knowledge and skills to transmit. They may weaken teacher authority in the professional sense of being responsible for most of the decisions of instruction, but they reinforce and even enhance that aspect of teacher authority which is of most concern to most teachers: control of the classroom. And, further, by directly linking teaching and testing, they provide a means to assure that what is tested is what has been taught.

As Cuban (1984) has made very clear, these concerns, particularly for classroom control, are paramount for teachers. They are, based on his earlier research, the primary factors which have limited the effect of earlier efforts to bring about some of the changes in teaching practice which are consistent with the uncommonsense positions adopted throughout this book. Cuban's history of the modifications that teachers have made in progressive, student-centered practices to fit them into the existing dynamics of classroom practices makes instructive reading for any of us advocating similar changes. He concludes his book by saying: "No longer should the central issue about instruction be: how should teachers teach? Based on my experience and study of classrooms over the last century, I believe the central question is simply: how can what teachers already do be improved?" (p. 268).

For Cuban there are five major components of classroom life that have limited the power of attempts to change schools and have ensured that classrooms have stayed more similar than not during the last century. They can serve as a kind of summary of the common sense of teaching.

1. *Schooling as social control and sorting:* Since schooling functions mostly as a system for preparing students for bureaucratic and industrial work, it is important to stress obedience, punctuality, uniformity, and so on, and, therefore, if students don't learn much academic content, there is little public concern as long as they learn to act like good workers.

2. *School and classroom structures:* Physical space, furniture, forty minute periods for learning, and so on, together with a transmission model of teaching, particularly in high schools (and, of course, universities) have dictated efficient and convenient (for teachers and/or their supervisors) use of rows, whole-class teaching, standardized tests, skills-and-drills instruction, and so on.

3. *The culture of teaching:* Conservatism is its chief ethos. This is rooted in the type of people recruited into the profession [like me, as illustrated in Chapter II!]: people who reaffirm, rather than challenge, the role of schools, who intuitively absorbed lessons of how to teach as they watched their teachers, from kindergarten through the university, during over 15,000 hours of classroom instruction, and who survive by learning from their colleagues what *works*, a process of lore accumulation which reinforces what *is*, rather than nourishing skepticism and inquiry.

4. *Beliefs: individual and shared:* Deeply embedded ideas, many of them developed while teachers were students and preservice teachers, about teaching and learning which include such things as "knowledge must be transmitted to young people; the role of the school is to develop the mind and instill social values; students learn best in well-managed, noiseless classrooms where limits are made plain, academic rigor is prized, and where rules are equitably enforced by the teacher; and the teacher's authority, rooted in institutional legitimacy and knowledge, must be paid respectful attention" (Cuban 1984, p. 245).

5. *Feckless implementation of reform:* That is, reforms and attempts at reform were badly put into place, either imposed from

above without teacher participation in choice or implementation, or presented as new techniques which were then domesticated within the school culture without the necessary change of the underlying beliefs of teachers or structures of schooling. (All five based on Cuban 1984, pp. 240–246.)

While granting his view that "there are definite limits to any reforms aimed at altering classroom behavior" (p. 260), I would also argue that fundamental to the common sense of teaching is the view that *teaching is supposed to enhance learning*. If teachers are, as I believe they are, finally more concerned with student learning than with anything else, then it seems at least plausible to suppose that a change in teacher beliefs about the nature of learning, about the relationship between teaching and learning both in general and in specific curricular areas, and a new conception of such notions as power, authority, and control could have profound effects on the way business is conducted in classrooms.

I'm certainly not suggesting that a change in belief structures is easy to accomplish. The power of long-held constructs which have the virtue of working pretty well in the commonsense context of schools makes them resistant to change, in part because there seems to be little need to do so. And those teachers who are more concerned with their own comfort and control in the classroom than they are with anything else are not likely to be worried by explicit or implicit questions about whether or not traditional classroom routines are actually promoting the kinds of learning they are intended to. And, like Cuban, I know that even teachers who are concerned with student learning won't adopt an approach to classroom management which seems to promise only chaos and confusion.

Determining Teacher Competence

During the early 1970s, in a rather late response to concerns about the quality of teachers originally raised a decade earlier in the Sputnik crisis, many national and state agencies concerned with teacher education and certification attempted to use the teacher-licensing process to specify the abilities beginning teachers ought to have. The idea was that if such capacities could be specified in detail, then teacher education programs would know exactly what they had to do and would have appropriate criteria on which to assess the certifiability of prospective teachers. Called Competency Based Teacher Education (CBTE), this approach was intended to guarantee employers high-quality beginning teachers, to give substance to the previously rather vague course requirements which

had typified state licensing procedures, and to make teacher education more rigorous and therefore more immune to attacks from
those who saw it as mickey mouse stuff.

It was a hard idea to argue with since by appropriating the
term *competence,* anyone opposing it seemed to be in favor of incompetence. Further, it certainly seemed sensible enough to explore in
detail what beginners did need to know and be able to do, and to
use that knowledge to enrich teacher education programs and to
make sure that they did prepare beginners adequately. But when it
was attempted by my colleagues and me at New York University,
and in thousands of other teacher education programs around the
country, it just didn't work, either practically or conceptually. Practically, most institutions got bogged down in the nearly endless
lists of "competencies" teachers were expected to master; conceptually, the lists themselves just didn't capture the heart of the
matter. Trying to do so did help some of us come to understand
teaching better, however, so it wasn't a total loss, and that is why
I'm looking at the effort again here.

CBTE was also sometimes referred to as PBTE (Performance
Based Teacher Education) because the goal was to specify those
things that teachers had to be able to *do* in order to succeed in classrooms. This alternative label revealed more clearly the behaviorist/
positivist roots of the enterprise, since the criteria for success were
all to be specified in observable terms. This led some early developers of such programs to look carefully at what successful teachers
did and then write down lists of all of the observable behaviors they
manifested. (The criteria for identifying such successful teachers
were never made very clear, but this was only the beginning difficulty such programs faced.) The lists rapidly mushroomed to nearly
unmanageable proportions as thousands of behaviors were identified, and the list makers were never able to specify very well which
behaviors were essential to good teaching and which were not.
While "competencies" like: "writes clearly on the blackboard" or
"speaks loudly enough to be heard in the back of the room" didn't
seem to capture the essence of good teaching, they weren't irrelevant either, but the system provided no criteria which could rank
the relative importance of any of the identified "competencies."

The practical problems posed by such huge lists were not the
real weakness, however. That was revealed when we began to ask
the question *why* about various teacher behaviors, and, further,
began to explore what teachers had to *know* in order to *perform* in
appropriate ways. What had been lacking, in fact, in the conceptual
collapsing of Competency and Performance Based standards for
judgment was an understanding of the distinction between *competence* and *performance* in an almost exact parallel to that developed

by Chomsky for the study of language. That is, competence is a mental state which underlies and is enacted in performance, but because the structure of competence is so complex, as are the contexts which influence and affect how it is employed, that *performance itself does not unambiguously reflect or reveal competence.* One cannot, therefore, determine competence by *only* observing performance.

This may seem counterintuitive, and certainly runs counter to common sense, so let's look at two brief examples of teacher performance to see how it works.

In example one, we see a teacher sitting in a classroom reading a book. His feet are up on the desk, and he is smiling and chuckling to himself as he turns the pages. He occasionally glances up at the students, and from time to time responds to questions either from students who approach his desk or call out from their seats, but other than to respond to student questions he says nothing.

In example two, we see a teacher standing in front of the chalkboard. He is delivering a lecture to the students and from time to time writes *key* words or phrases on the board. One or two students raise their hands and are called on with what turn out to be questions which he tries to answer. He moves *actively* about the front of the room and has a *dynamic* manner *which helps to emphasize the points that he is making.* His voice is deep and clear, and he *often makes eye contact* with individual students as he is talking. His manner is *authoritative* but *informal* and *seems to encourage student questions which he listens to carefully.*

Can we determine from watching these two teachers whether or not one or both are competent? We certainly get some clues, but even they are often as much in the mind of the beholder as they are in the observed behavior. I italicized some words and phrases in the second description to emphasize how even behavior descriptions often involve interpretation. (Try eliminating them or substituting less interpretive—less subjective? less biased?—descriptions and see what is gained and lost.)

But that is part of the point; just as texts do not directly transmit their meanings which have to be, instead, reconstructed by the reader, so too, *behavior does not directly reveal its meaning without interpretation by the observer.* Movements can be charted, language recorded and transcribed, but doing so will not reveal their meaning until we bring our interpretive systems to bear.

The interpretive systems we bring to making sense of our observations derive, of course, from our sense (common or uncommon) of what competent teaching looks and sounds like. If I were to tell you that the second example was a university class in applied linguistics, you might nod your head and say, yes, I thought as much, and it seems quite competent in that circumstance. But what if I place the first teacher in the same context? For many people familiar with higher education it will seem at least strange, and at least raise doubts about the competence of the teacher. Maybe that would be true in any case. He certainly isn't doing much which looks like typical commonsense teaching except answering questions.

But would it seem less strange if the students were ten-year-olds? How about if they were fifteen? Would the second type of teaching fit equally well with ten- or fifteen-year-olds? How would we decide?

We are back, in effect, to the same question: *How does performance reveal competence?* And we have, in essence, two ways to determine the answer. The first is to rely on our own constructs and beliefs about what effective teaching looks like and to judge what we see on the basis of the interpretation of behavior that those constructs permit; the second is to ask the teacher why he was doing what he did. Either solution clearly violates the conditions for limiting oneself to observable evidence, which is at the core of the behaviorist position which underlies this approach, but the first preserves the illusion of objectivity so dear to its advocates because, since we make our interpretations unconsciously, we can claim that we are simply decoding the behavior in a neutral fashion. The second explicitly violates behaviorism, because it recognizes that behavior is only the surface manifestation of underlying beliefs and attitudes, and, further, because it emphasizes that why teachers choose to behave in the ways they do is centrally involved in determining their competence.

The central criterion which bears on the relationship of teacher choice of performances and competence is that of its effect on student learning. We could go performance-based teacher evaluators one better and say that teacher performance, as such, doesn't matter, since the bottom line is whether or not the students are learning. This position is taken by developers of teacher-proof curricula and their accompanying tests. If student test performance is the sole criterion by which we are going to judge teachers, then we need never look inside their classrooms at all; the only relevant evidence we need will be test scores. And this has been generally the line of retreat (or they would call it advance) taken by C/PBTEers when the conceptual foundations of their approach were challenged. In this case, therefore, all we'd need to do to determine whether teacher one and teacher two were competent would be to see how their students did on the test.

But this just won't do. Even if we can agree that student learning is the bottom-line criteria by which to evaluate competence in teaching, we have to remember that learning is not a theory-neutral, value-free concept in terms of either means or ends. Further, as already discussed in this chapter, the tests we have available are extremely limited in what and how they can test learning, and they are, for the most part, strongly influenced by the profound confusion between teaching and learning. That is, most tests test whether or not a student has successfully engaged in an instructional sequence, not whether or not he has learned the more global and integrated abilities that such instructional sequences are intended to promote but very often do not. So tests just won't do any more than observation will to reveal teacher competence in objective, unambiguous, interpretation-free terms.

We come closer to being able to make such judgments if we consider an integrated complex of factors including teacher intentions, the activities and performances of *both* students and teachers in the classroom—failing to observe and understand what students were doing was another flaw in PBTE, and further revealed the teacher-centered bias of the enterprise—and a variety of broad-gauged measures of whether or not students are learning. And this was where Harold Vine and I ended up with our attempt to develop a CBTE system. We sharply distinguished competence from performance and developed what we called a teaching act model to illustrate the complexities of the process. (See Figure 9–1.)

Our concern was to show both that what was actually observable in classrooms was only the tip of the competence iceberg, and, even more important, that the crucial determinants of teaching

Figure 9–1   Teaching Act Model

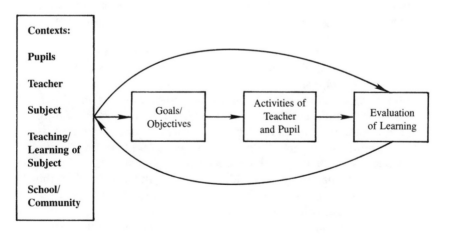

Note: These contexts are the *teacher's* construal/image/perception/
mental model of the teaching situation. (After Mayher
and Vine, 1974.)

competence were the teacher's *mental* activities, since they determined the instructional choices which set the goals, paced the
activities, and determined the ways the learning would be evaluated. While observers could see only what happened, a more ethnographic perspective, including asking the teacher why he did what
he did and/or how it fit with his understanding of the context in
which he was working, would be needed in order to make competence judgments. And, of course, such judgments would inevitably
be subjective as well, since they would depend on the observer's
constructs of the situation, which would determine her interpretation of the appropriateness of the teaching act.

While absolute competence judgments cannot be achieved
by such a process, it has the great advantage of making otherwise
hidden systems more public and therefore open to examination,
reflection, criticism, and, potentially at least, to negotiation and
change. In that sense, it is analogous to the earlier discussion about
the importance of making student assessment criteria public and
explicit.

In the case described briefly above of the first teacher, if we
can understand why he is spending his time reading at his desk,
we may make a different judgment about his competence than if
we must interpret his behavior solely from our own frame of reference. If he told us, for example, that he believed his pupils had had
too little experience of seeing anyone read for pleasure, that might
help to justify the activity if we shared or could come to share his
perception of the class. Or he might tell us, further, that he believed
that children needed time to read on their own, which is what we
had noticed them doing but not attended to because of our earlier
focus on teaching, because that is a crucial factor in learning to read.
Or he might even tell us that he doesn't really approve of what he
was doing, but the school had mandated a silent reading program,
and he was doing his best to accommodate the school's demands.

Whatever he said would and should influence our interpretation of the activity, but it would also initiate a professional dialogue which could continue to enrich not only our understanding
of the situation as observers, but the teacher's understanding as
well. Where we disagreed we could have a shared context to discuss our disagreements and to explore alternative beliefs and practices. Where change seemed desirable from the teacher's or the
observer's perspective, such changes could be investigated not only
as alternative activities—the usual framework for teacher change—
but in terms of the relationship of activities to the underlying structure of knowledge and belief that gives meaning and purpose to the
activities. And in such a framework, real teacher concerns for such
things as classroom control and authority can be recognized and
respected without making them rigid roadblocks to change.

The other crucial feature of the diagram—represented by the curved arrows—is the emphasis on the intimate connection between the teacher's mental model of the situation and the processes and results of the evaluation of student learning. The top arrow illustrates the fact that the underlying purpose of all teaching acts is to enhance student learning. The bottom one shows that such evaluations should be providing continual feedback to the teacher's construal of the situation which, ideally, will result in modification of that construal in ways which will permit ever more successful teaching acts. This process of feedforward and feedback is characteristic of what Donald Schön (1983) characterizes as "being in conversation" with the situation "so that his own models and appreciations are also shaped by the situation. The phenomena he seeks to understand are partly of his own making; he is *in* the situation he seeks to understand" (p. 151, his italics).

In terms of assessing teacher competence, Harold Vine and I came to the conclusion that the capacity to use such feedback was the key ingredient. As experienced teachers ourselves, we knew that we were still growing and changing as teachers, and we could hardly expect the beginning teachers we were working with to have thoroughly mastered all of the capacities they would eventually need when they began to practice. What we did think we could identify, however, was the one essential ingredient they would need to keep on getting better: *the capacity to learn from their teaching by being in continual conversation with it.* We would bet on a teacher who had that capacity for the future; those who did not would be dubious candidates for success. So we ended up with a CBTE program based on one competency, essentially that of the reflective practitioner—although we didn't use that term—but that "one" competency is itself complex and is embedded in a highly complex vision of the teaching/learning situation. (See Mayher and Brause [1985] for additional explanation of the process.)

Learning Teachers: Reflective Transactions

Central to this view of teaching is the idea we first saw in the opening chapter that professional teachers are, in Schön's (1983) terms *reflective practitioners.* Schön defines reflective practice as "transactional" (p. 150) in much the same sense derived from John Dewey (Bentley and Dewey 1949), that we earlier defined the process of meaning making through reading and writing and speaking and listening as transactional: that the inferential processes we use to interpret the text/situation simultaneously change it and us.

Schön goes on to point out that experience of acting in a situation can bring increasing pressures toward rigidity, toward taking our mental model of the situation as the reality of the situation itself. Nowhere in the professions is this more of a problem than in teaching since, as we've already seen, our commonsense concept of teaching has been solidified through more than 15,000 hours of observing teachers while we were students. This certainly makes it harder to maintain the "double vision" necessary for reflective practice, but without it we will continue to be condemned to doing tomorrow essentially what we did today. Not only is such a prospect boring, but by severely hampering our capacity to listen to the back talk of our teaching situation, we are, as the curved lines of the teaching model illustrate, robbing ourselves of the major source of information we need to ensure that our teaching becomes steadily more successful.

The structure of this book has been built, in a sense, on this notion of double vision. By counterposing common- and uncommonsense constructs of the contexts of teaching acts—of pupils and their ways of learning, of the nature and role of teachers, of the subjects of language education, of the ways those subjects can be most effectively taught and learned, and of the influences of the school and community on the rest—I have tried to provide the basis for alternative ways of construing teaching acts. Doing so will not, of course, provide definitive recipes for action. The uniqueness of each teacher and each teaching context makes that impossible and gives the lie to the idea that there can be teacher-proof curricula. But what it can do is provide an alternative frame for "reflection-in-action," as Schön calls it, whereby teachers can continue to grow by inquiring into their own practice.

Such inquiry into our own practice, however, may seem to bring even more extensive threats to our already shaky sense of our authority and competence. As we have already seen, Cuban (1984) has shown that many earlier attempts to introduce learner-centered reforms into the classroom have failed because they did not sufficiently accommodate legitimate teacher concerns for the control of their classroom situation. And at a time when teacher autonomy has been seriously under attack, teachers anxious to hang onto the few vestiges we have may be even more fearful of any approach which seems to undermine them further. My sense, however, is that teachers will never be sufficiently autonomous to free ourselves from the packagers and the testers until we can demonstrate to each other and to the public that we know what we are doing. Reflective practice involving inquiry can provide the strongest possible basis for such an assertion.

As Schön (1983) points out, it will involve changes in our stance, and we must give up "the rewards of unquestioned authority, the freedom to practice without challenge to our competence, the comfort of relative invulnerability, the gratification of deference" (p. 299). Since I have been arguing that, as teachers, we have very few of those rewards, freedoms, comforts, or deference in the real world anyway, we have much less to lose than many other professionals and consequently much more to gain.

The new satisfactions open to [us] are largely those of discovery—about the meanings of [our] advice to our clients [both students and the public, including parents], about [our] knowledge-in-practice, and about [ourselves]. *When a practitioner becomes a researcher into his own practice, he engages in a continuing process of self-education.* When practice is a repetitive administration of techniques to the same kinds of problems [as in the drills of teacher-proof curricula], the practitioner may look to leisure as a source of relief, or to early retirement; but when she functions as a researcher-in-practice, the practice itself is a source of renewal. The recognition of error, with its resulting uncertainty, can become a source of discovery rather than an occasion for self defense. (Schön 1983, p. 299, my italics.)

A further advantage for teachers of abandoning the "expert" role for that of the reflective practitioner is that it can allow us to be in control of the process of change in our own classrooms: to become responsible for our own teaching (Lester and Mayher 1987). Rather than reforms being imposed upon us from without— whatever their purpose, progressive or reactionary—we can regain control of our own turf by insisting that only reflective professionals can really understand the teaching and learning situation well enough to determine what should go on in it. This may make the process of change slower than some reformers might like— including me in my more evangelical frame of mind—but it will be the only way of really answering Cuban's final question, "How can what teachers already do be improved?" cited earlier in this chapter.

Since I am convinced that teachers *want* to improve the ways they help their students learn, employing a reflective practitioner stance toward their teaching within the framework of the teaching act model should enable them to do so. It will mean living with more uncertainty than some of us find comfortable, since we will no longer be able to demand unquestioned authority or to be sure that what we are doing is the best way to act. But it will continue to allow us to act on the basis of the best we know at any given moment, while using our double vision to ensure that we continue to learn from the situation in ways that will make us better able to act effectively in comparable situations (Brause and Mayher 1984).

Those teachers who have already begun to inquire into their own practice by becoming teacher researchers have learned the benefits that such activities can bring in terms of both improving their teaching and adding satisfaction to what they are doing. Such a stance will not be a panacea for our problems and will undoubtedly make for some new ones, as teachers become increasingly resistant to the bureaucratic restraints on teacher autonomy which we've already explored. Autonomous professional teachers will not fit neatly into the pigeonholes of packagers and testers, but they are as essential to the education of children.

Toward Uncommonsense Teaching Competence: A Summary

In addition to the capacity to keep on learning through performing as reflective practitioners in conversation with our teaching situation, based on the teaching act model, competent uncommonsense language teachers will need to have developed a usable and internally consistent set of constructs about that situation. It should be emphasized that these constructs are not always or even normally used consciously, and in some cases we may not even be aware that we hold them. They should be open to conscious reflection, however, partly because this will enable us to participate in ongoing professional dialogues about the means and ends of our teaching, and partly because once we have reflected on our beliefs, we are more likely to be able to modify them through our ongoing professional reading and other transactions with our colleagues. These constructs also need to be sufficiently flexible to permit change as our construal of the effectiveness of our teaching changes through our continuing observation.

In terms of our mental model of our *pupils*, what we need is the best information we can get about them, derived both directly from our observations and indirectly through our understanding of the richest theories of social and individual development we can have access to. Such theories need not be limited to anthropology, sociology, or psychology, of course, since they can also be derived from the arts, particularly from literature, and, with appropriate cautions, from our own experiences as learners, particularly as learners in out-of-school contexts. If, as Frank Smith (1973) has suggested, the best rule for teaching reading (or, I would suggest, nearly anything else) is to "respond to what the child is trying to do," then we need to have useful and productive lenses for understanding what that is. As Lindfors (1984) pointed out, continuing to confuse what we are trying to do as teachers with what children are trying to do as learners can lead to a continuing misinterpretation of what children have already achieved and of what they need to do next.

Our means of observing our students, therefore, depend directly on our understanding of both developmental learning theories and theories about the role that children's sociocultural environments play in their development. Our assumptions about how children learn, or about whether or not some children—boys or girls, rich kids or poor kids, black kids or white kids, native or non-native speakers of English—have the same potential to learn as others derive from our tacit theories, and they function as lenses or filters through which we see the actual children we are teaching. Since our observations of them, filtered through these lenses, directly determine what we think they need to learn, we'd better be as sure as we can be that our lenses don't cause myopia.

Our view of our students must also be influenced by our recognition, consistent with the transactional theory of language use, that they must be the ones who make their own meanings, and that they are, in fact, finally responsible for their own learning. Beyond recognizing their active role as meaning makers for themselves, our conception of them must also permit us to recognize that while they are learning from and with us, so we are learning from and with them. Without such an active role in their learning experiences in school, they will never be able to continue to be active, self-motivated learners after they leave school.

Our understanding of ourselves as *teachers* involves our conceptions of our roles and responsibilities, as well as our sense of our individual talents and abilities, our personality and communicative style, and our attitudes toward children, our subject, and other adults, both within and without the school context. All of these derive, of course, from our experience, but in terms of our sense of ourselves, *as teachers*, our own schooling and whatever prior experience we've had in teaching will be the most crucial factors.

I recognize that the reflective practitioner role is not familiar for many teachers and may seem in conflict with traditional conceptions of the teacher as authority, a conception which has seemed to be essential to maintaining professional mental health. While I grant that it is unfamiliar, I have tried to argue that it can, in fact, be a source of renewal of authority and control, and therefore a bulwark and not a threat to security and confidence. It does take time to make the shift, and our own and others' expectations of what teachers do will have to change, including, of course, those of students and parents, as well as administrators and colleagues. But once we adopt such a stance and become reflective teacher inquirers, we can find, as Schön has suggested, a whole new source of both confidence and pleasure in what we do. It seems far more desirable to me to have my authority and control as a teacher derive from within the context of my classroom as my students come to recognize my legitimacy within the teaching-learning transaction, rather than to have to depend on external mandates of authority and external means of ensuring it like making seat assignments, giving homework and tests, and taking attendance. I know that many of these power-maintaining measures are not directly within our control, and compromises will have to be made along the way about some of them, but if we know where we want to go and how we want to *be* in our classrooms, many of them can be renegotiated to be helpful and meaningful to our students, rather than harmful.

The reflective practitioner/teacher-learner stance will still permit a wide variety of teaching approaches and be congenial with a diverse set of personalities and teaching styles. I am certainly no more an advocate of homogenizing teachers and teaching than I am of sameness of curricula, tests, and so on. Diversity is clearly to be cherished and encouraged, providing it is diversity within the universe of authentic learners. Authentic learners are the models children need to become learners themselves, to initiate them, in Frank Smith's (1987) term, into "the learning club." And authentic learners will be the kind of teachers who recognize that however good they get at teaching, they can always get better.

I haven't talked very much about the *subject* context in this chapter because it is indirectly the subject of the whole book. What is required in this context is to notice that the teacher's conception of her subject must be congruent with the other contexts explored here, particularly in the sense that it must become more fluid than has usually been the case. The traditional dichotomy that elementary teachers teach children and secondary teachers teach a subject, for example, is both counterfactual and counterproductive: Both teach both. But what they think about what they are doing clearly influences what they do and how they do it, and that must be one area where reflective teachers must examine their beliefs. Like our beliefs about learners, so too our construction of our subject can have a direct effect on the goals we identify for them to learn, and so being both clear and flexible about our definitions can keep us from attempting to teach things that won't help students learn.

This context also covers the notion that teachers must have specialist knowledge of the content of the subject they teach. We saw in Chapter II that one of the "reforms" advocated in response to the Sputnik crisis was to teach teachers more content, and similar pressures have emerged in response to *A Nation at Risk*. While there is no doubt that language teachers will benefit from, say, having read more literature, or knowing more linguistics, there is substantial reason to doubt that these are the solutions to the education crisis, or even to making teachers appear more professional, unless such learning is integrated into the processes of helping children learn. And, as we saw in Chapter II, when such content is taught in ways which make it actually inaccessible or useless to children and adolescents—obfuscating and mystifying the processes of reading literature for one example, teaching grammar, whether traditional or modern, for another—then teachers may actually be better off without it. Or at least their pupils will be.

This makes the distinction between teacher's construal of their subject and of the *teaching and learning of that subject* hard and perhaps impossible to draw. When Harold Vine and I originally proposed distinguishing them we did so because we were concerned that the continuing focus on the *what* of English (and language education) was clouding concern with the *how* of English (and language education). I'm more and more convinced that they are really two sides of the same coin, and one cannot effectively consider one without the other in terms of their implications for teaching practice.

The final context, that of the *school and community*, has been one of the major themes of this chapter in terms of their effect on teacher autonomy, or the lack thereof. The issues already raised are important ones, but there are others as well that should be attended to more fully, including, especially, the role of teachers in a democratic society. There has been a long tradition in American education that schools should be politically neutral, by which it is usually meant that schools should not play a direct role in partisan politics. The same tradition has kept schools religiously neutral, partly in response to the First Amendment's prohibition against the establishment of religion, and partly in response to the long and healthy tradition of religious toleration which is one of the cornerstones of our democracy.

In recent years, however, both traditions have come under scrutiny and, in some cases, direct attack. The attack has taken a variety of forms, including the continuing effort to censor books as either unsuitable to children—because they contain language deemed offensive, or because they paint such a harsh picture of life that some feel children should be protected from—or for the ideas they contain—of which the creationist challenge to the Darwinian theory of evolution has been the most prominent, but which has recently been expanded to include a threat to the very notion of religious neutrality itself. All of these efforts seriously undermine both the freedom of teachers to teach and of children to learn, but the last is particularly damaging because it has managed to define the absence of the advocacy of a religious belief, in particular the absence of a Christian religious belief, as a "religion." According to a logic that strikes me as particularly twisted, it is argued that if you are trying to be neutral among and tolerant of all religions, that means you are a secular humanist, that secular humanism is a religion, and therefore schools that endorse (preach?) it have an established religion.

James Moffett, whose own textbooks have undergone some of the most aggressive censorship, has reflected on what all this means. In a talk at the NCTE convention in 1987, he called for our attention to the underlying common spirituality we share as human beings, a sense of the worth of the individual and of each individual's human spirit, which can transcend sectarian concerns and give us a sounder basis for helping children and adolescents make choices as to what they should read. He also pointed out, however, that many of the books and ideas which are available are challenging to the beliefs of those who want to keep their children isolated from the larger society and safely tucked in a dogmatic cocoon. Such beliefs are threatened by open choices and by reading which doesn't conform to their narrow doctrines. Moffett's only hope was to try to go beyond these narrow confines and to find a universal human spirit to counteract them.

While I am reasonably confident that such narrow ideas will not prevail in the larger context of American life, they do have strong support among a substantial fraction of the population, and in some schools and school districts that can include a majority, or close to a majority, of the parents and other community members. In such cases, teachers and the principles of freedom to learn and inquire have come under strong attack, and such threats are not likely to soon diminish. In the area of censorship, there have already been some notable victories for the forces of thought control, either in instances where books have been banned or, even more commonly, where books believed to be "controversial" have been avoided to keep trouble from starting. This is hardly a new problem, since I was told by my department chairman at my first English department meeting as a high school teacher that we were not only not to teach *The Catcher in the Rye*, but that we were never to write it down on a list of recommended books. And the power of the Gablers, a couple in Texas actively involved in attempting to get books censored, to influence the whole country by demanding changes in texts proposed for adoption by the Texas Department of Education is well known. They have been able to have such influence because Texas adopts books on a statewide basis and no publisher wants to put out one set of books for Texas and one set for the rest of the country, so what the Gablers want is what the rest of us get whether we want it or not.

These threats to the freedom to learn and teach in elementary and secondary schools are important to understand, not only because they limit our freedom of action as teachers, but more crucially because they seriously limit the freedom of children and adolescents to learn. Or, worse, they help to teach children that ideas are dangerous, that criticism is risky business, and that open-minded inquiry and curiosity are not worth the trouble they bring on. I don't want to suggest that learning and inquiry are value-free processes, and in some sense open inquiry is a risky and a dangerous business. As we've seen in the case of all language transactions, our values play a major role in the meanings we make through language use, and my values are clear in endorsing and reaffirming what I take to be the major significance for education of the First Amendment's guarantees of freedom of religion, speech, and the press. That is, that the role of education in a democratic society is to make those guarantees operable: to both enact them within the classroom and to ensure that learners will develop the powers of critical literacy necessary to continue to enact them after they leave school.

In order for teachers to play a leadership role in achieving and protecting such democratic classrooms, we must develop a political conception of our role and adequate sociopolitical theories to understand the forces that would limit our power to teach. This does not mean taking partisan political stands as much as it means becoming what Aronowitz and Giroux (1985) and Giroux and McLaren (1986) call "transformative intellectuals." This they define as one who recognizes that issues affecting teaching and learning are political issues directly concerned with "the struggle for meaning and the struggle over power relations . . . Teachers who assume the role of transformative intellectuals treat students as critical agents, question how knowledge is produced and distributed, utilize dialogue, and make knowledge meaningful, critical, and ultimately emancipatory" (Giroux and McLaren 1986, p. 215, based on Aronowitz and Giroux 1985, especially Chapter 2).

Without such a stance, which is part of what is required to be a reflective practitioner, teachers will continue to have our autonomy curtailed and our professionalism threatened. As Israel Scheffler has put it, teachers should not be seen as "performers professionally equipped to realize any goals that are set for them. Rather [we should] be viewed as free men and women with a special dedication to the values of the intellect and the enhancement of the critical powers of the young" (Scheffler 1968, p.11). Continuing to accept the first definition of our role is to continue to be powerless to oppose the imposition of teacher-proof curricula and their accompanying tests, and to remain vulnerable to the censors and others who want to use schools to serve special economic or political interests. Only by entering the political struggle will we be able to play a role in assuring that the second definition becomes the cultural norm.

And, of course, we do not do so for ourselves alone. We do it because we are convinced that unless we are free to inquire and to learn, we will not be free to teach our students to become the kind of critical learners and citizens which are essential to a democratic society. We will, in other words, be failing the kids and the future.

References

Ahlberg, Janet and Allan. 1986. *The Jolly Postman or Other People's Letters.* London: Heinemann; Boston: Little, Brown.

Allen, David. 1980. *English Teaching Since 1965: How Much Growth?* London: Heinemann.

Apple, Michael. 1986. *Teachers and Texts: A Political Economy of Class and Gender Relations in Education.* New York: Routledge & Kegan Paul.

Applebee, Arthur. 1974. *Tradition and Reform in the Teaching of English: A History.* Urbana, IL: NCTE.

Applebee, Arthur. 1978. *The Child's Concept of Story.* Chicago: University of Chicago Press.

Arnold, Matthew. 1873. *Literature and Dogma.* London: Ermintrude.

Aronowitz, Stanley, and Giroux, Henry A. 1985. *Education Under Seige: The Conservative, Liberal and Radical Debate over Schooling.* So. Hadley, MA: Bergin and Garvey.

Atwell, Nancie. 1987. *In the Middle: Writing, Reading, and Learning with Adolescents.* Portsmouth, NH: Boynton/Cook.

Barnes, Douglas. 1969/revised 1986. In *Language, the Learner, and the School.* Britton, James; Barnes, Douglas; and Rosen, Harold, eds. (1st ed.; Mike Torbe replaced Rosen in the 2nd ed.). Harmondsworth: Penguin.

Barnes, Douglas. 1976. *From Communication to Curriculum.* Harmondsworth: Penguin.

Barnes, Douglas, and Todd, Frankie. 1977. *Communication and Learning in Small Groups.* London: Routledge & Kegan Paul.

Baron, Dennis E. 1982. *Grammar and Good Taste: Reforming the American Language.* New Haven: Yale University Press.

Barr, Mary. 1983. "Language in Learning: From Research into Practice." Unpublished dissertation, New York University.

Bates, Elizabeth. 1976. *Language and Context: The Acquisition of Pragmatics.* New York: Academic Press.

Bell, Martha. 1977. "Toward a Model of Reading Acquisition." Unpublished dissertation, New York University.

Bellack, Arno, and others. 1966. *The Language of the Classroom.* New York: Teachers College Press.

Bentley, A. F., and Dewey, John. 1949. *Knowing the Known.* Boston: Beacon Press.

Berger, Peter, and Luckmann, Thomas. 1966. *The Social Construction of Reality.* New York: Doubleday.

Berkenkotter, Carol. 1983. "Decisions and revisions: The planning strategies of a publishing writer." *College Composition and Communication* 34:2, May.

Berthoff, Ann E. 1988. *Forming/Thinking/Writing: The Composing Imagination;* 2d Ed. Portsmouth, NH: Boynton/Cook.

Bickerton, Derek. 1981. *The Roots of Language.* Ann Arbor, MI: Karoma.

Bissex, Glenda. 1980. *Gnys at Wrk.* Cambridge, MA: Harvard University Press.

Blau, Sheridan. 1988. "Teacher development and the revolution in teaching." *English Journal* 77:4, April.

Bloom, Allan. 1987. *The Closing of the American Mind: How Higher Education Has Failed Democracy and Impoverished the Souls of Today's Students.* New York: Simon & Schuster.

Bloome, David, ed. 1987. *Literacy and Schooling.* Norwood, NJ: Ablex.

Bloomfield, Leonard, and Barnhart, Clarence. 1961. *Let's Read: A Linguistic Approach.* Detroit: Wayne State University Press.

Bluestone, Barry, and Harrison, Bennett. 1982. *The Deindustrialization of America.* New York: Basic Books.

Boomer, Garth, ed. 1982. *Negotiating the Curriculum: A Teacher-Student Partnership.* Sydney: Ashton-Scholastic.

Boyer, Ernest. 1983. *High School.* New York: Harper & Row.

Braddock, Richard; Lloyd-Jones, Richard; and Schoer, Lowell. 1963. *Research in Written Composition.* Urbana, IL: NCTE.

Brannon, Lil, and Knoblauch, C. H. 1982. "On students' rights to their own text: A mode of teacher response." *College Composition and Communication* 33:2.

Brause, Rita S., and Mayher, John S. 1983. "Learning through teaching: The classroom teacher as researcher." *Language Arts* 60:6, September.

Brause, Rita S., and Mayher, John S. 1984. "Learning through teaching: Asking the right questions." *Language Arts* 61:5, September.

Britton, James. 1970. *Language and Learning.* Harmondsworth: Penguin.

Britton, James. 1980. "English teaching: Prospect and retrospect." presented at the IFTE Conference, Sydney, and in *Prospect and Retrospect.* 1982. Pradl, G. M., ed. Portsmouth, NH: Boynton/Cook.

Britton, James. 1982. *Prospect and Retrospect: Selected Essays.* Pradl, Gordon M., ed. Portsmouth, NH: Boynton/Cook.

Brown, Roger. 1977. "Introduction" to Catherine Snow and Charles Ferguson, eds. *Talking to Children: Language Input and Acquisition*. Cambridge: Cambridge University Press.

Bruner, Jerome. 1975. "The ontogenesis of speech acts." *Journal of Child Language* 2:1–19.

Bruner, Jerome. 1983. *Child's Talk*. New York: Norton.

Bruner, Jerome. 1986. *Actual Minds, Possible Worlds*. Cambridge, MA: Harvard University Press.

Cheney, Lynne V. 1987. *American Memory: A Report on the Humanities in the Nation's Public Schools*. Washington, DC: National Endowment for the Humanities.

Chomsky, Carol. 1970. "Reading, writing, and phonology." *Harvard Educational Review* 40:2.

Chomsky, Carol. 1974. "Stages in language development and reading exposure." *Harvard Educational Review* 42:1, February.

Chomsky, Noam. 1965. *Aspects of the Theory of Syntax*. Cambridge, MA: MIT Press.

Chomsky, Noam. 1972. *Language and Mind*. (enlarged edition.) New York: Harcourt Brace Jovanovich.

Chomsky, Noam. 1984. "Chomsky writes to Mrs. Davis about grammar." *English Education* 16:3, October.

Chomsky, Noam. 1986. *Knowledge of Language: Its Nature, Origin and Use*. New York: Praeger.

Commission on English. 1965. *Freedom and Discipline in English*. New York: College Entrance Examination Board.

Cuban, Larry. 1984. *How Teachers Taught: Constancy and Change in American Classrooms, 1890–1980*. New York: Longman.

Dewey, John. 1933. *How We Think: A Restatement of the Relation of Reflective Thinking to the Educative Process*. Boston: D. C. Heath.

Dixon, John. (1967, 2nd ed. 1969, 3rd ed. 1975.) *Growth Through English*. Oxford: Oxford University Press for NATE; Urbana, IL: NCTE.

Donaldson, Margaret. 1978. *Children's Minds*. London: Fontana/Croon Helm.

Douglas, Wallace. 1976. "Rhetoric for the Meritocracy." In Richard Ohmann. *English in America*. Oxford: Oxford University Press.

Duckworth, Eleanor. 1987. *The Having of Wonderful Ideas and Other Essays on Teaching and Learning*. New York: Teachers College Press.

Dyson, Anne Haas. 1983. "The role of oral language in early writing processes." *Research in the Teaching of English* 17:1, February.

Eagleton, Terry. 1983. *Literary Theory: An Introduction*. Minneapolis: University of Minnesota Press.

Elbow, Peter. 1973. *Writing Without Teachers*. Oxford: Oxford University Press.

Emig, Janet. 1971. *The Composing Process of Twelfth Graders*. Urbana, IL: NCTE.

Fish, Stanley. 1980. *Is There a Text in this Class?: The Authority of Interpretive Communities*. Cambridge, MA: Harvard University Press.

Flesch, Rudolf. 1955. *Why Johnny Can't Read . . . and What You Can Do About It*. New York: Harper & Row.

Fox, Geoff. 1979. "Dark watchers: Young readers and their fiction." *English in Education* 13:1, Spring.

Gardner, Howard. 1983. *Frames of Mind: The Theory of Multiple Intelligences.* New York: Basic Books.

Gazzinaga, Michael. 1985. *The Social Brain.* New York: Basic Books.

Geertz, Clifford. 1983. "Common Sense as a Cultural System." In *Local Knowledge.* New York: Basic Books.

Gilligan, Carol. 1982. *In a Different Voice: Psychological Theory and Women's Development.* Cambridge, MA: Harvard University Press.

Giroux, Henry, and McLaren, Peter. 1986. "Teacher education and the politics of engagement: The case for democratic schooling." *Harvard Educational Review* 56:3, August.

Givon, Talmy. 1979. *On Understanding Grammar.* New York: Academic Press.

Goodlad, John. 1984. *A Place Called School.* New York: McGraw-Hill.

Goodman, Kenneth. 1986. *What's Whole in Whole Language.* Portsmouth, NH: Heinemann.

Gould, Stephen Jay. 1981. *The Mismeasure of Man.* New York: Norton.

Green, Judith, and Wallat, Cynthia, eds. 1981. *Ethnography and Language in Educational Settings.* Norwood, NJ: Ablex.

Grice, H. Paul. 1967/Forthcoming. "Logic and Conversation" (In *William James Lectures* —delivered 1967, to be published by Harvard University Press.)

Grice, H. Paul. 1975. *Logic and Conversation* in Cole, P., and Morgan, J. eds.: *Syntax and Semantics, Vol. 3: Speech Acts.* New York: Academic Press.

Halliday, Michael A. K. 1975. *Learning How to Mean: Explorations in the Development of Language.* London: Edward Arnold.

Halliday, Michael A. K. 1978. *Language as Social Semiotic: The Social Interpretation of Language and Meaning.* London: Edward Arnold.

Hampel, Robert. 1986. *The Last Little Citadel: American High Schools Since 1940.* Boston: Houghton Mifflin.

Hancock, Joelie and Hill, Susan, eds. 1988. *Literature-based Reading Programs at Work.* Portsmouth, NH: Heinemann.

Hardy, Barbara. 1975. *Storytellers and Listeners.* London: Athlone Press.

Hartwell, Patrick. 1985. "Grammar, grammars, and the teaching of grammar." *College English* 47:2, February.

Hayes, J. R., and Flower, Linda. 1980. "Identifying the Organization of the Writing Process." in L. W. Gregg and E. R. Steinberg, eds. *Cognitive Processes in Writing.* Hillsdale, NJ: Erlbaum.

Heath, Shirley Brice. 1983. *Ways with Words: Language, Life and Work in Communities and Classrooms.* New York: Cambridge University Press.

Herndon, James. 1968. *The Way It Spozed to Be.* New York: Simon & Schuster.

Hillocks, George. 1986. *Research on Written Composition: New Directions for Teaching.* Urbana, IL: NCRE/ERIC.

Hirsch, E. D. 1967. *Validity in Interpretation.* New Haven: Yale University Press.

Hirsch, E. D. 1977. *The Philosophy of Composition.* Chicago: University of Chicago Press

Hirsch, E. D. 1987. *Cultural Literacy: What Every American Needs to Know.* Boston: Houghton Mifflin.

Holland, James F., and Skinner, B. F. 1961. *The Analysis of Behavior: A Program for Self-instruction.* New York: McGraw-Hill.

Holt, John. 1964. *How Children Fail.* New York: Dell.

Hook, J. N. 1979. *A Long Way Together.* Urbana, IL: NCTE.

Hull, Robert. 1985.*The Language Gap: How Classroom Dialogue Fails.* London: Methuen.

Hull, Robert. 1988. *Behind the Poem: A Teacher's View of Children's Writing.* London: Routledge.

Humboldt, Wilhelm von. 1836/1988. *On Language: The Diversity of Human Language—Structure and Its Influence on the Mental Development of Mankind.* (Translated by Peter Heath.) Cambridge: Cambridge University Press.

Iser, Wolfgang. 1978. *The Act of Reading: A Theory of Aesthetic Response.* Baltimore: Johns Hopkins University Press.

Jespersen, Otto. 1924. *The Philosophy of Grammar.* New York: Norton.

Johnson, Mark. 1987. *The Body in the Mind: The Bodily Basis of Meaning, Imagination and Reason.* Chicago: University of Chicago Press.

Johnson-Laird, Phillip. 1983. *Mental Models: Toward a Cognitive Science of Language, Inference, and Consciousness.* Cambridge, MA: Harvard University Press.

Kaye, Kenneth. 1982. *The Mental And Social Life of Babies: How Parents Create Persons.* Brighton, Sussex: The Harvester Press.

Kelly, George. 1955. *The Psychology of Personal Constructs.* New York: Norton.

Klima, Edward, and Bellugi, Ursula. 1979. *The Signs of Language.* Cambridge, MA: Harvard University Press.

Kohl, Herbert. 1967. *36 Children.* New York: New American Library.

Kozol, Jonathan. 1967. *Death at an Early Age.* Boston: Houghton Mifflin.

Kuhn, Thomas. 1961. *The Structure of Scientific Revolutions.* Chicago: University of Chicago Press.

Labov, William. 1972a. "The logic of non-standard English." In *Language in the Inner City.* Philadelphia: University of Pennsylvania Press.

Labov, William. 1972b. "The Linguistic Consequences of Being a Lame." In *Language of the Inner City.* Philadelphia: University of Pennsylvania Press.

Labov, William, and Waletsky, Joshua. 1967. "Narrative Analysis." In *Essays on the Verbal and Visual Arts.* June Helm, ed. Seattle: University of Washington Press.

Lakoff, George. 1987. *Women, Fire, and Dangerous Things: What Categories Reveal about the Mind.* Chicago: University of Chicago Press.

Lakoff, George, and Johnson, Mark. 1980. *Metaphors We Live By.* Chicago: University of Chicago Press.

Langer, Judith, and Applebee, Arthur. 1987. *How Writing Shapes Thinking.* Urbana, IL: NCTE.

Lester, Nancy B., and Mayher, John S. 1987. "Critical professional inquiry." *English Education* 19:4, December.

Lester, Nancy B., and Onore, Cynthia S. 1985. "Immersion and distancing: A model for inservice education." *English Education* 17:1, February.

Lester, Nancy B., and Onore, Cynthia S. 1990. *Learning Change: One School District Meets Language Across the Curriculum*. Portsmouth, NH: Boynton/Cook.

Lindfors, Judith Wells. 1984. "How children learn or how teachers teach: A profound confusion." *Language Arts* 61:6, October.

Loban, Walter. 1976. *Language Development: Kindergarten through Grade Twelve*. Urbana, IL: NCTE.

Lowth, Robert. 1762. *A Short Introduction to English Grammar*. London: J. Hughs.

Marshall, John. 1987. "Language Learning, Language Acquisition, or Language Growth." In Modgil, S. and Modgil, C., eds. *Noam Chomsky*. Philadelphia: Falmer Press.

Martin, Nancy; D'Arcy, Pat; Newton, Bryan; and Parker, Robert. 1976. *Writing and Learning Across the Curriculum: 11–16*. London: Ward Lock.

Mathiesen, Margaret. 1975. *The Preachers of Culture*. London: Allen and Unwin.

Mayher, John S. 1968. "Transformational Grammar in Action." In Suhor, C.; Mayher, J. S.; and D'Angelo, F. J., eds. *The Growing Edges of Secondary English*. Urbana, IL: NCTE.

Mayher, John S. 1970. "Linguistics for English Teachers: What, Why, and How They Should Know about Language." Unpublished dissertation, Harvard Graduate School of Education.

Mayher, John S. 1982. "Another journey through the looking glass: New lenses for old problems." *Arizona English Bulletin* 24:3, May.

Mayher, John S., and Brause, Rita S. 1985. "Learning through teaching: A structure for inquiry and change." *Language Arts* 62:3, March.

Mayher, John S.; Lester, Nancy B.; and Pradl, Gordon M. 1983. *Learning to Write/Writing to Learn*. Portsmouth, NH: Boynton/Cook.

Mayher, John S., and Lester, Nancy B. 1983. "Putting learning first in writing to learn." *Language Arts* 60:6, September.

Mayher, John S., and Vine, Harold A., Jr. 1974. "The teaching act model." *NYU Education Quarterly*. Fall.

McCracken, Nancy M. 1985. "Teacher's Response to Student Writing: A Description of the Process as Teaching, Problem-solving and Composing." Unpublished dissertation, New York University.

McLuhan, Marshall. 1964. *Understanding Media: The Extensions of Man*. New York: McGraw-Hill.

McNeil, Linda M. 1986. *Contradictions of Control: School Structure and School Knowledge*. New York: Routledge & Kegan Paul.

Meek, Margaret. 1983. *Achieving Literacy: Longitudinal Studies of Adolescents Learning to Read*. London: Routledge & Kegan Paul.

Meek, Margaret, and Miller, Jane, eds. 1984. *Changing English: Essays for Harold Rosen*. London: Heinemann.

Mellon, John. 1969. *Transformational Sentence-Combining*. Urbana, IL: NCTE.

Moffett, James. 1968a. *Teaching the Universe of Discourse*. Boston: Houghton Mifflin.

Moffett, James. 1968b. *A Student Centered Language Arts Curriculum: Grades K–13*. Boston: Houghton Mifflin.

Murray, Donald M. 1978. "Internal Revision: A Process of Discovery." In Cooper, C. R., and Odell, L. *Research on Composing: Points of Departure*. Urbana, IL: NCTE.

Murray, Lindley. 1790/American Ed. 1800. *English Grammar Adapted to Different Classes of Learners with an Appendix Containing Rules and Observations*. Boston: Manning and Loring (1st Am. Ed.).

National Commission on Excellence in Education. 1983. *A Nation at Risk*. Washington: U.S. Government Printing Office.

Neel, Jasper. 1988. *Plato, Derrida, and Writing*. Carbondale, IL: Southern Illinois University Press.

Newman, Judith M., ed. 1985. *Whole Language: Theory in Use*. Portsmouth, NH: Heinemann.

Newport, E. L.; Gleitman, H.; and Gleitman, L. 1977. "Mother I'd Rather Do It Myself: Some Effects and Noneffects of Maternal Speech Style." In Snow, C.E. and Ferguson, C. eds. *Talking to Children*. Cambridge: Cambridge University Press.

Newport, E. L. 1977. "Motherese: The Speech of Mothers to Young Children." In Castellan, N.; Pisoni, D.; and Potts, G., eds. *Cognitive Theory*. Hillsdale, NJ: Erlbaum.

North, Stephen M. 1987. *The Making of Knowledge in Composition: Portrait of an Emerging Field*. Portsmouth, NH: Boynton/Cook.

Oakes, Jeannie. 1985. *Keeping Track: How Schools Structure Inequality*. New Haven: Yale University Press.

Ohmann, Richard. 1976. *English in America: A Radical View of the Profession*. New York: Oxford University Press.

Onore, Cynthia S. 1983. "Students' Revisions and Teachers' Comments: Toward a Transactional Theory of the Composing Process." Unpublished dissertation, New York University.

Ornstein, Robert. 1986. *Multimind*. Boston: Houghton Mifflin.

Ortony, Andrew, ed. 1979. *Metaphor and Thought*. Cambridge: Cambridge University Press.

Paley, Vivian Gussin. 1981. *Wally's Stories*. Cambridge, MA: Harvard University Press.

Paley, Vivian Gussin. 1988. *Bad Guys Don't Have Birthdays: Fantasy Play at Four*. Chicago: University of Chicago Press.

Pathways of Language Development. 1987–88. A curriculum project of the Education Department, Tasmania, Australia.

Peitzman, Faye. 1981. "The Composing Process of Three College Freshmen: Focus on Revision." Unpublished dissertation, New York University.

Perkinson, Henry. 1968. *The Imperfect Panacea: American Faith in Education, 1865–1965*. New York: Random House.

Perl, Sondra. 1975. "Five Writers Writing: The Composing Processes of Unskilled College Writers." Unpublished dissertation, New York University.

Perry, William G. 1970. *Forms of Intellectual and Ethical Development in the College Years*. New York: Holt, Rinehart & Winston.

Piaget, Jean. 1967. *Six Psychological Studies*. New York: Random House.

Polanyi, Michael. 1958. *Personal Knowledge*. Chicago: University of Chicago Press.

Polanyi, Michael. 1966. *The Tacit Dimension*. New York: Doubleday.

Postman, Neil, and Weingartner, Charles. 1969. *Teaching as a Subversive Activity*. New York: Delacorte.

Powell, Arthur G.; Farrar, Eleanor; and Cohen, David K. 1985. *The Shopping Mall High School*. Boston: Houghton Mifflin.

Pradl, Gordon M., ed. 1982. *Prospect and Retrospect: Selected Essays of James Britton*. Portsmouth, NH: Boynton/Cook.

Pradl, Gordon M. 1987. "Close encounters of the first kind: Teaching the poem at the point of utterance." *English Journal* 76, 2, February.

Pradl, Gordon M., and Mayher, John S. 1985. "Reinvigorating learning through writing." *Educational Leadership* 42:5, February.

Radway, Janice A. 1984. *Reading the Romance: Women, Patriarchy, and Popular Literature*. Chapel Hill: University of North Carolina Press.

Ravitch, Diane, and Finn, Chester. 1987. *What Do Our 17-year-olds Know? A Report on the First National Assessment of History and Literature*. New York: Harper & Row.

Read, Charles. 1971. "Pre-school children's knowledge of English phonology." *Harvard Educational Review* 41, 1, February.

Reddy, Michael. 1979. "The Conduit Metaphor." In Ortony, A., ed. *Metaphor and Thought*. Cambridge: Cambridge University Press.

Reid, Ian. 1984. *The Making of Literature*. Adelaide: Australian Association for the Teaching of English.

Rist, Ray. 1970. "Student social class and teacher expectations: The self-fulfilling prophecy in ghetto education." *Harvard Educational Review* 40:3, August.

Rorty, Richard. 1979. *Philosophy and the Mirror of Nature*. Princeton: Princeton University Press.

Rosen, Harold. 1984. *Stories and Meanings*. London: National Association for the Teaching of English.

Rosenblatt, Louise M. 1938, rev. 1968. *Literature as Exploration*. New York: Appleton Century.

Rosenblatt, Louise M. 1978. *The Reader, the Text, the Poem: The Transactional Theory of the Literary Work*. Carbondale, IL: Southern Illinois University Press.

Sacks, Oliver. 1985. *The Man Who Mistook His Wife for a Hat and Other Clinical Tales*. New York: Summit.

Salmon, Phillida. 1985. *Living in Time: A New Look at Personal Development*. London: J. M. Dent.

Sapir, Edward. 1921. *Language* New York: Harcourt Brace.

Sauer, Edward. 1961. *English in the Secondary School*. New York: Holt, Rinehart & Winston.

Scheffler, Israel. 1968. "University scholarship and the education of teachers." *Teacher's College Record* 70:1.

Schön, Donald A. 1983. *The Reflective Practitioner*. New York: Basic Books.

Schön, Donald A. 1987. *Educating the Reflective Practitioner*. San Francisco: Jossey-Bass.

Sedlak, Michael W.; Wheeler, Christopher W.; Pullin, Diana C.; and Cusick, Philip A. 1986. *Selling Students Short: Classroom Bargains and Academic Reform in the American High School.* New York: Teachers College Press.

Sherwin, Stephen. 1969. *Four Problems in Teaching English: A Critique of Research.* New York: International Textbook Co.

Sinclair, Hermine. 1987. "Language: A Gift of Nature or a Home-made Tool?" In Modgil, S., and Modgil, C., eds. *Noam Chomsky.* Philadelphia: Falmer Press.

Sizer, Theodore. 1984. *Horace's Compromise: The Dilemma of the American High School.* Boston: Houghton Mifflin.

Skinner, B. F. 1971. *Beyond Freedom and Dignity.* New York: Knopf.

Skinner, B. F. 1948. *Walden Two.* New York: Macmillan.

Smith, Frank. 1973. "Twelve Ways to Make Learning to Read Difficult and One Difficult Way to Make It Easy." In *Psycholinguistics and Reading.* New York: Holt, Rinehart & Winston.

Smith, Frank. 1986. *Insult to Intelligence.* New York: Arbor House.

Sperber, Dan, and Wilson, Deirdre. 1986. *Relevance: Communication and Cognition.* Oxford: Basil Blackwell.

Squire, James, et al. 1961.*The National Interest and the Teaching of English.* Urbana, IL: NCTE.

Squire, James, et al. 1964. *The National Interest and the Continuing Education of Teachers of English.* Urbana, IL: NCTE.

Suhor, Charles. 1988. "Content and Process in the English Curriculum." In Brandt, R. S., ed. *Content of the Curriculum: 1988 ASCD Yearbook.* Washington, DC: ASCD.

Sulzby, Elizabeth. 1986. "Writing and Reading: Signs of Written and Oral Language Organization in the Young Child." In Teale, W. H. and Sulzby, E., eds. *Emergent Literacy: Writing and Reading.* Norwood, NJ: Ablex.

Tannen, Deborah. 1986. *That's Not What I Meant: How Conversational Style Makes or Breaks Relationships.* New York: Morrow.

Terrace, Herbert. 1979. *Nim: A Chimpanzee Who Learned Sign Language.* New York: Knopf.

Thomson, Jack. 1987. *Understanding Teenagers Reading: Reading Processes and the Teaching of Literature.* North Ryde, NSW: Methuen; Australia and New York; Nichols.

Torbe, Mike, and Medway, Peter. 1981. *The Climate for Learning.* Portsmouth, NH: Boynton/Cook.

Trelease, Jim. 1982. *The Read-Aloud Handbook.* New York: Penguin.

Vygotsky, Lev S. 1962. *Thought and Language.* Cambridge, MA: MIT Press.

Vygotsky, Lev S. 1978. *Mind in Society.* Cambridge, MA: Harvard University Press.

Warriner, John. 1986. *Warriner's Grammar and Composition (Liberty Edition).* Orlando, FL: Harcourt Brace Jovanovich.

Watson, Ken. 1981.*English Teaching in Perspective.* Sydney: St. Clair Press.

Wells, Gordon. 1986. *The Meaning Makers: Children Learning Language and Using Language to Learn.* Portsmouth, NH: Heinemann.

Whorf, Benjamin Lee. 1956. *Language, Thought and Reality: Selected Papers of Benjamin Lee Whorf.* Carroll, J. B., ed. Cambridge, MA: MIT Press.

Ziv, Nina D. 1981. "The Effects of Teacher Comments on the Writing of Four College Freshmen." Unpublished dissertation, New York University.

Index